International Auditing Standards in the United States

International Auditing Standards in the United States

Comparing and Understanding Standards for ISA and PCAOB

Asokan Anandarajan and
Gary Kleinman

BEP BUSINESS EXPERT PRESS

International Auditing Standards in the United States: Comparing and Understanding Standards for ISA and PCAOB

First published in 2015 by
Business Expert Press, LLC
222 East 46th Street, New York, NY 10017
www.businessexpertpress.com

ISBN-13: 978-1-60649-612-1 (paperback)
ISBN-13: 978-1-60649-613-8 (e-book)

Business Expert Press Financial Accounting and Auditing Collection

Collection ISSN: 2151-2795 (print)
Collection ISSN: 2151-2817 (electronic)

Cover and interior design by Exeter Premedia Services Private Ltd., Chennai, India

First edition: 2015

10 9 8 7 6 5 4 3 2 1

Printed in the United States of America.

Abstract

International auditing of publicly owned corporations is governed largely by either U.S. Public Company Accounting Oversight Board (PCAOB) auditing standards or International Standards on Auditing (ISA) established by the International Federation of Accountants (IFAC). In some respects, the U.S. PCAOB and ISA are similar, but in other ways they are not. In this book, we describe key differences between PCAOB auditing standards and ISA. Our goal in doing so is to provide students, managers, and researchers with a clear, concise guide to the major differences between PCAOB and ISA standards. Understanding these differences will provide the reader with a greater appreciation of the differences in the auditing process between nations, and a greater understanding of what the audit opinion means as issued in different parts of the world.

Keywords

convergence between ISA and GAAS, divergence between PCAOB and IAS, generally accepted auditing standards (GAAS), international standards on auditing (ISA), PCAOB auditing standards, public corporation accounting oversight board (PCAOB)

Contents

Preface

There has been a great deal written on the topic of the globalization of business operations and finances over the last 30 years. Increasingly, corporations in one nation set up offshore operations in another nation. Further, corporations in one state invest in, or extend credit to, corporations in another state. In addition, capital markets that individual and institutional investors invest in are global in that capital can be disinvested from one firm in State A and almost immediately invested in another firm in State B within moments. The importance of accounting information in facilitating these initial investment decisions and in providing the information investors/creditors need to monitor the outcome of these decisions cannot be understated. The problems encountered by investors in making these initial decisions and in monitoring the results of these decisions mirror those that initially gave rise in the United States to the U.S. requirements that first financial statements in proxy statements be audited (i.e., as codified in the Securities Act of 1933) and then that financial statements of all publicly listed firms in the United States be audited by independent auditors (as codified in the Securities Exchange Act of 1934). While figures may not lie, liars do figure. These acts were passed due to President Franklin Delano Roosevelt's recognition that, as part of the need to restore public confidence in the security markets in the United States during the Great Depression, investors and creditors needed to have confidence in the information that they were provided by firms seeking funds or else they would not invest. That confidence, of course, was provided by requiring independent auditors to audit the numbers provided by firm management on their financial statements using audit methodologies. At that time, of course, the amount of international investment was small compared to today. The size of domestic, let alone international, financial markets and cross-market investing was small as well.

Since World War II, the size of the domestic U.S. financial market has grown much larger, as have the financial markets of the European Union,

China, Japan, and the emerging economies elsewhere. Given this, and the growing level of cross-national investment, investors and creditors need to be concerned with the "fairness of presentation" of domestic U.S. financial statements as well as whether those of overseas firms reflect a *true and fair view* of the underlying economic reality that the financial statements claim to represent. They also need to have some understanding of what the auditor's report, which will accompany the U.S. or non-U.S. financial statements, means and, given that it is very important, how the auditor came to his or her conclusion. In order to help with this, we discuss the background of auditing and the different sets of laws that are relevant to the practice of auditing. We also compare the auditing standards used domestically for publicly listed corporations in the United States with those used internationally. Our goal in doing so is to provide students, managers, and researchers with a clear, concise guide to the major differences between these standards. Given the global environment within which we live, we believe that understanding these differences will promote additional study of the standards and greater understanding of the relevant (to this book) differences between financial statements audited within as opposed to outside the United States.

Auditing standards themselves are standards or guidelines that auditors follow when conducting a financial audit of a company's financial statements. As such, they cover such areas of concern to students of auditing as ethically correct behavior, the legal environment of auditing, and what ethical behavior is supposed to be, given the auditing standards in force. Accordingly, it becomes clearer for the auditors which practical actions are to be undertaken to provide an accurate audit report on the financial statements and stay within the ethical rules and laws within which the auditor works. Standards, though, are the key focus of this book. International Standards on Auditing (ISA) are the standards to be followed in those jurisdictions that have adopted ISA or some version of ISA. ISA covers much ground. Each jurisdiction designates specific responsibilities of an auditor including how to plan an audit; how to evaluate and conclude on the adequacies of internal controls; how to evaluate audit evidence and draw conclusions from it, and how to write an audit report. The ISA also puts out ethical standards and quality control standards for auditors and audit firms to follow. It is not enough to set forth standards, the auditor also has to feel internally obligated (i.e., being ethical) to live up to the standards, and the audit firm has to monitor the quality of its members' compliance with the standards.

The United States, on the other hand, has its own auditing standards: the so-called Generally Accepted Auditing Standards (GAAS) set forth by the American Institute of Certified Public Accountants (AICPA) for use in private company audits; and the Public Company Accounting Oversight Board (PCAOB) standards, which apply to the audits of publicly owned corporations. The problem for both practitioners and students is that the auditing principles of the ISA and the AICPA are not identical, even though they are now converged. This problem is compounded because of the significant differences between the standards of the ISA and PCAOB, sets of standards that are not moving towards convergence. ISA standards generally cover audits of clients that are both publicly owned and privately owned. In the United States, the AIPCA's auditing standards for privately owned clients cover audits of firms that are typically, but not always, small. There are many larger private organizations, governments, and universities that are subject to audits using AICPA auditing standards. Auditing standards for publicly owned firms in the United States are set by the PCAOB. These are typically much larger firms. In this book, we focus on the differences between PCAOB auditing standards and the ISA. In doing so, we maximize the usefulness of this book to its users since the typical reader is very unlikely to read the financial statements, let alone see the audit report, for a small—or even a larger—privately owned client firm.

Accordingly, while books have been written on both the PCAOB standards and the ISA, here we plan to focus on the differences between the PCAOB standards and the ISA. We will cover the important differences and similarities in a clear and concise way. This should be of importance to students of auditing, researchers, and managers in the United States and internationally.

Acknowledgments

Asokan Anandarajan dedicates this book to his wife and son, Krishni and Rajkrishna for their patience and much support during the writing of this book. He is also thankful to the New Jersey Institute of Technology for allowing his sabbatical leave to work on this book. Dr. Kleinman gratefully acknowledges the supportiveness of his family during the writing of this book.

CHAPTER 1

International Auditing: A History and Introduction

This chapter discusses important background elements of auditing.

- Background of the Auditing Standards Board (ASB) and Public Company Accounting Oversight Board (PCAOB) of the United States, and International Auditing and Assurance Standards Board
- Determination of international auditing standards and ASB and PCAOB standards. A brief description of how an audit is conducted
- Implications for researchers, practitioners, and students

Introduction

Millions of individuals have had their financial futures negatively affected by corporate fraud and other malfeasance in the last 30 years. Management of corporations bear the responsibility for creating the financial statements that many stockholders and creditors use to ascertain whether a firm should receive their investments or loanable funds. Regrettably, recent financial scandals have raised questions regarding whether corporations can be trusted to produce accurate financial statements, that is, financial statements that reflect the actual success of the firm in generating revenue. Auditors and audit firms have, since the early 1930s in the United States at least, served the function of investigators of the compliance of corporate management-prepared financial statements with financial accounting standards. Financial accounting standards are the rules adopted within each nation to spell out how corporate transactions are to be analyzed and recorded. Based on the their investigation, auditors produce an opinion as to whether the recording of economic events or transactions that impact the financial statements adequately reflect the underlying economic reality facing the firm in compliance with the applicable reporting framework.

The importance of accurate auditing has been highlighted by recent events in the United States and abroad. In the United States, the WorldCom, Xerox, Health South, Bristol Myers, Citibank, Kmart and NextCard, and Enron scandals in the recent past, (and prior to that, Lincoln Savings and Loan, Penn Square, Sunbeam, Regina, ZZZZ Best, Crazy Eddy, Waste Management, Cendant, Livent, and Mattel), led to important changes in the auditing environment. Europe too had their equivalent of the Enron scandal such as the frauds at Ahold, Parmalat, and Comroad; in Japan, it was the bank Resona; in Australia, it was the insurance company HIH. The failure of these companies, and the inability of the auditor to recognize fraud and notify the public in their audit reports were the prime motivating forces that resulted in the significant regulatory changes we evidence today.

In the United States, for example, the key change in regulation is the Sarbanes-Oxley Act (SOX) of 2002. In Europe, the equivalent to SOX is the European Council Commission Directive 84/253/EEC (EU Eighth Company Law Directive), also referred to as European Commission's (EC) Eighth Directive on statutory audits effective from 2006. Similar regulatory action was taken in Russia, Japan, China, and other countries. Scandal was not the only reason for changes in the auditing environment. The exponential growth of investing and raising capital in the global markets has also contributed to the changes in both the auditing environment and in international accounting as well. The changes in the auditing environment affected three aspects of the auditing profession: the nature of the regulation of auditing practice, the nature of the standards that auditors must use in performing the audit, and the ethics of the profession. In this book, we focus on the two main sets of standards that govern audits in most of the globe. These are the PCAOB standards that govern public company audits in the United States and the International Standards for Auditing (ISA) set by the International Auditing Assurance Standards Board (IAASB) of the International Federation of Accountants (IFAC).

The three aspects of auditing previously mentioned are impacted by the standards set by the PCAOB and IAASB. We also discuss and describe the role of the American Institute of Certified Public Accountants (AICPA) of the United States in setting private company auditing standards. We believe this is important in helping to understand the complexity of the auditing environment given the importance of appreciating the demands of a changing business environment.

With respect to the international environment, two important sets of standards have emerged; one is in accounting and the other in auditing. These are the international accounting standards, known as the International Financial Reporting Standards (IFRS), developed by the International Accounting Standards Committee (IASC) and the auditing standards, known as ISA, developed by the IAASB. Many global multinational corporations that are headquartered outside the United States prepare their financial statements in accordance with international accounting standards and have them audited in accordance with international auditing standards. Auditing is a process of checking or evaluating whether the financial statements, for example, are prepared in accordance with a given set of criteria. For financial statements prepared in accordance with IFRS, therefore, an auditor checks whether IFRS was correctly applied to financial transactions accurately collected and summarized in the company's financial statements. Just as financial data collection and financial statement preparation needs to follow rules of IFRS, the auditor must follow rules for auditing.

International standards on auditing (a major focus of this book) are promulgated by the IAASB. It follows a due process procedure in which research or other information suggestive of the need for new standards or for redrafting of old standards is analyzed. Once it has been decided that a new standard or revision of an old standard is required, then drafts of the proposed auditing standard are made available for public comment and discussion. Only after comments with respect to proposed standards are received and digested are final versions of the standards issued by the IAASB.

The first core set of international standards on auditing was completed and released in 1994. This has subsequently been regarded as *work in progress* and is being constantly refined and enhanced. Although various national adaptations of the ISA exist because nations adapt the ISA to mesh better with local laws and customs, we focus only on the standards as promulgated by the IAASB.

The purpose of this book is to focus purely on the changes in international auditing standards and the way these changes impinge on U.S. auditors in the performance of their auditing duties in the international arena. Internationally, the IAASB is the main auditing standards setting body. As such, it is equivalent to the AICPA's ASB in the United States with respect to private company auditors or PCAOB with respect to public company auditors. All three standards setting bodies use the due process procedure outlined above, although the PCAOB also must have the U.S. Securities Exchange Commission approve the standards it adopts before they can have the force of law. Although all three auditing standard setting bodies work to set standards for the audits of financial statements and internal controls in their respective jurisdictions, they work independent of the financial accounting standards setting bodies.

In this book, we examine these key international auditing standards in detail and compare and contrast the requirements of IAASB standards with, predominantly, the PCAOB standards as well as the AICPA's ASB standards where they are of particular interest. However, the convergence of the AICPA and IAASB standards has largely removed the need to compare AICPA and IAASB standards. These comparisons should provide U.S. auditors, and managers of U.S. businesses with the skills needed to comprehend the differing requirements of auditing standards set by these different bodies. Accounting students will benefit from having a resource for understanding the differences between the standards, both as they move through the accounting curriculum and as they enter their professional careers. Researchers, of course, may be interested in having comparisons of audit practice in the United States versus other parts of the world available. Having a clear, concise, guide to key differences between, predominantly, PCAOB and IAASB standards should ease the difficulties in making the comparison.

The research for this book was primarily obtained from three sources. First, we analyzed the relevant PCAOB standards and equivalent ISA and studied convergences and divergences with special emphasis on the divergences. Second, we obtained complementary information where possible from an AICPA website entitled "Substantive differences between the international standards on auditing and generally accepted auditing standards" (www.aicpa.org/FRS). Finally, to a lesser extent but equally important, we found useful information in a research project conducted by the Maastricht accounting, auditing, and information management research center entitled (EU project No Markt/2007/15/F lot 2) "Evaluation of the differences between international standards on auditing (ISA) and the standards of the US Public Company Accounting Oversight Board (PCAOB)" which was published five years ago. Discussions that are still relevant were assessed against our findings where possible and included in our discussions.

Brief History of International Auditing

The history of auditing can be traced back to ancient China and Egypt going back to circa 3000 BC. The treatment of auditors was quite harsh in both countries because the auditors, in fact, served the Chinese emperors and the Egyptian pharaohs. It is reported that, in ancient Egypt, the Pharaoh used auditors to provide *checks* against fraud. For example, an auditor counted goods prior to their being stored. Another auditor then counted the goods stored. The Pharaoh's supervisor was responsible for reconciling the two counts. If a material difference existed that could not be explained, both auditors were sacrificed to the gods as punishment.

The practice of modern day auditing, however, began when corporations started being set up after the industrial revolution. The divergence between owning the corporation and managing it had the potential to cause major problems for the owners should the managers take advantage of the owners' lack of knowledge of the business's actual operations. Thus, there was an intensified need for auditors to verify for the owners the management's claims with regard to business progress. The profession realized that there was a need for auditing to have some standardized elements in order to better ensure that it was being done well. The first steps at providing such guidance to auditors were initiated in Scotland in 1853 with the formation of the Society of Accountants in

Edinburgh. Initially, similar competing *regulatory* bodies cropped up all over the United Kingdom. However, it was realized that the only way these competing bodies could be effective was if they worked in conjunction with each other. These competing bodies subsequently consolidated in 1880 to form the Institute of Chartered Accountants of England and Wales (ICAEW). The advantage of having a single body to provide guidance to and regulation of auditors was recognized and resulted in the formation of similar bodies by other countries in the Western world.

Internationally, the spur to the growth and development of audit standards arose as a result of several well publicized fraud cases where it was felt that the auditors, in their role as *watchdogs*, had not performed their tasks adequately. The British Companies Acts, passed in the latter half of the 19th century, attempted to set standards and provide guidelines to auditors. In the United States, the first auditing standards were issued in 1917. The first major development in international accounting and auditing was the formation of the IFAC on October 7, 1977, in Munich, Germany, at the 11th World Congress of Accountants Conference. Specifically, IFAC was established to strengthen the worldwide accounting profession in the public interest by:

- developing high quality international standards and supporting their adoption and use;
- facilitating collaboration and cooperation among its member bodies; and
- collaborating and cooperating with other international organizations and serving as the international spokesperson for the accounting profession.

(For further information, please visit the IFAC website at IFAC.org.).

The formation of the IFAC was the first major attempt at global international standards. The IFAC is currently a global organization that works with 155 member accounting boards in 118 countries. As of January 2014, the IFAC claims that 126 nations around the world have adopted IAASB standards to some degree (IAASB, 2014) The IFAC's objective in creating these standards is to protect public interest by encouraging high quality practices among the world's accountants.

The ISA have come a long way since the start of their development in 1994. They started as guidelines under the harmonization process of IFAC and its member bodies, one of which is the AICPA. The IFAC itself has been charged with the responsibility to enhance and expand the worldwide use of auditing standards with the objective of improving the quality and uniformity of international practice (Roussey 1999). The IFAC's responsibilities include:

- issuing international standards on auditing;
- issuing guidance on the application of such standards;
- promoting the adoption of the committee's pronouncements as the primary source of national standards and as guidance in cross border offerings;
- promoting the endorsement of the standards by legislators and securities exchanges; and
- promoting debate with practitioners, users, and regulators throughout the world to identify user needs for new standards and guidance.

The importance of international auditing standards at the present moment cannot be understated. Roussey notes that there has been growing acceptance of ISA by:

- a number of large international accounting firms as the basis for their worldwide auditing practices;
- global public companies reporting outside their national borders;
- companies involved in issuing securities in cross-border transactions;
- companies using securities in domestic financing transactions;
- regulatory bodies accepting financial statements audited using the ISA for regulatory filings in their countries or requiring the use of ISA by including them in company law;

- global organizations, such as the Organization for Economic Cooperation and Development, that have endorsed ISA for use in auditing financial statements in their jurisdictions; and
- national accountancy bodies that have used ISA as the basis for their national auditing standards.

A significant number of countries around the world have taken substantial steps to harmonize their auditing standards with the ISA. Among these countries are the Netherlands, the United Kingdom, The European Commission through the Fédération des Experts Comptables Européens, as well as Canada, and South Africa. Some nations adopt the ISA word-for-word, others adapt the ISA to their own preferences based on local considerations.

In the United States, there are two sets of auditing standards, as already noted. The AICPA's auditing standards are used in audits of companies whose stocks are not traded above a certain market capitalization level on any U.S. stock exchange or are not traded at all on any stock exchange. (Market capitalization refers to an estimation of the value of a business that is obtained by multiplying the number of shares issued by the current price of a share.) AICPA auditing standards, like those of the IAASB, are often considered to encourage greater reliance on the auditor's professional judgment and skepticism than do the PCAOB standards. We also note that one of the big differences between accounting standards in the United States versus the international arena is the idea of rules-based versus principles-based standards. Rules-based accounting is basically a list of detailed rules that must be followed when preparing financial statements. Many accountants favor the prospect of using rules-based standards because, in the absence of rules, they could be brought to court if their judgments of the financial statements are incorrect. When there are strict rules that need to be followed, the possibility of lawsuits is diminished. Having a set of rules can also increase accuracy and reduce the ambiguity that can trigger aggressive reporting decisions by management. Principles-based accounting is a simple set of key objectives to ensure good reporting. The fundamental premise is that its broad guidelines can be practical for a variety of circumstances. However, lack of guidelines may result in unreliable and inconsistent information.

Both the IAASB and the AICPA have moved towards the harmonization of their respective sets of standards. For example, the AICPA's ASB has established a number of action plans to implement key initiatives as set forth in its report *Horizons for the Auditing Standards Board.* These include establishing a standing subcommittee of the ASB on international auditing standards, promoting opportunities for joint projects and initiating an effort for reporting on the credibility of information. Importantly, IFAC states that the AICPA's ASB has chosen to use the IAASB's ISA as the basis for its own standards with the aim of having minimal if any differences between AICPA Statements on Auditing Standards (SASs) and the requirements of the IAASB's ISA.* We note that there is now convergence as noted by the IAASB in its publication, Implementation of the Clarified International Standards on Auditing (IAASB 2014)

The PCAOB came into existence with the passage of the SOX of 2002 by the Congress of the United States. It was set up with the responsibility of setting auditing standards—subject to SEC review—for publicly owned companies. PCAOB audits are required to cover both a company's internal controls over financial reporting and its financial statements. While all auditing standards claim to rely on auditor professional judgment, the PCAOB standards impose more detailed guidelines with respect to how audits of financial statements are supposed to be undertaken. Unlike the AICPA's ASB, the PCAOB does not overtly seek to harmonize its standards with those of the IAASB.

The first standard issued by the PCAOB was the so-called Auditing Standard (AS) 1. This auditing standard adopted all then existing AICPA ASB standards as its own. These AICPA ASB standards, which then—for public company audits—were dubbed "interim standards" retain the status of standards public company auditors should follow until the PCAOB replaces them with its own standards. We will frequently refer to these interim standards as standards "under the aegis of the PCAOB," or use similar wording. Since the effective date of the PCAOB's AS 1, April 16, 2003, the PCAOB has adopted an additional 17 standards, gradually replacing many, but not all, of the original interim standards.

---

* http://www.ifac.org/webfm_send/1966

Most recently in 2014, the PCAOB issued AS 18 dealing with related parties and significant unusual transactions. Since April 16, 2003, the AICPA has remained as the setter of auditing standards for privately owned companies in the United States. It has revised many of its earlier standards and engaged in a rewrite of these standards and has clarified their presentation. We refer to these standards occasionally but only to highlight more important points regarding the PCAOB standards and the ISA that are the focus of this book. However, please also note that the PCAOB is currently proposing a framework for reorganizing the existing interim (AU) and PCAOB issued standards (AS) into a single integrated numbering system based on subject matter. Hence, the numbers we cite may not be the final numbers and may be revised depending on the final decision (PCAOB release 2013-13 of March 26, 2013).

In the next section, we discuss what auditing is, the objectives of an audit, and the key components of auditing from the perspective of international standards on auditing. The different types of audit and auditors, the principles governing an audit, the limitations of an audit, and the risks faced by auditors are then examined. The generally accepted *model* of an audit is reviewed. Thus this section provides a broad description of what an audit is, the different types of audits, the requirements for becoming a certified or chartered accountant, and an overview of the auditing process to help you understand the more detailed information in the chapters that follow. In other words, it provides with a framework for understanding the rest of the book. In presenting this framework for understanding auditing, we refer heavily to the ISA to more simply illustrate the interplay between auditing standards and what an auditor does than would be achievable by reference to both the ISA and the PCAOB standards. However, later in the book, we also compare PCAOB standards with ISA.

What is an Audit?

Interestingly, there is no actual definition of what constitutes an audit in the ISA. The closest we come as authors to finding a definition of standards is in ISA 200. ISA 200 states that an auditor should conduct an audit sufficiently to enable him/her to express an opinion whether the financial statements *present a true and fair view* or *present fairly, in all material respects* the financial health of a company in accordance with an identified financial reporting framework. Hayes et al. (2005) point outs that while the great majority of audit work today is financial auditing, that is, checking the fundamental accuracy of a firm's financial statements, operational auditing and compliance auditing are also very important. However, this definition does not cover these important types of auditing. Operational auditing involves examining the operational efficiency and effectiveness of an organization, while compliance auditing involves examining a firm's compliance with other, nonfinancial rules, regulations, and laws. These two forms of audit, though, are not of concern here.

Objectives of an Audit

If we go back a century, Dicksee (1900) in *Auditing: A Practical Manual for Auditors*, states that an objective of an audit is three fold, namely:

- The detection of fraud
- The detection of technical errors
- The detection of errors on principle

The detection of fraud, according to Dicksee, was the most important part of the auditor's duties. As Hayes et al. note, however, gradually the auditor's duties began to change, with fraud detection becoming less and less of a priority. What was the reason for this development away from fraud? Several reasons have been given for this phenomenon, but the most important reasons according to Hayes et al. are:

- the acceptance that the audit of the financial statements on behalf of the third parties is an art in its own way
- the acceptance that an investigation aimed at finding any kind of fraud is extremely laborious expensive and not practical, considering the increases in size and complexity of the companies, as well as their improved self or internal controls

By the late 1950s, fraud detection became merely a responsibility and not a primary objective of auditing. Commencing in the late 1970s and continuing through the 1980s, however, the public, which was dissatisfied with this interpretation, imposed pressure on the auditing profession to take a more aggressive stance towards fraud detection. This resulted in the appointment of several commissions including the Cohen Commission (1978), the Treadway Commission (1987), and the Dingell Committee (1987) in the United States. Similar pressure internationally resulted in the Davison and Benson Committees in the United Kingdom. In the United States, due to the pressures imposed by the findings of the committees referred to earlier, the ASB implemented the Statement on Auditing Standards (SAS) No. 99 *Consideration of Fraud* in *a Financial Statement Audit* effective from October 2002. It is now under the aegis of the PCAOB, AU 316 under the same name, Consideration of fraud in a financial statement audit. Under AU 316 auditors have to implement very extensive procedures to detect fraud. AU 316 describes a process in which the auditor (1) has to gather information needed to identify risks of material misstatement as a result of fraud, (2) assesses these risks after taking into account evaluation of the entity's programs and controls, and (3) has to respond to the results. Under SAS 99 auditors will have to gather and consider much more information to assess fraud risks than in the past.

The current position of the IAASB with respect to fraud detection is described in ISA 240. According to the ISA 240, fraud is defined as "sophisticated and carefully organized schemes designed to conceal acts such as forgery, deliberate failure to record transactions and intentional misrepresentations being made to the auditor." The responsibility for the prevention and detection of fraud and error rests primarily with management and those charged with governance under ISA 240. The PCAOB has now taken the requirements of SAS 99 under its aegis, and it is now the PCAOB's AU 316 entitled *Consideration of fraud in a financial statement audit.*

Key Components of Auditing

An audit, as discussed in ISA 200, is an independent and expert examination involving evaluation of evidence in order to ascertain whether the financial statements present a *true and fair view* of the underlying economic reality of the client firm. It is in effect, a systematic approach that employs a structured, well documented plan for analyzing accounting records, using a variety of methodologies to acquire relevant evidence, to find out the relationship between the financial statements and the underlying economic reality of the firm. An audit is expected to be conducted without prejudice or bias. A term commonly used is that it must be conducted objectively, meaning that auditors are required to be impartial when evaluating evidence. The auditor is expected to collect sufficient evidence to determine whether the financial statements present a true and fair view of the underlying economic reality of the firm and evaluate that evidence without bias (referred to as reliability). The auditor has to ensure sufficiency and reliability by critically evaluating the internal controls to determine what type of tests should be done (referred to as nature of testing), the level of tests (extent), and when each test should be conducted (timing).

Auditors are also required to evaluate what is referred to as assertions of management. Assertions are assumptions about economic actions and events made by management. These assertions either explicitly or implicitly are embodied in the financial statements. An example of an assertion is that all assets reported on the balance sheet actually exist and are not fictitious. Furthermore, the company actually owns these assets, and they do not belong to anybody else. The assumption that assets on the balance sheet are real is referred to as the existence assertion. The assumption that the assets reported in the balance sheet are actually owned by the company and does not belong to anybody else is referred to as the rights and obligations assertion. The auditor is required to examine these assertions. The auditor is required to test these assertions by inquiring and physically observing (on a test or sampling basis) whether the assets exist and checking documentation to ensure that a transaction has occurred and physical ownership exists. By testing or sampling basis, we mean that *not every* transaction is checked to see if it occurred, but rather a sufficient number of, preferably randomly selected, transactions are checked. Based on this testing basis, the auditor is allowed to draw a reasonable conclusion about the account balances affected by that kind of transaction. In the case of assets such as accounts receivable, the auditor has to send confirmation of balances notices to customers (debtors) of the entity being audited.

The customers are asked to respond with respect to the correctness of the balance shown on the balance notice. The auditor's comparison of these two numbers (the number on the client's books and the number that the client provides to the auditor) is referred to as ascertaining the degree of correspondence between assertions and criteria. The auditor also has to check whether, in reporting the assets (and liabilities), local standards, regulations, and laws are observed.

The ultimate goal of an audit is to communicate the results to parties referred to as interested users. The auditor has to express an informed opinion in a written report. The communication of the auditor's opinion is called attestation. In layman's terms, it is referred to as the auditor's report. The auditors must state whether they believe that the financial statements give a *true and fair view* or *present fairly in all material respects* the financial position of the company. If, as in PCAOB audits, the auditor is giving an opinion on the effectiveness of the client's internal control over financial reporting, the auditor will state whether or not material weaknesses exist in the internal control system. Please note that the auditor is not providing an opinion about the internal control system that includes all controls. The auditor is focused on the key internal controls specific to financial reporting. The auditor's report may lend credibility to the financial statements if the auditor states he/she believes the statements present a *true and fair view*. On the other hand, if the auditor has sufficient reason to doubt that is true, the credibility of the financial statement is reduced.

In this book, we almost solely focus on financial statement audits. There are, though, several types of audits. We describe each of these in the following paragraphs.

Types of Audits

Financial Statement Audit

The purpose of financial statement audits is to examine the financial statements of companies to ensure that they present a true and fair view. The auditor also determines whether the accounts are in conformity with GAAP if the audit is conducted in the United States and IFRS if the audit is conducted in Europe and other Western countries. ISA and the PCAOB auditing standards were developed to guide auditors in the conduct of financial statement audits, including audit effort related to the client firm's internal controls over financial reporting. In some respects, ISA audits of financial statements are similar to U.S. audits of financial statements. There is, however, a major difference related to internal controls. As discussed in a later chapter, the PCAOB requires an audit of internal controls. The objective is to express an opinion as to whether a company's internal controls over financial reporting are effective. If the report indicates weaknesses, then the audit of the financial statements has to take this into account with respect to substantive testing, and so on. There is no equivalent for ISA; in general, that means there is no requirement for an auditor to render an opinion on the client's internal controls. However, the ISAs do specify some auditor responsibilities related to internal control over financial reporting. This is a major difference and will be discussed in a later chapter.

Operational Audits

The purpose of an operational audit is to study one specific operation or subdivision of a company and to make a report on the performance of the operation or subdivision that was audited. The operation under study can be any aspect of the client company, including, but not limited to, marketing management, production methods, and information technology (IT). In particular, the auditor is expected to examine the objectives of the company and then evaluate how effective the relevant procedures are in helping attain those objectives. The auditor is expected to critically audit the procedures in place in terms of efficiency and effectiveness to carry out relevant operations under study. The audit report generally comprises recommendations to management on areas of improvement with respect to the operations that were studied.

Compliance Audits

The purpose of a compliance audit is to study whether the company under audit has adopted the rules and procedures set out by top management.

The purpose of a compliance audit is to critically examine if the company is complying with the procedures they are expected to follow based on the prevalent laws. In general compliance audits are conducted by government auditors and internal auditors. The audit report comprises comments on deficiencies in compliance procedures and is sent to the manager of the division being audited.

Operational and compliance audits are internal reports. To the best of our knowledge they are not provided to investors in any way under either PCAOB or ISA rules.

Types of Auditors

There are two basic types of auditors: internal auditors and independent external auditors, whose work is our focus.

Internal Auditors

The purpose of internal auditors is to investigate the effectiveness of the operations of the company and report to company management. The paramount responsibility of an internal auditor is the critical review of the efficiency of internal controls. The main task of internal auditors is operational audits, financial audits, and compliance audits. It is generally accepted that the external auditor should, as part of their duties, review the work of the internal auditor especially in those areas where perceived lack of adequate control could, potentially, jeopardize the quality of financial information generated by the company's accounting systems.

The internal auditor, can hopefully act as if they are independent of the board of directors and the heads of departments for whom they conduct the audit. The majority of internal auditors of public companies report to the audit committee or, alternatively, to the Chief Financial Officer (CFO). However, this is easier said than done; it is accepted that total independence is not possible because, in effect, the internal auditors are employees of the company and do work for the company. One advantage (among others) of having internal auditors is that they could provide direct assistance to the external auditor during the course of the audit. It is required that external auditors assess the competence of internal auditors by reviewing their educational backgrounds and experience. External auditors are also required to assess the potential *objectivity* of the internal auditor. For example, if the status of the internal auditor on the organizational chart is relatively *low*, then their objectivity could be questioned because they might not be able to protect themselves from the managers their reports criticize.

External Auditor

The primary function of the external auditor is to perform an effective and independent audit and provide what in technical terms is referred to as an attest function. We are solely interested here in the work of the external auditors. The attest function requires that the external auditor deliver an opinion as to whether the company's financial statements and management assertions provide, in the United Kingdom for example, what is called *a true and fair view* of the state of the company's affairs. In the United States, the opinion states whether the financial statements *present fairly* the company's financial affairs. Depending on the country, independent auditors are certified by a professional organization or by a government agency.

The background discussed in the preceding paragraphs regarding internal versus external auditors applies to the United States and internationally.

The final result of an audit is the expression of an opinion. Internationally, this is governed by the company laws of each country. In most cases, the law of each country applies to the country as a whole. However, in the United States and Canada, individual states and provinces, respectively, have authority over regulating the attest function.

Principles Governing the Audit of Financial Statements

In the international arena, auditors are expected to follow ISA 200, which emphasizes that auditors conform to the Code of Ethics for Professional Accountants issued by IFAC. The ethical principles, as in the United States, relate to the auditor's independence, integrity, objectivity, professional competence, due care, confidentiality, professional behavior, and technical standards. What are the standards or guiding characteristics in the United States? In the United States, the auditor is expected to conduct the audit in accordance with the auditing standards promulgated by the PCAOB for publicly owned companies and the AICPA's ASB for privately owned companies. Internationally, ISA 200 requires that the auditor conduct the audit in accordance with the ISA. Both ASB and ISA have strong similarities. In both cases, the auditor is required to plan and perform the audit with an attitude of professional skepticism. Professional skepticism implies that the auditor should not take the honesty of the client for granted; rather, the auditor should recognize that under certain circumstances, the financial statements could be materially misstated. (Professional skepticism is defined by the PCAOB's AU 230's *Due professional care in the performance of work* as an attitude that includes a questioning mind and a critical assessment of audit evidence. The ISA defines professional skepticism as an essential attitude that enhances the auditor's ability to identify and respond to conditions that may indicate possible misstatement. So essentially in both definitions the key tenets are the adoption of an attitude enabling critical assessment of evidence. Hence, there is little difference in this respect.)

Both the ASB standards and the ISA give a lot of leeway to the auditor's professional judgment. The PCAOB standards, however, are more likely to require *check the box* types of procedures. That is, the PCAOB provides less leeway for individual auditor professional judgment than do the ASB standards or the ISA. Just as with the ASB standards and the ISA, however, the PCAOB standards also requires that the auditor plan and perform the audit with an attitude of professional skepticism.

Limitation of the Audit

As Hayes et al. (2005) note, there are certain inherent limitations in an audit that affect the auditor's ability to detect material misstatements. These limitations result from such factors as the use of testing or sampling, the inherent limitations of any accounting and internal control system, and the fact that most evidence is persuasive rather than conclusive. Furthermore, the process of obtaining evidence to form an opinion is matter by judgment. Judgment is required to determine the nature and extent of audit evidence and the drawing of conclusions based on the audit evidence gathered. Because of these factors, an audit is no guarantee that the financial statements are free of material misstatement. In the United States, the auditor's opinion states that the audit provides 'reasonable assurance', not complete assurance, that the statements are free of material misstatement.

ISA audit reports state the same. For both, it goes without saying that collusion by clients is a limitation because collusion enables the colluding parties to overcome internal controls

Risks Faced by Auditors

Business Risk and Audit Risk

Whereas a company may face a plethora of business-related risks, management is primarily responsible for understanding and mitigating the effects of these risks. The auditor's primary concern relates to risks associated with the financial statements. The most important risk (frequently referred to as type 1 risk) is the risk of giving an erroneously clean, that is a "good" or "unqualified", opinion in undeserving circumstances do not. The newest revision of ISA 200 requires the auditors to adequately plan and perform their audit to reduce type 1 risk to the lowest acceptable level possible. Type 2 risk is the risk that the auditor will erroneously give a *bad* or *qualified* or *adverse* opinion to financial statements that deserve a *good* or *unqualified* opinion. A key problem with a type 1 opinion is that investors may be more likely to invest in shares of a company that has received the erroneous *good* opinion. When the truth about the company comes out, and the investors realize that the company's value may be less than they had thought, the stock price may drop and investor wealth may decline. If, though, the auditors gave the client firm an erroneous *qualified* or *bad* opinion, investors may sell off their holdings of the firm's shares, with the result that the stock price will drop when, had the auditor given a correct opinion, the stock price would not have fallen. Thus shareholder wealth would be diminished for a wrong reason.

We have now discussed the objectives of the audits, we the qualifications of auditors, the types of audits, and the types of opinions. It is important now to describe briefly the audit process model. The audit ends with an opinion (*good* or *bad*). However, many things must happen before the opinion can be given. We discuss the audit process next.

Standard Audit Process Model

The phases of the audit according to international auditing standards are:

- client acceptance preplanning;
- planning and design of an audit approach;
- administering the tests for evidence; and
- completion of the audit and issuance of an audit report.

We discuss each of these stages in turn.

Client Acceptance

Client acceptance is covered in ISA 210 under *Terms of audit engagements*. For recurring audits, ISA 210 paragraph 13 says that the auditor should assess whether the circumstances that exist at that time require the terms of the engagement to be changed. Also, paragraph 13 states that the auditor should consider whether the client needs to be reminded of the terms of the audit engagement.

It is assumed that, unless an untoward incident has occurred (e.g., finding that the client engages in fraud), then the status quo is maintained and the related risk associated with the client is the same as it was the previous year. With respect to new clients, the auditor is required to determine the business risk by investigating the background, financial statements, and the nature and type of the industry of the client.

Planning and Design of an Audit Approach

Planning is covered in ISA 300. It is required that the audit firm plan the work such that the audit is both timely and efficient. The plan is contingent on the nature of the industry and the business environment of the client. The auditor should develop a plan after studying the business environment of the client, the types of control (including an understanding of the entire control environment and control procedures), and the client's accounting system. The auditor is required to conduct analytical procedures to test the control procedures. The results of the analytical procedures help to determine overall riskiness of the client because the ratio analyses involved, including analyses of how specific ratios changed from one year to the next, help direct the auditor's attention to potential problem areas. With this and other information in hand, the auditor is then required to set materiality levels based on assessed risk. For example, the combination of risk and materiality assessment might dictate where the auditor allocates work time. So if materiality is high but risk is low, the auditor may do less work. Similarly, if materiality is low but risk is high, the auditor may do more work. The auditor is then required to prepare a plan (also referred to as an audit program) outlining the nature, type, and extent of audit procedures that are required overall and for each account type to gather evidence.

ISA 300 emphasizes the importance of evaluating the client's internal control structure in the planning stage. The auditor is required to assess if: (1) the client's internal control structure is adequate to generate reliable data and (2) the client's internal control is adequate to safeguard assets. The evidence subsequently required to be tested is contingent on these results. If the tests reveal weak internal controls, then auditors are required to obtain relatively more evidence because there is a greater likelihood that problems in financial reporting will not be *caught* and corrected by the internal control system and, therefore, the problems will be included in the financial statements themselves. Guidance for this is provided in ISA 315. ISA 315 also covers the computer information systems environment, a very important factor, given the computerization of the business environment.

Tests for Evidence

ISA Sections 500 and 501 provided guidance on types of tests and evidence required. These sections require that the audit be performed and the report prepared with *due professional care* by persons who have adequate training, experience, and competence in auditing. The auditor is required to act with *due professional care*. This means that the auditor acts independently and adheres to international ethics by keeping the results confidential. *Due professional care* also means that the auditor should perform the audit diligently, obtain sufficient evidence before arriving at an opinion, maintain a complete set of working papers, and prepare an audit report that is appropriate to the state of the client's affairs.

Tests of controls are tests designed to obtain reasonable assurance that the financial system controls are in place and are effective. This is discussed in PCAOB's Auditing Standard No 5 entitled *An audit of internal control over financial reporting that is integrated with an audit of financial statements*. The auditor is required to test controls for the purpose of reducing risk and then, based on the results, determine the extent of substantive tests. (The purpose of substantive tests is to obtain evidence of the completeness, accuracy, and validity of the data provided by the accounting system.) Analytical procedures (discussed in detail in ISA 520) are used to identify significant discrepancies between the results the auditor expected to find and the actual results. Based on this, further substantive tests are determined. If the analytical procedures do not indicate significant discrepancies, then the substantive tests can be reduced.

Completion of an Audit and Issuance of an Audit Report

This is discussed in ISA 550, 560, 570 and 580. The auditor is required to first assess the following:

- Has the financial information been the result of acceptable accounting policies?
- Have the acceptable accounting policies been consistently applied?
- Has the company complied with relevant regulations and statutory requirements in the preparation of the financial information?
- Does the financial information present a view that is congruent with the auditor's knowledge of the entity based on other sources and the auditor's experience?
- Has all material information been adequately disclosed?

The auditor must perform final audit procedures before the audit report can be written. These are described in ISA Sections 600 and 620. As described in these sections, the auditor is required to obtain legal letters and identify subsequent events that could potentially adversely or favorably affect the company. The auditor should then report to the board of directors and obtain a management representation letter. Guidance relating to obtaining the representation letter is provided in ISA 580.

Conclusion and Implications for Researchers, Manager, and Students

This chapter introduced the reader to the role of the auditor in the validation of financial statements prepared by corporate management. In doing so, we focused on international standards when describing the audit process. The chapter begins by describing the different sources of auditing standards used by an auditor, depending on whether they are auditing organizations based in the United States and which have their stocks sold on U.S. Exchanges or whether they are auditing organizations whose clients are headquartered in countries that have adopted international auditing standards. It then describes the different types of audits and, based on the international auditing standards, leads the reader through the audit process. This information provides a quick guide to the role that different standards setting bodies play in the public audit, depending on the location of the client firm. The topics in this chapter are deeply explored as we go into further discussion of auditing and a comparison of the differences between ISA and PCAOB auditing standards.

CHAPTER 2

The International and U.S. Audit Environments

This chapter discusses factors influencing legal liability of auditors in the United States and abroad. This chapter focuses on:

- legislation and law in the United States that could affect the liability of auditors;
- legislation internationally that could affect the liability of auditors;
- liability to third parties, criminal liability under statutory law in the United States and in Europe;
- important differences in legislation that could affect the liability of U.S. auditors working in a European environment.

Introduction

Many parties rely on audited financial statements. The parties include, but are not limited to, stockholders, trade creditors, bankers, customers, employees, state governments, and the federal government. All these parties could be adversely affected by inappropriate audit opinions and, hence, could potentially sue the auditor. To what extent is the auditor liable to each of these parties? This is a difficult question to answer. In the United States, the nature and extent of liability could vary from state to state. To understand legal liability, we have to first understand laws that affect the auditor when carrying out the audit function on behalf of the client. The audit firm, as an institution, has a duty to enforce compliance of its personnel to the relevant law and the individual auditor, regardless of the activities or preferences of their firm, has the obligation to follow the law. Auditors, both as audit firms and as individuals working in the audit firms, in the United States are affected by common law and statutory law. Laws in the United States and certain other countries (e.g., the United Kingdom) can be classified as either common law or statutory law. Common law is based on precedent or case law. Under common law, new laws are created through decisions made by judges. The judges in turn make decisions using earlier cases as precedents. If there are no prior cases that can be used as precedents, then whatever the judge decides becomes law. Statutory law, in contrast, is written law decided by the legislature or, with a grant of authority from the legislature through a provision in legislation, a government agency. These laws are not based on lawsuits that have been heard in a court of law, but rather are issued to meet the needs of citizens or to formalize existing law or to resolve an outstanding issue that the courts refer to the government.

The auditor could face either civil or criminal liability under statutory law. They also face liability as members who should be acting according to professional standards, but who are believed not to be doing so. That is, failure to meet professional standards in the conduct of an audit may subject the auditor to punishment under statutory law. In this chapter, regulation, which affects auditors in the United States and other countries (mainly Europe), and the background to the regulation is discussed. This is important because applicable laws and regulations vary by country. Further, in some countries only the auditor signing the contract (engagement letter) is liable, whereas in others all partners are liable. Some countries have laws which allow third parties to even sue the assistants who worked on the audit. Liability to third parties can vary. Finland is the extreme case where even *statutory representatives* of the auditor (banks, etc, which give information to the auditor) could be sued. There is usually a limit to the amount of time after a legal violation that the offense can be brought to court and ultimately punished, called the statute of limitations. The statute of limitations for law suits varies by country from 5 to 20 years. Further liability *caps* (the maximum amount for which the auditor can be sued) varies with specified amounts in some countries to unlimited amounts in others. In some countries, auditors are allowed to limit liability by including it in the contract signed with the company being audited. In other countries, this is not permissible. Thus, it is vital for auditors from the United States to be aware of these differences. We first discuss relevant regulation that affects auditors in the United States. Then we do a comparative analysis with other countries. This chapter then concludes by discussing the Sarbanes-Oxley Act in the United States and its comparable equivalent in Europe and the implications of these new laws for auditors.

Legal Liability in the United States

A client, as a plaintiff or *injured* party, can bring action against an auditor in the form of breach of contract; injured third parties can bring a tort action for negligence. A tort in common law is a civil wrong, which unfairly causes someone else to suffer loss or harm resulting in legal liability for the person who commits the tortious act. Whereas crimes may be torts, the cause of legal action is not necessarily a crime; the harm may be due to negligence that does not amount to criminal negligence. The victim of the harm can recover their loss as damages in a lawsuit. In order to prevail, the plaintiff in the law suit must show that the actions or lack of action was the legally recognizable cause of the harm.

In the United States, Certified Public Accountants (CPAs) have both common law liability and statutory law liability. Common law liability arises from negligence, breach of contract and fraud. Statutory law liability is the obligation that comes from a certain statute or law. The sources can be summarized as follows:

- **Privity:** CPAs and their clients enter into a contract to perform certain services. Liability occurs when there is a breach of contract. This would apply when the CPAs do not perform what they stated in the engagement letter.
- **Negligence:** Negligence can be thought of as *failure to exercise professional care*. This can arise from a wrongful act, injury, or damage for which a civil action can be brought. Negligence in turn is dichotomized into *ordinary* and *gross*. Ordinary negligence is defined as failure of duty in accordance with applicable standards and gross negligence occurs when there

is an apparent lack of concern for the likelihood that injuries will result.

- **Fraud:** Fraud is the misrepresentation of a material fact by a people who are aware of their actions and its consequences. There is the intention of misleading the other party, and the other party suffers injury as a result.
- **Statutory liability:** CPAs have statutory liability under both federal and state security laws. Under statutory law, an auditor can be held civilly or criminally liable.

Tort actions are the most common because the monetary awards are substantially higher. Liability can be incurred under common law if a plaintiff can prove that the auditor did not discover financial statement fraud or employee fraud because they were negligent when conducting their audit. The injured party can be a client who has contracted with the auditor for an audit performed according to professional standards and who subsequently feels that contract has been breached by the auditor's (alleged) failure to perform, or the injured party can be a third party or both the client and a third party. The right of the client itself to sue for breach of contract has long been settled law. The right of others, third parties, to sue in the event of an alleged failed audit has evolved over the years. Although this right of third parties has long been contested by auditors on the grounds of lack of privity of contract with the auditor— that the auditor never directly contracted with these parties to perform the audit—the auditor's position in this regard has eroded over the years. We discuss the evolution of auditor liability to third parties, first in the United States and then in key European nations and the European Community (EC).

Common Law Sources of Auditor Liability in the United States

In this section, we discuss the evolution of auditor liability to third parties, first in the United States and then in key European nations and the European Community (EC). In most engagements, the auditor does not know specifically who will be using the financial statements but is aware that *third parties*, that is individuals or organizations other than the client organization and the auditor themselves, will be using them. Generally, the courts have held auditors liable to injured third parties when the auditor has been found guilty of fraud. The fundamental question, however, is who exactly is a third party? Whereas a third party is defined as an outsider who takes action (either investing or lending) based on the auditor's report, there are different types of third parties. The courts differ as to which third party the auditor should be liable to. Overall the rule is *forseeability*, namely, could the auditor have foreseen that a specific party would be adversely affected as a result of an inappropriate opinion?

Forseeability and Negligence in Common Law

The fundamental issue is what a third party must prove to be successful in obtaining damages from an auditor. Overall, third parties must prove that:

- they suffered a loss;
- the loss was due to reliance on misleading financial statements;
- the auditor knew, or should have known, that the financial statements were misleading.

However, courts have varied the standard or burden of proof by the plaintiff, depending on the likelihood that an auditor could reasonably foresee that a user might have relied upon the financial statements or other attestation services provided by the auditor. Generally, less foreseeable plaintiffs have a greater burden in proving that the auditor had a duty to them. However, the courts are not uniform on this issue. Overall, common law is based on court decisions. The most important case in the United States was the Ultramares case (1931).

The Ultramares Case: The Third Party Beneficiary Test

The landmark case of *Ultramares Corporation v. Touche* set the precedent for auditor liability to third parties. It was decided by the New York Court of Appeals in 1931. Judge Cardoza, writing the unanimous decision, expressed concern about expansive auditor liability to third parties. The court held that auditors are liable to third parties for fraud and gross negligence but not for ordinary negligence unless the plaintiff is part of the contract. A third party beneficiary must be specifically identified in the engagement letter as a user for whom the audit is being conducted. That specific identification makes the user a "known" user. For example, assume that a bank requires that an audit be conducted as part of the loan approval process and the name of the bank is specifically mentioned in the engagement letter. If the bank approved the loan based on a *clean* (unqualified) report and circumstances subsequently showed that an unqualified report was inappropriate, then the auditor may be held liable to the bank for ordinary negligence. If the bank had not been named in the engagement letter, however, such liability would not exist. And the auditors could not be sued by the bank as an injured third party.

The precedent set in the Ultramares case dominated judicial thinking for many years and is still followed in many jurisdictions. For example, in 1992, the California Supreme Court upheld the precedent set in the Ultramares case in the case of *Bily v. Arthur Young and Co.* A third party who had dealings with the Osborne Computer Company, which subsequently filed for bankruptcy, sued the auditor on the basis that they had taken action based on a clean opinion provided by the auditor. The plaintiff, Bily, noted that there was no impending warning in the auditor's report to indicate the possibility of the company subsequently failing. The California Supreme Court upheld the Ultramares precedent. It concluded that extending auditor liability to other third parties "raises the spectre of multibillion dollar professional liability that is distinctly out of proportion to: (1) the fault of the auditor; and (2) the connection between the auditor's conduct and third party's injury." However, in the 1980s the Ultramares precedent was amended by what was referred to as the *foreseen user* and *foreseeable user* tests. These are discussed below.

Expansion of Ultramares: The Identified (Foreseen) User Test

In the 1985 case of *Credit Alliance Corp v. Arthur Andersen and Co*, the New York Court of Appeals broke away from the Ultramares precedent and extended auditor liability for ordinary negligence to what they described as *identified users*. An identified user was defined as "a specific third party who the auditor knows will use the audited financial statements for a particular purpose, even though the identified user is not named in the engagement letter". This is also referred to as the foreseen user test because the auditor is expected to foresee that these users would be impacted by negligence on the part of the auditor.

Expansion of Ultramares: The Foreseeable User Test

Some courts subsequently extended auditor liability to foreseeable users of audited financial statements. This was based on the notion that the environment had changed considerably since 1931. A foreseeable user is a third party who the auditor, in hindsight, could foresee as depending on the auditor's report. In *Rosenblum Inc. v. Adler*, the New Jersey Supreme Court noted that the nature of the economy had changed since the Ultramares case and that auditors act as if a number of potential users rely on their audit opinion. The New Jersey court made it clear, however, that to have a valid claim, foreseeable users must have obtained the financial statements from the client for proper business purposes. This view is upheld by the Wisconsin Supreme Court as well. In *Citizens State Bank v. Timm, Schmidt and Co*, the Wisconsin Supreme Court extended auditor liability to creditors who could foreseeably use the audited financial statements as well. However, it must be noted that this does not apply equally in all states in the United States. Different rules apply in different jurisdictions.

Auditor Civil Liability under Statutory Law

Most countries have statutory laws that affect the civil liabilities of auditors. Securities laws, for example, may impose strict standards on professional accountants. In the United States, the Securities Act of 1933 created the Securities and Exchange Commission (SEC), and the subsequent 1934 Act regulates the trading of securities after their initial issuance. The Securities Act of 1933 requires a company to register with the Securities and Exchange Commission. In order to complete registration, the company must include audited financial statements and numerous other disclosures. If the registration statement is found to be materially misstated both the company and its auditors may be held liable. Plaintiffs need only prove that they suffered a loss because the registration statement was misleading. However, it must be noted that, in order to complete registration, the company must include audited financial statements along with numerous other disclosures. In order to avoid liability, the auditor must prove that the audit was performed with due diligence; that the plaintiff's losses were not caused by misstated financial statements; and that the plaintiffs knew of the misstatement at the time the securities were purchased. The Securities Exchange Act of 1934 requires all public companies under SEC jurisdiction to file an annual audit and have quarterly review of financial statements. A review of financial statements is a much less detailed look at the process that generated the financial statements than would be found happening in an audit. It involves making inquiries of management and using analytical procedures (analyses of the relationships between numbers on the financial statements, for example) to acquire a limited assurance that the financial statements are not misstated.

Further, the Securities and Exchange Act of 1934 in the United States requires every company with securities traded on national and over the counter exchanges to submit audited financial statements annually. These are the most common periodic reports:

- **Annual reports to shareholders and 10Ks:** 10Ks are corporate annual reports filed with the SEC. Both contain audited financial statements as well as other descriptive information on the company.
- **Quarterly financial reports to shareholders and 10Qs:** 10Qs are quarterly reports filed with the SEC. 10Qs must be filed within 45 days of the end of each of the first three quarters and must be reviewed by the auditors.

The Act sets out (Rule 10b-5) criminal liability conditions if the auditor employs any device, scheme, or artifice to defraud or make any untrue statement of a material fact or omits to state a material fact, that is, the auditor intentionally or recklessly misrepresents information for third party use. The SEC also has authority to sanction or suspend an auditor from doing audits for SEC-registered companies.

These laws established the first statutory civil recovery rules for third parties against auditors. The liability provisions in these laws are similar to common law. The act explicitly makes it unlawful to make any untrue statement of a material fact or to omit to state a material fact that is necessary for understanding the financial statements. In *Herzfeld v. Laventhol, Krekstein, Howarth and Howarth* (1974) the auditors were found liable under the 1934 act for failure to fully disclose the facts and circumstances underlying their qualified opinion. Judge Friendly stated that the auditor cannot be content merely to see that the financial statements meet minimum requirements of GAAP but that the auditor has a duty to inform the public if adherence to GAAP does not fairly portray the economic results of the company being audited.

Under the 1934 act, an auditor may also be held liable for fraud in the purchase or sale of any security. Original purchasers of securities of a newly registered company making a public offering have recourse against the auditor if the financial statements are false or misleading under the Securities Act of 1933. Anyone who purchased securities described in the registration statement (S1) may sue the auditor for material representations or omissions in financial statements published in the S1 if they depended on the auditor's report for their decision to purchase. (The registration statement has key information including, but not limited to: the nature of the business; rights of different classes of securities issued; directors and officer names; material contracts, balance sheets, and income statements covering three preceding fiscal years; any further financial statements which the SEC may deem necessary.) The auditor has the burden of demonstrating that reasonable investigation was conducted or all the loss of the purchaser of securities (plaintiff) was caused by factors other than the misleading financial statements. If the auditor cannot prove this, the plaintiff wins the case.

Criminal Liability under Statutory Law

Rittenberg, Schwieger and Johnstone (2008) note that a professional accountant may be held criminally liable under the laws of a country or district that makes it a criminal offense to defraud another person through knowingly being involved with false financial statements. As an illustration, in the *United States v. Natelli* (1975) two auditors were convicted of criminal liability for certifying the financial statements of National Marketing Corporation that contained inadequate disclosures pertaining to accounts receivable. In *United States v. Weiner* (1975), three auditors were convicted of securities fraud in connection with their audit of Equity Funding Corporation of America. Rittenberg et al. note that the fraud that the company perpetrated was so massive and the audit work so substandard that the court concluded that the auditors must have been aware of the fraud. In *ESM Government Securities v. Alexander Grant and Co* (1985), management revealed to the audit partner that the prior years' financials were misstated and the partner agreed to say nothing in the auditor's report. The partner was convicted of criminal charges for his role in sustaining the fraud and was sentenced to a 12-year prison term.

Auditor legal liability depends on the outcome of the court case. The plaintiff has to prove the case against the auditor in order to establish that liability. Specifically, in order to win a case, the plaintiff must prove the following:

- The auditor has been negligent.
- The auditor owes a duty of care to the plaintiff.
- The plaintiff incurred losses because of the negligence of the auditor.
- The plaintiff can quantify the extent of the loss suffered as a result of the auditor's negligence.

The action taken against the auditors can vary depending on the perceived extent of the negligence. The sanction can be a fine, a reprimand (oral or written), a suspension for a limited period of time, or in the worst case scenario, a lifetime ban from the profession.

In the United States, these trials can be public and the verdicts too are made public, especially if the verdict is severe such as a suspension or life time ban. The auditor has the right to appeal against the verdicts.

The issues discussed in the preceding section can be summarized as follows:

Applicable Laws and Regulations

In the United States, auditors are liable under contract law, common law, and statutory law. Under contract law, liability is based on breach of contract. Under common law, liability concepts are developed from court decisions such as those discussed above. Under statutory law, liability is based on federal securities laws primarily. To the auditing profession, the most important of these statutes are the Securities Act of 1933 and the Securities Exchange Act of 1934. These have been discussed earlier.

Who is Liable

There is a general misconception that an audit partner who signed the audit report is solely liable. This is not true. The audit report is signed with the name of the audit firm, for example, EY. Although the partner who oversees the audit is responsible for ensuring that the audit is carried out in accordance with professional standards, all partners jointly have to bear the losses in the event of a lawsuit.

To Whom May the Auditor Be Liable

The auditors can be held liable to clients in accordance with the terms of the contracts between them (usually the engagement letter). Auditors can be held liable to clients under contract law for breach of contract and can be sued by the client under the concepts of negligence, gross negligence, and fraud. Auditors can also be held liable by an approach established in the Ultramares case to assess the liability of an auditor for negligent misrepresentation. Prior to the Ultramares test, it was held that an accountant may be liable to any person whom the accountant could reasonably have foreseen would obtain and rely on the accountant's opinion. Thus, the auditor's liability was broad. The Ultramares test limits a CPAs liability. This limits the accountant's liability to a noncontractual third party who relied on an inaccurate financial statement to his or her detriment only if the accountant was aware that the report was to be used for a particular purpose. If the auditor was not aware or could not have foreseen the user(s), then the auditor is not liable.

Liability Cap

There are no caps on liability. Thus the auditor can be sued for an unlimited amount, though in practice, the court rules what they determine to be a justifiable amount.

Limitation Period (Statute of Limitations)

A statute of limitations refers to an enactment in a common law legal system that sets the maximum time after an event that legal proceedings can be initiated. The limitation period for an auditor (i.e., the period in which to sue an auditor) varies by state. In New York, for example, the Civil Practices Act requires that law suits must be commenced within two years after the event. In California, the time limit favors the plaintiff by stating that the statute does not begin when the event took place but rather when a victim realizes that the accountant's incorrect advice (clean audit report which was not justified, for example) was the cause of the suffering.

Legal Liability in Europe

We now consider legal liability in Europe. In Europe, individual shareholders, creditors, and prospective purchasers of the audited company are all in a position to rely on the statutory auditor's report and, as a result, suffer damages. It must be noted that the extent of auditor's duty of care, the amount and nature of the damages that can be granted, and the time period to file a law suit against the auditor (statute of limitations) are different from the United States and can vary by country in Europe. The discussion that follows is based on a report published by the European Economic Commission in 2005 entitled *A study on systems of civil liability of statutory auditors in the context of a single market for auditing services in the European Union* (hereafter referred to as the EEC Report).

According to the EEC report the basis for legal liability varies by country and this is a matter that auditors in the United States should be keenly aware of. In some countries, there are no specific statutory regulations (e.g., Denmark, Ireland, Luxemburg, Netherlands, and the United Kingdom). Hence, in these countries, only general rules civil liability are applied to auditors. Some countries have specific statutory regulations that apply only to auditors (Austria, Belgium, Finland, Germany, Greece, Portugal,

Table 2.1 Comparison of auditor liability by country in the European Union and elsewhere

Country	To audited (client) entities	To third parties
Austria	Contractual	Contractual/Tort
Belgium	Contractual/Tort	Tort
Denmark	Contractual	Tort
Finland	Tort	Tort
France	Tort	Tort
Germany	Contractual/Tort	Contractual/Tort
Greece	Contractual	Tort
Ireland	Contractual/Tort	Tort
Italy	Contractual	Tort
Luxemburg	Contractual	Tort
Netherlands	Contractual	Tort
Portugal	Contractual/Tort	Contractual/Tort
Spain	Contractual	Tort
Sweden	Contractual	Tort
UK	Contractual/Tort	Tort
United States	Contractual/Tort	Contractual \ Tort

Spain and Sweden). A summary of the EEC Report in 2005 is provided in Table 2.1. Table 2.1 shows, by nation, whether auditors are subject to liability for torts, contractual breaches, or both. The definition of torts is the commission of a civil (noncriminal) wrong that unfairly causes others to suffer damage or harm, including losses. Committing a tort results in legal liability for the person who committed that act. Torts may be due to negligence and may not necessarily constitute a crime. Torts, unlike criminal acts, are provable by a preponderance of the evidence. They do not require evidence showing guilt beyond a reasonable doubt. Contractual liability, in contrast, exists when a contract exists between individuals and one of the parties to the contract fails to perform his or her obligations under the contract. This is often called breach of contract. A key difference between tort law and contract lawsuits is the way damages are awarded. The purpose of damage awards in breach of contracts law suits is to restore the parties to their position before the breach occurred. In a torts claim, in contrast, the damages awarded serve to compensate the victims for the harm they suffered.

The EEC report notes that every country, except Finland and France, bases liability towards the audited company on the contract entered into between the auditor and the audited company. This situation is justified by the fact that the mission, though statutory in nature, arises from a contractual relationship between such parties.

The law concerning civil liability of statutory auditors in the various member states of the EU is summarized in the following section. (All information shown here is obtained from the EEC Report.)

Austria

Applicable Law and Regulations

Auditors are liable contractually and by tort. Contractual liability is based on the general rule as modified by Section *275 of the Handelsgesetzbuch* (HGB). Tortious liability is governed by the general rules set forth in court cases.

Who is Liable

Not only the statutory auditor (either an individual or an audit firm) but also all his assistants as well as the statutory representatives of the auditing firm are directly liable to the injured party. All liable parties are jointly and severally liable.

To Whom May the Auditor Be Liable

The plaintiff in a suit brought under HGB Section 275 may be the audited company (i.e., the contracting party) or a company affiliated with the audited company as set forth in HGB Section 228.3. Liability towards third parties, which is possible under restrictive conditions, is based in tort, unless the court recognizes the existence of an implied contract between the third party and the auditor or of a contract with protective effects towards the third party.

Liability Cap

Under this specific statutory provision of HGB Section 275, liability cannot be waived nor limited. However, the liability of all possible defendants who did not act intentionally is limited to an amount of 364,000 Euros per audit

Limitation Period

The statute of limitations is five years from the occurrence of the damage, instead of three according to the general rules for civil liability applicable in the case of tort liability.

Belgium

Applicable Laws and Regulations

In addition to the general rules of civil liability, the liability of statutory auditors falls within a specific legal framework. Article 64 of the Loi coordomnee sure les societes commerciales (LCSC) describes the duties of the auditor and the conditions of his liability.

Who is Liable

The statutory auditor, whether an audit firm or an individual, may be liable. The signing persons and the associates may also be jointly and severally liable.

To Whom May the Auditor Be Liable

Auditors may be liable towards the audited company and third parties. The liability towards the audited company is based either on the contract between the company and the statutory auditor, or in tort, the liability towards third parties is based in tort.

Liability Cap

There is no legal liability cap, and the parties cannot limit the amount of damages nor reduce the scope of auditor liability in the contract in a separate agreement.

Limitation Period

The limitation period for both contractual and tortious actions is five years from the occurrence of the damage.

Denmark

Applicable Law and Regulations

The liability of auditors arises from the general rules of liability to which reference is made in Section 141 of the Danish Companies Act as developed by case law.

Who is Liable

Both the individual statutory auditor in charge of the audit and the audit firm are liable. Associates who participated in the audit will not be liable under Danish law.

To Whom May the Auditor Be Liable

The statutory auditor's liability to the audited company also extends to third parties from a breach of duty in tort.

Liability Cap

There is no statutory liability cap, but the auditor and the audited company may reduce the obligations of the statutory auditor by contract and set a liability cap. Such an agreement has no effect on third parties.

Limitation Period

The action can be brought within five years from the discovery of negligence. This period can be reduced by contract. Any such reduction is effective only between the statutory auditor and the audited company.

Finland

The auditor is liable under specific liability provisions based on Section 44 of the Act on Auditing Tilimtarkastuslaki (TTL). This act does not include any provisions on specific issues such as the calculation of damages, causation, or the level of breach of duty or contributory negligence of the plaintiff. In this regard, general principles of civil law are applied to damages caused in a contractual relationship.

Who is Liable

An action in tort under TTL 44 can be brought against the statutory auditor, whether an individual or an audit firm. In this case, the signing person is also liable. The associates may also be held liable.

To Whom May the Auditor Be Liable

The action in tort under TTL 44 is available to the audited company, its shareholders and members, and to any third party. As a consequence, the action in contract is of lesser interest because a wide variety of third parties can sue the auditor.

Liability Cap

There is no statutory liability cap, and contractual limitations to the statutory auditor's liability do not exist in Finland, although they are possible in theory.

Limitation Period

The limitation period depends on the plaintiff. The limitation period is three years from the signature of the report if the plaintiff is the audited company and ten years from the occurrence of the damage if the plaintiff is a third party.

France

Applicable Law and Regulations

The statutory auditor's liability is governed by a specific provision contained in Article 234 of the Company Law. This provision is considered to be no more than an application of the general civil liability rules of Article 1382 of the Civil Code, the concepts of fault, damages, and causation being the same.

Who is Liable

The statutory auditor, whether an audit firm or an individual qualified auditor, may be liable. If the appointed auditor is a firm, the signatory of the report is jointly and severally liable with the other partners of the firm. The associates cannot be liable under the specific provision of the company law.

To Whom May the Auditor Be Liable

The auditor is liable towards the audited company, its shareholders, and any third parties.

Liability Cap

There is no legal liability cap, and the parties cannot limit the amount of damages nor reduce the scope of the auditor's liability in the contract or in a separate agreement.

Limitation Period

The action must be brought within three years from the damage-causing event.

Germany

Applicable Law and Regulations

Statutory auditors liability arises from the general rules for civil liability in tort as well as from specific statutory provisions for statutory auditors as contained in Article 323 of the law, which provides for contractual liability of auditors. Some of the statutory provisions applicable to auditor liability are also found in the professional rules contained in the Act on the Profession of Auditors (Wirtschaftspriferordnung).

Who is Liable

Under Section 323, not only the statutory auditor but also all his assistants as well as the statutory representatives of an auditing company participating in the audit are directly liable to the injured party. All liable parties are jointly and severally liable.

To Whom May the Auditor Be Liable

The plaintiff in a suit brought under article 323 of the law can be the audited company or a company affiliated to the audited company. An action may not be brought by the audited company in tort if the auditor fails to meet his contractual obligations under Article 323. The liability towards third parties, which is possible under restrictive conditions, is based in tort (unless the court recognizes the existence of an implied contract between the third party and the auditor).

Liability Cap

Under the specific statutory provision of Article 323, liability can neither be waived nor limited. An auditor's contractual liability is limited to 4 million deutsche marks (1 million to 4 million deutsche marks depending on the circumstances).

Limitation Period

Action in contract should be brought within five years from when all elements of claim exist. The statute of limitation for an action in tort is three years from discovery of damages and the liable party.

Greece

Applicable Law and Regulation

Greek law distinguishes between common auditors and chartered auditors, who have specific professional responsibilities. Liability arises from general rules of law (civil code, penal code) and specific provisions, which include:

- Codified law 2190, which sets forth civil liability of auditors towards the company.

- Presidential decree 226/1992 concerning the establishment, organization and operation of the Corps of Chartered Auditors. Article 19 of the Decree also contains special provisions, which limit the civil liability of chartered auditors.

Who is Liable

The appointed statutory auditor and the statutory auditor's associates are liable for the damages caused by the conduct of the audit. If the appointed auditor is a firm, the signatory of the report is jointly and severally liable along with the firm.

To Whom May the Auditor Be Liable

The statutory auditor's liability to the audited company arises from the existence of a contract and to any third parties from a breach of duty in tort.

Liability Cap

The parties cannot limit the legal liability of the auditor by contract. The liability cap is either the quintuple of the annual salary (salaries) or the total amount of fee received by the chartered auditor during the previous fiscal year, whichever is higher.

Limitation Period

For the audited company, the limitation period is two years and starts when all elements of claim exist. Third parties should sue the auditor within five years from the discovery of the damages and the liable party and, in any case, within twenty years from the commission of the act.

Ireland

Applicable Law and Regulations

Liability arises from the general common law rules for civil liability (breach of contract, breach of statutory duty or tort) but claims could be raised if the auditors fail to meet their statutory obligations contained in the Companies Act of 1963 and 1990. Section 163 of the Companies Act of 1963 and Sections 193 and 194 of the Companies Act 1990 state the scope of the auditor's work and his main duties.

Who is Liable

If the statutory auditor is an individual, the action will be brought against that person. If the statutory auditor is a partnership, each partner is jointly and severally liable. The associates may also be liable, but there has not been any instance where this has occurred.

To Whom May the Auditor Be Liable

The audited company may bring an action in contract or in tort against the auditor, depending on the duty breached. Third parties may bring an action in tort under restrictive conditions.

Liability Cap

There is no legal liability cap, and the parties cannot limit the amount of damages nor reduce the scope of auditor liability in the contract or in a separate agreement.

Limitation Period

The limitation period is six years from the breach of contract and or from the occurrence of damage for both contractual and tort actions.

Italy

Applicable Law and Regulations

Statutory auditor's liability is governed by specific provisions, which set forth two different liability systems applicable, respectively, to the Board of Auditors or to the auditing firm. Article 2407 of the Civil Code provides for the liability of the Board of Auditors, based on the duty of diligence of an agent. The liability of auditing firms is governed by Article 164 of the Legislative Decree of February 24, 1998, which refers to Article 2407 of the Civil Code.

Who is Liable

The appointed auditor (firm or individual) is liable. If the statutory auditor is a firm, the signatory of the report is also liable. The auditor member of the Board of Auditors is liable for the damages caused by his associates, whereas the associates of an auditing firm are jointly and severally liable with the firm.

To Whom May the Auditor Be Liable

The statutory auditor's liability to the audited company arises due to being under contract, and to any third parties from a breach of duty in tort. A tort, in common law jurisdictions, is a civil wrong which unfairly causes someone else to suffer loss or harm. This results in legal liability for the party that commits the tortious act.

Liability Cap

There is no legal liability cap, and the parties cannot limit the amount of damages nor reduce the scope of auditor liability in the contract or in a separate agreement.

Limitation Period

The action against the Board of auditors should be brought within five years from discovery of the damage. The limitation period of the actions against auditing firms is either 10 years (if the damage is suffered by the audited company) or five years (if the plaintiff is a third party).

Luxembourg

Applicable Law and Regulations

The general legal rules for liability set forth in Article 1142 (contractual liability) as well as in Articles 1382 and 1383 (tortious liability) govern the liability of statutory auditors.

Who is Liable

In case of a breach of the contract, the appointed auditor only is liable, whether the appointed auditor is a firm or an individual person. In tort, the appointed auditor is liable together with the signing person and the associates for the damages they caused in the course of the audit.

To Whom May the Auditor Be Liable

The statutory auditor's liability to the audited company arises due to being under contract and to any third parties from a breach of duty in tort.

Liability Cap

There is no legal liability cap. The audited company and the appointed auditor may set forth such a limitation by contract. However, this does not affect the tortious liability of the auditor towards third parties.

Limitation Period

The limitation period is five years from the signature of the report.

The Netherlands

Applicable Law and Regulations

There is no specific provision in the Dutch Civil Code, which deals with the liability of statutory auditors. General rules of civil liability, as enforced by the courts are, thus, applicable.

Who is Liable

In case of a breach of contract, the appointed auditor only is liable, whether the auditor is a firm or an individual person. In tort, the committer of the tort is liable together with the associates and the signing person, if any, for the damages they caused in the course of the audit.

To Whom May the Auditor Be Liable

The appointed auditor is liable towards the company for any breach of contract. Tortious liability towards third parties is not automatic. It requires specific circumstances showing breach of a duty of care that the auditor owes to a third party.

Liability Cap

There is no statutory liability cap, but the auditor and the audited company may include a clause in the contract reducing the liability. Such an agreement has no effect on third parties.

Limitation Period

The action should be brought within five years from the discovery of the damage and the liable party and, in any case, within 20 years from the event that caused the damage.

Portugal

Applicable Law and Regulations

The general rules of civil liability apply to statutory auditors. Tortious liability is governed by Article 483 of the civil code. There are, however, specific statutory provisions, the most important of which are:

- Articles 78, 81, and 82 of the Codigo das Sociedades Comerciais (CSC), which establish the auditor liability towards the audited company, the shareholders, and the creditors;
- Article 114 of Decreto Lie 487/99, dated 16 November 1999, which extends the scope of these provisions to the auditing firms;
- Article 10 of the Codigo de Mercado de Valores Mobiliarios, which aims to protect investors and third parties through an extended liability of stock listed company's auditors; and

- Article 13 of the Codigo de Processo Tributario, which governs the liability of the auditor if the company cannot pay off its taxes.

Even where these provisions apply, the general rules of liability of the Civil Code provide the rules applicable for civil liability because these specific provisions do not include a complete regime.

Who is Liable

The appointed auditor and, if the auditor is a firm, the signatory of the report are jointly and severally liable. There are three qualifications to this general rule:

- The managers of the auditing company (usually the partners) may be liable towards the creditors of the audited company.
- The partners of the audit firm appointed as auditor of a stock listed company may be jointly and severally liable.
- The associates who participated in the audit may be liable, but this has not occurred in practice.

To Whom May the Auditor Be Liable

The statutory auditor's liability to the audited company arises in contract or in tort and to any third parties mainly from a breach of duty in tort, some of which are legally defined as stated earlier.

Liability Cap

There is no legal liability cap, and the parties cannot limit the amount of damages nor reduce the scope of the auditor's liability in the contract or in a separate agreement.

Limitation Period

The action should be brought within a period of five years from the discovery of negligence.

Spain

Applicable Laws and Regulations

The civil liability of statutory auditors is provided for by Articles 11 and 12 of Law 19/1988 of 12 July 1988 on the Audit of Accounts (Ley de Auditoria de Cuentas) and Articles 42 and 45 of Royal Decree 1636/1990 of 20 December 1990 approving the regulation of the Audit of Accounts. There is also a specific reference to auditors liability in Article 211 of the law of public companies (Ley de Sociedades Anonimas) approved by Royal Legislative Decree 1564/1989 of 22 December 1989. However, these provisions do not contain a full and complete set of rules and it is generally acknowledged that they should be construed as a reference to the general provisions regulating civil liability under Spanish law, namely (1) Articles 1101 et seq. of the Civil Code for contractual liability and (2) Articles 1902 et seq of the Civil Code for tortious liability.

Who is Liable

The statutory auditor, whether an individual or a firm, may be liable. The audit firm and the partner in charge of the work are jointly and severally liable. Once the remedies are exhausted against them, the other partners of the firm are also jointly and severally liable. Auditors are liable for the damages caused by their associates.

To Whom May the Auditor Be Liable

The statutory auditor's liability to the audited company arises in contract. Their tortious liability towards third parties is subject to restrictive conditions.

Liability Cap

There is no statutory liability cap, but the auditor and the audited company may agree to a liability cap. Such an agreement has no effect on third parties.

Limitation Period

The audited company should bring the action within fifteen years from when all elements of claim exist. The statute of limitation for an action in tort is one year from discovery of damages.

Sweden

Applicable Law and Regulations

Civil liability for statutory auditors is specifically regulated in Chapter 15, Section 2 Swedish Companies Act. A statutory auditor may also be liable under the general damage rules of the Tort Liability Act. The damage suffered by the company or third parties in consequence of the acts or omissions of a statutory auditor will, however, usually be deemed pure financial damage (i.e., damage incurred without connection to bodily injury or property damage), which is in principle recoverable only if it is the result of a criminal offence.

Who is Liable

The appointed statutory auditor and, in case the auditor is an audit firm, the signatory of the report, are jointly and severally liable. The auditor is also liable for the damages caused by the associates.

To Whom May the Auditor Be Liable

The statutory auditor's liability to the audited company arises due to being under contract and to any third parties from a breach of duty in tort.

Liability Cap

There is no legal liability cap, and the parties cannot limit the amount of damages nor reduce the scope of the auditor's liability in the contract or in a separate agreement.

Limitation Period

For the audited company, the limitation period is five years from the end of the fiscal year. The third parties should sue the auditor within ten years from the occurrence of the damage.

United Kingdom

Applicable Law and Regulations

In the absence of applicable statutory provisions, liability arises from general rules of common law for civil liability.

Who is Liable

The statutory auditor (an individual or an audit firm) and, if the firm is a partnership, any or all of the partners, may be liable for the damages they as well as their associates caused. If the statutory auditor is not an audit firm, the signatory of the report is also liable.

To Whom May the Auditor Be Liable

The statutory auditor's liability to the audited company arises concurrently in contract and in tort. The auditor may be liable to third parties under restrictive conditions.

Liability Cap

There is no legal cap, and the parties cannot limit the amount of damages nor reduce the scope of the auditor's liability in the contract or in a separate agreement.

Limitation Period

In principle, the action must be brought within six years after the occurrence of the damage-causing event (the breach of contract if the claim is based on contract, the date when damage is suffered if the action is based on tort).

Recent Developments in Auditor Regulation in the United States and Elsewhere

The Sarbanes Oxley Act of 2002 in the United States: The accounting scandals begun by the Enron collapse and extending to such giant companies as WorldCom, Xerox, and Tyco caused a backlash in the United States, resulting in legislation being signed into law by the U.S. president in July 2002. The Sarbanes Oxley Act (SOX) is the first accounting law passed by the United States since the Securities and Exchange Act of 1934. The SOX was named after sponsors Paul Sarbanes and U.S. Representative Michael G. Oxley.

The act has new requirements for audit firms and audit committees. Auditors must report to the audit committee, not management. The lead audit partner and audit review partner must be rotated every five years. It is believed that periodic rotation of partners helps bring a fresh approach to audits and minimize bias that may result from long term contacts with client management. To help assure auditor independence SOX prohibits registered public accounting firms from performing certain services for public company audit clients. The law prohibits the following:

- Bookkeeping or other services related to the accounting records or financial statements of the audit client
- Financial information systems design and implementation
- Actuarial services
- Internal audit outsourcing services
- Management functions or human resources
- Broker or dealer, investment adviser, or investment banking services
- Legal services and expert services unrelated to the audit

SOX requires that the audit committee of a public company be responsible for assessing an audit firm's independence prior to hiring that firm. In addition, it requires that any nonaudit services to be performed by its audit firm must be preapproved by the audit committee (and also be approved after the fact) unless such services, in the aggregate, amount to less than 5 percent of the total amount paid to its audit firm during the year. To emphasize, the after the fact approval relates to amounts less than five percent. Nonaudit services not banned by the Act must be pre-approved by the audit committee. Rittenberg, Schwieger, and Johnstone (1998) note that the AICPA's Code of Professional Conduct allows public accounting firms to perform services not specifically prohibited for non-public audit clients if the firm determines that independence will not be compromised.

In the United States, the SEC approved updated New York Stock Exchange (NYSE) listing standards in November 2003. According to the NYSE, listed companies MUST maintain an internal audit function to provide management and the audit committee with ongoing assessments of the company's risk management processes and system of internal control. In Europe, there is a duty assigned to the board and its audit committee by article 41 of the EU 8th Directive. This directive puts internal auditing as part of the *cornerstone* of corporate governance because audit committees can look to the internal audit department for assurance of good organizational governance.

The directive states that the firm is advised to establish an understanding with the client that the client is responsible for:

- designating management level individuals to be responsible for overseeing the services being provided;
- evaluating the adequacy of the services performed and any resulting findings; and
- making management decisions related to the service.

SOX required the SEC to create a Public Company Accounting Oversight Board (PCAOB). The PCAOB is empowered to regularly inspect registered accounting firms' operations and investigate potential violations of securities laws, standards, consistency, and conduct. The Board oversees and investigates the audits and auditors of public companies and sanctions both firms and individuals for violations of laws, regulations, and rules. The PCAOB has a wide ambit including not only auditors based in the United States but any firm registered with the SEC, irrespective of whether such a firm is headquartered in the United States or not. In essence SOX created the new requirements listed above and then created the PCAOB to establish additional oversight and rules.

The SOX act requires auditors to report on internal control. Hayes et al. note that support for reporting lies in the belief that users of financial information have a legitimate interest in the condition of the controls over the accounting system and management's response to the suggestions of the auditors for correction of weaknesses. This issue is not without dispute. Opponents argue that requiring companies to evaluate and report on controls significantly increases the costs of audits without significantly enhancing the quality of financial reporting. Section 404 of the SOX and PCAOB Audit Standard No. 5 requires each annual report of a company to contain a report from the management, which has to state in clear words that (a) management takes responsibility for establishing and maintaining adequate internal controls and (b) makes an assessment of and comments on the effectiveness of the internal controls. The report also has to have a report by the auditors on management's report on the internal control over financial reporting.

Non-United States Equivalents to SOX of the United States

Australia

In Australia, the Corporate Law Economic Reform Program Act 1999 established a new body, the Financial Reporting Council (FRC), with the responsibility for the broad oversight of the accounting and auditing standard setting process. The FRC is also required to review developments with respect to international accounting and auditing standards. The FRC is required to review these standards, and, if in their opinion the changes in the standards are relevant to Australia, make changes to Australian standards to ensure that these standards are up to date with those of the rest of the world.

Europe

In 2004, the Commission of the European Union proposed a major revision of the Eighth Company Directive, setting out a new structure for audit and corporate governance. Hayes et al. (2005) note that the proposal is the consequence of a reorientation of the EU policy on statutory audit that started in 1996 with a Green Paper on the role and responsibility of the statutory auditor in the EU. The proposal considerably broadens the scope of the existing Eighth Council Directive that basically deals with the approval of auditors. With reference to publicly listed companies, the proposal:

- Clearly explains the role and duties of statutory auditors (the term statutory auditor is another term for auditor used in Europe).
- Clearly explains the role required of auditors to maintain their independence and also provides ethical guidelines to auditors. Basic principles of professional ethics and auditor independence are defined. With respect to the role required by auditors to maintain their independence, the issues outlined follow closely the guidelines established by SOX discussed earlier.
- Creates an audit regulatory committee to ensure public oversight over the audit profession (equivalent to the PCAOB established by SOX in the United States).
- Identifies the steps to enhance audit quality within the EU. These steps include auditors being required to constantly enhance their knowledge with the latest developments in the auditing world.
- Sets forth requirement that all auditor firms wanting to conduct audits involving EU countries be registered with the EU. Further, an audit firm in any country within the EU can audit a firm in any other country within the EU without any hindrance. However, clear rules are provided to prevent *low balling*. This means preventing audit firms from other EU countries entering a member EU country and offering audit services and nonaudit services at much lower fees relative to the home country. All companies are required to state clearly in the notes to the financial statements the amount of audit fees and fees for nonaudit services provided to the auditor. Management is required to sign that all information provided is accurate.
- Sets forth that auditors should use international auditing standards for audits in EU countries (not U.S. auditing standards).

- Sets forth that common rules for all EU countries for the appointment and termination of statutory auditors. Companies are also required to document all communication with their auditors.
- Sets forth that, in the case of disciplinary actions having to be taken against an auditor, the local rules in an EU country where the violation has occurred are used to sanction or punish the auditors.

This chapter provided a summary of legal liability of auditors both in the United States and Europe. It is important for auditors to be aware of what criteria are used in different countries to establish liability as this can vary between countries. We described the differences in rules and regulations and discuss liability and limitations to liability pertinent to auditors operating in a global arena.

Implications for Researchers, Managers, and Students

This chapter has described features of the legal system in various countries that affect the auditor with respect to their responsibility to the client. For example, this chapter discussed different criteria used in different countries to establish liability. Understanding the sources of auditor legal liability is important to a manager because it helps raise the manager's awareness of the auditor's responsibility. Accordingly, when the auditor does not seem to fulfill that responsibility, the manager can search for a remedy. Also, in learning about the different kinds of legal liability of an auditor, the manager understands why the auditor may insist on certain things that may appear unnecessary to the manager during the audit. The brief summary of applicable legal considerations in this chapter would be of help to the researcher in the pursuit of their own research agenda. This chapter provides the student of business what they need to know about the auditor's legal liability and thus the auditor's role and actions, which in turn, may be useful in the student's own studies or research. This information can also be used as a starting point for further exploration.

CHAPTER 3

Ethics for International Auditors

Introduction

It is vital that auditors in the United States understand the minimum set of ethical rules required by The International Federation of Accountants (IFAC) and the differences between these ethical standards set forth by the International Ethics Standards Board of Accounting (IESBA) component of the IFAC— standards that set the minimum standards that member organizations are permitted to formulate and enforce upon their own members—and the ethical standards enforced on public company auditors in the United States by the Public Company Accounting Oversight Board (PCAOB). Auditors must always comply with the ethical standards of their licensing body (e.g., a state board of accountancy in the United States) even if they are performing an audit in a jurisdiction (say Great Britain) that follows ISA. It is impossible to explore all the various combinations of ethical standards and sets of auditing standards (e.g., ISA) that can be encountered in practice. Accordingly, here we make a simplifying assumption that auditors in the United States, on public company audits, must follow PCAOB ethical standards while auditors in Great Britain must follow IFAC's IESBA ethical standards. In this chapter we:

- define ethics and discuss the key components of ethics;
- discuss relevant international ethical standards with special focus on standards that are
  - ○ required to maintain an auditor's independence; and
  - ○ demonstrate key differences between international and U.S. standards on ethics.

Definition of Ethics

Hayes et al. (2005) define ethics as a set of moral principles, rules of conduct, or values. Ethics apply when an individual has to make a decision about various alternatives, with the alternatives having different moral consequences. The IFAC Code of Ethics for Professional Accountants states "The objectives of the accountancy profession are to work in the highest standards of professionalism, to attain the highest levels of performance and generally to meet the public interest" (p.16). The guidance is incorporated into the code (accessible at http://www.ifac.org). This code, which is specifically developed by the IESBA component of the IFAC, is intended to serve as a model on which to base national ethical guidance. It sets minimum standards for ethical codes of conduct that member organizations of the IFAC are permitted to use in setting standards for professional accountants who belong to those organizations. It seeks convergence between the IESBA's standards and those of other national ethics-setting boards, with member organizations of the IFAC required to employ ethics standards at least as stringent as those contained in the IESBA's code. Thus, an auditor who is licensed by a member organization of IFAC must comply with that member organization's ethical standards. Given that standards of member organizations of IFAC must be at least as strict as those of IFAC's IESBA itself, that auditor must comply with the stricter of the two sets of ethical standards. Similarly, an auditor who is both licensed by a state board of accountancy in the United States and is performing a PCAOB-related audit must follow the stricter of two sets of ethical rules, the state board's ethics rules or the PCAOB's ethics rules. As of June 1, 2014, 117 nations contained at least one accounting organization, which belonged to the IFAC. Some nations had more than one organization as a participating IFAC member. In the United States, both the American Institute of Certified Public Accountants (AICPA) and the Institute of Management Accountants were member organizations of the IFAC. Additional organizations, some in countries that had organizations that were members of the IFAC, were *associated* with the IFAC, and other countries contained organizations that were *affiliated* to the IFAC. As of June 1, 2014, the PCAOB was neither a member, associate, nor an affiliate of the IFAC.

IFAC member organizations are required to demonstrate that they are taking steps to remain in good standing, while associate member organizations are required to demonstrate that they are making progress towards membership (see www.ifac.org/about-ifac/membership/compliance-program). The IFAC states that its "…member organizations are required to apply ethical standards *at least as stringent* as the Code. Convergence to a single set of standards can enhance the quality and consistency of services provided by professional accountants throughout the world and can improve the efficiency of global capital markets. The Code requires professional accountants to comply with five fundamental principles: integrity; objectivity; professional competence and due care; confidentiality; and professional behavior." Each member organization is required to provide and regularly update evidence of the steps it is taking to remain in compliance with the code in order to remain in good standing. Assuming compliance with this requirement and the effectiveness of the compliance monitoring program, it would appear that all member organizations in each of the 117 nations have ethics codes at least as stringent as those of the IFAC. How well these codes are actually enforced in a membership that girdles the globe is a different matter, one beyond the limits of this book. IFAC itself notes that, with respect to business ethics, "application of business ethics differs depending on the country, culture, and traditions, as well as the level of maturity in terms of regulation and enforcement of organizations' legal responsibility and the expectations and duties of directors." While this IFAC statement specifically addresses business ethics as opposed to professional accounting ethics, it has clear applicability to the accounting field as well (e.g., Kleinman, Lin, and Palmon 2014).

Understanding how well or poorly even ethics codes that have been converged between IFAC member organizations function is one thing; understanding how uniformly and effectively these consistent ethics codes have been or are being enforced on the individuals who belong to the IFAC member organizations is another. That latter task is beyond what can be accomplished here. Kleinman, Lin, and Palmon (2014), for example, note the many ways that accounting regulation's effectiveness may differ between countries due to national culture, religion, and other factors despite the overall similarity of regulatory structure. We take the approach that the IFAC standards are followed by the member organizations and that the member organizations enforce these standards on individuals who are their members. The PCAOB, though, is neither a member nor an associate of the IFAC and, therefore, is not required to have its ethics code converge with that of the IFAC's code, as set forth by the IESBA. Accordingly, the rest of the chapter proceeds with a comparison between the IFAC's own code and the ethics rules used by the PCAOB. Given that the PCAOB, with its Auditing Standard 1, adopted on April 16, 2003, adopted as its own the then extant AICPA ethics standards, there may be few differences between the IFAC standards and the PCAOB standards.

Familiarity with both IFAC's IESBA Code of Ethics for Professional Accountants (IESBA Code), in addition to the AICPA Code of Professional Conduct (AICPA Code), is very important for auditors. According to Allen (2010) writing in the Journal of Accountancy, the IESBA and AICPA codes are quite similar. However, some differences are significant. It is important to briefly review these differences. Some key differences are:

- **Presentation of Code:** The IESBA Code is divided into three parts: Part A applies to all professional accountants; Part B to persons in public accounting; and Part C to everyone who is not in public practice. The AICPA does not currently apportion its principles and rules in this manner. This is true in both the old AICPA Code of Ethics and the revised AICPA Code of Ethics issued on June 1, 2014, with an implementation date of December 15, 2014. The revised AICPA code notes that members in practice should consult other relevant sets of ethics rules in carrying out their responsibilities, whether as auditors or as accountants in business settings. Among the sets of ethics rules that the AICPA Code mentions are the ethics rules set forth by the PCAOB. Accordingly, we focus here on the PCAOB ethics rules for auditors, rules which are binding on all auditors on PCAOB audits, whether or not they are members of the AICPA. The AICPA notes, in the preamble to the new set of ethics rules issued on June 1, 2014, that "By accepting membership, a *member* assumes an obligation of self-discipline above and beyond the requirements of laws and regulations" (AICPA 2014). Thus, AICPA members consulting this book should be aware that they are responsible for adhering to the strictest of PCAOB or AICPA rules. This book, though, is geared to researchers, managers, and students. Accordingly, we focus on comparing ISA ethics rules with PCAOB ethics rules and do not dwell on whether or not the auditor is a member of the AICPA. The PCAOB has not, as yet, changed its own set of ethics rules to fit with those just released (6/1/14) by the AICPA.

- **Principles versus Rules:** The IESBA Code is often referred to as a principles-based code. A principles-based code is used as a conceptual basis for accountants. A simple set of key objectives are set out. Common examples are provided as guidance to explain the objectives. In contrast, the PCAOB code is considered to be more rules based. Rules-based accounting is basically a list of detailed rules that must be followed. The bulk of the IESBA Code provides detailed descriptions on how a principles-based code applies in specific situations. It provides, for example, an illustration of how providing nonassurance services to an audit client may threaten an accounting firm's independence. The code provides many other examples.
- **Differences in Approach:** The IESBA uses a principles-based code to evaluate ethical conduct; the AICPA, on the other hand, only requires members to use this approach if the rules do not address their situation.
- **Topics Addressed:** Both standards address the same topics. However, the IESBA code includes three areas not specifically addressed by AICPA in its ethics code. The first of these, ethical considerations related to the acceptance and continuance of client engagements, is addressed by the PCAOB in the PCAOB's quality control standards, using the AICPA's standards in place before April 16, 2003, that is, the so-called Interim Standards. The second of these, ethical considerations related to the provision of a second opinion on the application of auditing and reporting standards, is addressed in the

PCAOB's AU 625. Finally, the third of these, ethical considerations relating to holding client assets, is not addressed by the PCAOB.

- **Comparing Independence:** The IESBA Code discusses certain potential independence matters that do not appear in the AICPA independence rules. Examples include long association of senior personnel with the client and size of audit fee (namely, how would these affect an auditor's independence).
- **Split Level Independence:** The IESBA splits independence requirements into two sections: Section 290, which provides strong prescriptions for audits and reviews of financial statements, and Section 291, which applies to all other assurance engagements. The AICPA code does not separate its independence standards. The PCAOB adopted the AICPA's AU 220 as it existed as of April 16, 2003, as one of its interim standards.

Commonalities between IESBA and AICPA codes

There are fundamental principles of ethics in these codes that are applicable to all accountants. They are:

- **Integrity:** Section 100.4 of the IESBA Code states that a professional accountant should be straightforward and honest in all professional and business relationships.
- **Objectivity:** The same section of the IESBA Code noted above states that a professional accountant should not allow bias, conflict of interest or undue influence of others to override professional or business judgments.
- **Professional competence and due care:** The same section of the IESBA Code notes that a professional accountant has a continuing duty to maintain professional knowledge and skill at the level required to ensure that a client or employer receives competent professional service based on current developments in practice, legislation, and techniques. The IESBA Code expects that a professional accountant should

act diligently and in accordance with applicable technical and professional standards when providing professional services.

- *Confidentiality:* The IESBA Code requires that a professional accountant should respect the confidentiality of information acquired as a result of professional and business relationships and should not disclose any such information to third parties without proper and specific authority unless there is a legal or professional right of duty to disclose. Confidential information acquired as a result of professional and business relationships should not be used for the personal advantage of the professional accountant or third parties.

When disclosure is authorized by the employer or client, the accountants should consider the interests of all the parties, including third parties who might be affected. Hayes et al. cite two examples that we reproduce here. One example is disclosure of client information required by law when the accountant has to produce documents or give evidence in legal proceedings. Another example is disclosure of infringements of the law to appropriate public authorities. In the United States, accountants may be required to give evidence in court, and in the Netherlands and UK, auditors may be required to disclose fraud to government appointed authorities. Confidentiality of information is part of statutory or common law and, therefore, requirements of confidentiality will depend on the law of the home country of the accountant.

- *Professional behavior:* The IESBA Code notes that a professional accountant should comply with relevant laws and regulations and should avoid any action that discredits the profession.

IFAC notes that an accountant may perform services in a country other than his or her home country. If differences exist between ethical requirements of the two countries, IFAC states that the following provisions should be applied when:

- the ethical requirements of the country in which the services are being performed *are less strict* than the IFAC Code of Ethics, then the ethical guidance of the IFAC should be applied;
- the ethical requirements of the country in which the services are being performed *are stricter* than the IFAC ethical guidance, then the ethical requirements of the country where the services are being performed should be applied; and
- the ethical requirements of the home country are mandatory for services performed outside that country and are stricter than set out in the preceding points, then the ethical requirements of the home country should be applied.

This is applicable to the AICPA Code as well. In this respect, the AICPA and the IFAC appear to have arrived at consistent judgments on this issue. This consistency reflects the AICPA's objective of ensuring commonality with the international code.

Ethical Standards Required by IFAC

The independence of the auditor from the firm that is being audited is one of the basic requirements to ensure public confidence in the reliability of the audit report. Independence adds credibility to the audit report on which investors, creditors, employees, government, and other stakeholders depend to make decisions about a company. Accordingly, we focus on ethics and auditor independence here. As Hayes et al. note that, across the world, national rules on auditors' independence differ in several respects. Differences cited by Hayes include:

- the scope of persons to whom independence rules should apply;
- the kind of financial, business, or other relationships that an auditor may have with the audit client;
- the type of nonaudit services that can and cannot be provided to an audit client; and
- the safeguards which should be used.

In the United States, the Sarbanes Oxley Act of 2002 provides limited independence requirements, requirements which are consistent with the preferences of the U.S. Securities Exchange Commission. The latter has the authority to approve or reject PCAOB independence-related requirements such as the PCAOB's *somewhat* recently adopted rules 3502 and 3521 to 3525. The European Commission Council Directive 84/253/EEC (EU Eighth Company Law Directive 2006) gives discretionary power to member states to determine the conditions of independence for a statutory auditor. To provide each EU country with a common understanding of this independence requirement, the European Union Committee on Auditing developed a set of fundamental principles. These are set out in a Commission recommendation called *Statutory Auditors' Independence in the EU: A Set of Fundamental Principles*. Most of the requirements are based on the rules set forth by IFAC which we now discus. We note that there are many commonalities There are many commonalities between ISA and PCAOB. However, we do not delve into this because addressing commonalities is not our focus. Rather, our focus is on focusing on divergences and implications thereon.

According to the IFAC Section 290.6, independence requires both (a) independence in mind and (b) independence in appearance.

Independence in Mind

According to Section 290.8, this refers to a state of mind that permits the expression of a conclusion without being affected by influences that compromise professional judgment, allowing an individual to act with integrity and exercise objectivity and professional skepticism.

Independence in Appearance

The avoidance of facts and circumstances that are so significant that a reasonable and informed third party, having knowledge of all relevant information, including safeguards applied, would reasonably conclude a firm's or an assurance team member's integrity, objectivity, or professional skepticism had been compromised.

Threats to Independence

Section 290 of ISA describes the threats to an auditor's independence. The following are considered to be threats that the auditor should be wary of.

Financial Interest Threats

Financial interest threats occur when an auditor could benefit from a monetary interest in an assurance client. Section 290.104 states that a financial interest in an assurance client may create a self-interest threat. When evaluating the type of financial interest, consideration should be given to the fact that financial interests range from those where the individual has no control over the investment vehicle or the financial interest held (e.g., a mutual fund, unit trust, or similar intermediary vehicle) to those where the individual has control over the financial interest (e.g., as a trustee) or is able to influence investment decisions. In evaluating the significance of any threat to independence, it is important to consider the degree of control or influence that can be exercised over the intermediary, the financial interest held, or its investment strategy. When control exists, the financial interest should be considered to be direct. Conversely, when the holder of the financial interest has no ability to exercise such control, the financial interest should be considered to be indirect.

Section 290.106 clearly states that, if a member of the audit team providing assurance services or their immediate family member has a direct financial interest or a material indirect financial interest in the client, the threat created would be so significant that the only safeguards available to eliminate the threat or reduce it to an acceptable level would be to dispose of the direct financial interest prior to the individual becoming a member of the assurance team. If a member of the audit team or their immediate family member has an indirect financial interest, then they should dispose of the indirect financial interest in total or dispose of a sufficient amount of it so that the remaining interest is no longer material prior to the individual becoming a member of the assurance team. The AICPA's Code of Ethics (2014) defines materiality as ownership of 5 percent or more of the outstanding shares of stock in a company or, say, a mutual fund (see, e.g.,

Section 1.240.010, entitled *Overview of Financial Interests* in the AICPA's revised ethics code). The PCAOB's Interim Standard AU 220 does not include this quantitative definition, leaving the notion of materiality to the auditor's prudent discretion.

Section 290.107 also notes that during the period prior to disposal of the financial interest or the removal of the individual from the assurance team, consideration should be given to whether additional safeguards are necessary to reduce the threat to an acceptable level. The safeguards suggested by Section 290.107 are:

- discussing the matter with those charged with governance such as the audit committee or
- involving an additional professional accountant to review the work done.

Section 290.110 also notes that consideration should also be given to partners and their immediate family members who are not members of the assurance team. Whether the interests held by such individuals may create a self-interest threat will depend on such factors as:

- the auditing firm's organizational, operating, and reporting structure; and
- the nature of the relationship between the individual who is an immediate family member and the member of the assurance team.

In order to prevent violation, and subsequent lawsuits, Section 290.11 in paragraph (a) recommends that:

- the firm have established policies and procedures that require all professionals to report promptly to the firm any breaches resulting from the purchase, inheritance, or other acquisition of a financial interest in the assurance client.
- the firm promptly notifies the professional that the financial interest should be disposed of; and

- the disposal occurs at the earliest practical date after identification of the issue, or the professional is removed from the assurance team.

Section 290.127 notes that a loan, or guarantee of a loan, from an assurance client that is a bank or a similar institution to a member of the assurance team or their immediate family would not create a threat to independence provided the loan is made under normal lending procedures, terms, and requirements. Examples of such loans include home mortgages, bank overdrafts, or car loans and credit card balances.

Advocacy Threat

This threat occurs when a member of the assurance team promotes, or seems to promote, an assurance client's opinion. Section 290.150 provides examples of such instances. In essence, the auditor seems to agree with the client's stance in a situation that creates doubts as to why the auditor should agree with the stance of the client. That is, the auditor agrees with the client in a situation in which there seems to be insufficient reason to support the client's stance as opposed to the available reasons to oppose the client's stance.

Familiarity Threat

This occurs when an auditor becomes too sympathetic to the client's interests because the auditor has a close relationship with an assurance client, its directors, officers, or employees. Examples of these threats are discussed in Section 290.135. This threat occurs when an immediate family member of a member of the assurance team is a director, an officer, or an employee of the assurance client and is in a position to exert direct and significant influence over the subject matter information of the assurance engagement. Threats can be removed by (reference provided in Section 290.138):

- Removing the individual from the assurance team
- Where possible, structuring the responsibilities of the assurance team so that the professional does not deal with matters that are within the responsibility of the close family member

- Policies and procedures to empower staff to communicate to senior levels within the firm any issue of independence and objectivity that concerns them

It must also be noted that, in some countries, the range of problematic relationships may be wider than a spouse or dependent (e.g., the child or its spouse, the parent or grandparent, parent-in-law, brother, sister, or brother-in-law or sister-in-law of the client). This could happen if the same senior personnel on an assurance engagement have been used over a long period of time. This could also happen if a member of the assurance team has an immediate family member or close family member who is a director or an officer of the assurance client. Another example is if the member of the assurance team has a close family member who is an employee of the assurance client and, hence, is in a position to significantly influence the subject matter of the assurance engagement. Acceptance of gifts is another indicator of the familiarity threat (unless the value is clearly insignificant).

Auditor payouts due to litigation hopefully can be minimized if the auditor takes certain safeguards. According to Section 290.153, these safeguards are:

- Rotating the senior personnel of the assurance team
- Involving an additional professional accountant who is not a member of the assurance team to review the work done by the senior personnel or otherwise as necessary
- Establishing independent internal quality reviews

In the case of a financial statement audit, Section 290.154 notes that using the same engagement partner or the same individual responsible for the engagement quality control review over a prolonged period may also create a familiarity threat. Accordingly, auditors may be better prepared to defend their work should litigation arise if the engagement partner and the individual responsible for the engagement quality control review are rotated after serving in either capacity or a combination thereof. Section 290.154 provides that the engagement partner and the individual responsible for the engagement quality control review should be rotated after having served for seven years and, upon rotation of the engagement, should not participate in any capacity in the audit until two years have elapsed. However, Section 290.156 provides some flexibility to auditors. If rotation has not occurred as required in Section 290.154, then the standard states that the auditor can still protect himself or herself if the auditor can prove the following:

- There is a situation when the person's continuity is especially important to the financial statement audit client
- Situations when, because of the size of the firm, rotation is not possible or it can be proved that such rotation does not constitute an adequate safeguard

Recency Threat

This occurs when a former officer, director or employee of the assurance client serves as a member of the assurance team. In the case of a financial statement audit engagement, Section 290.149 notes that if a partner or employee of a network firm were to serve as an officer or as a director on the board of the audit client, the threats would be so significant that no safeguard would reduce the threats to an acceptable level. The only course is for the auditor to withdraw from the audit engagement.

Self-review Threats

This relates to the provision of non-assurance services. Audit firms have traditionally provided to their clients a range of non-assurance services consistent with their skills and expertise. As discussed in Section 290.167, assisting a financial statement audit client in matters such as preparing accounting records or financial statements may create a self-review threat when the financial statements are subsequently audited by the firm. A self-review threat exists when an auditor may be reluctant to report a problem that problem originates because of the auditor's error. Self-review threats can also occur in the following situations as explained in Section 290.159:

- Auditor has the authority to execute or consummate a transaction or otherwise exercise authority on behalf of the assurance client.

- Auditor can determine which recommendation of the firm should be implemented.
- Auditor reports, in a management role, to those charged with governance.
- Auditor has custody of an assurance client's assets.
- Auditor has or can supervise assurance client employees in the performance of their normal recurring activities.
- Auditor has or can prepare source documents or originating data in electronic or other form, evidencing the occurrence of a transaction (e.g., purchase orders, payroll time records, and customer orders).

All these are self-review threats because the auditor is subsequently auditing transactions over which the auditor had authority and checking assets over which the auditor had custody or checking the work of employees whom the auditor supervised in the performance of their duties.

While allowing the above mentioned activities by the auditor, section 290.167 notes that, while it is the responsibility of financial statement audit client management to ensure that accounting records are kept and financial statements are prepared, they can request the audit firm to provide assistance for clients whose shares are not listed on a stock exchange. However, the section notes, that while this is acceptable, the auditors must not be in a position where they can influence management decisions for these unlisted clients. Noted examples of management decisions include:

- determining or changing journal entries and so the classification for accounts or transaction or other accounting records without obtaining the approval of the financial statement audit client;
- authorizing or approving transactions; and
- preparing source documents or originating data (including decisions on valuation assumptions) or making changes to such documents or data.

Section 290.169 notes that a self-review threat could also be created if the firm developed and prepared prospective financial information and subsequently provided assurance on this prospective financial information. Prospective financial information is material that gives management's view as to what the firm's financial information will look like in the future.

Nonaudit Services to Audit Clients Under the IFAC Ethics Code

Bookkeeping Services

If the client is *not listed* on a stock exchange, the audit firm may provide accounting and book keeping services including payroll services of a routine or mechanical nature. These include

- recording transactions for which the audit client has determined or approved the appropriate account classification;
- posting coded transactions to the audit client's general ledger;
- preparing financial statements based on information in the trial balance; and
- posting the audit client-approved entries to the trial balance.

According to Section 290.170, the significance of any threat created should be evaluated, and if the threat is other than clearly insignificant, safeguards should be considered and applied as necessary to reduce the threat to an acceptable level. Safeguards noted in the standard include:

- making arrangements so such services are not performed by a member of the assurance team;
- implementing policies and procedures to prohibit the individual providing such services from making any managerial decisions on behalf of the audit client;
- requiring the source data for the accounting errors to be originated by the audit client;
- requiring the underlying assumptions to be originated and approved by the audit client; or
- obtaining audit client approval for any proposed journal entries or other changes affecting the financial statements.

If the audit client *is* *listed* on a stock exchange, then bookkeeping services, including payroll services and the preparation of financial statements or financial information are prohibited.

Valuation Services

Valuation service is defined in Section 290.174 as comprising the making of assumptions with regard to future developments, the application of certain methodologies and techniques, and the combination of both in order to compute a certain value, or range of values, for an asset, liability, or a business as a whole. Section 290.176 notes that, if the valuation service involves the valuation of matters material to the financial statements and the valuation involves a significant degree of subjectivity, a self-review threat is created, and hence, such services are prohibited.

However, valuation services may be allowed under Section 290.177 if the services are neither separately nor in the aggregate material to the financial statements or do not involve a significant degree of subjectivity. This is because it is felt that this may create a self-review threat that could be reduced to an acceptable level by the application of safeguards. Noted safeguards could include:

- involving an additional professional accountant who was not a member of the assurance team to review the work done or otherwise advise as necessary;
- obtaining the audit client's acknowledgment of responsibility for the results of the work performed by the firm; and
- making arrangements so that personnel providing such services do not participate in the audit engagement.

Taxation Services

Taxation services according to Section 290.180 comprise a broad range of services, including compliance, planning, provision of formal taxation opinions, and assistance in the resolution of tax disputes. Such assignments are allowed because they are not seen to be threats to independence.

Provision of Internal Audit Services to Financial Statement Audit Clients

Section 290.182 defines internal audit services as services involving an extension of the procedures required to conduct a financial statement audit in accordance with international standards on auditing. This is not considered to impair auditor's independence and is allowed. However, performing a significant portion of the financial statement audit client's internal audit activities may create a self-review threat. While this is still allowed, Section 290.185 states that adequate safeguards should be applied in all circumstances to reduce the threats created to an acceptable level. Noted safeguards include the following:

- The audit client, the audit committee, or the supervisory body approves the scope, risk, and frequency of internal audit work.
- The audit client is responsible for evaluating and determining which recommendations of the firm should be implemented.
- The findings and recommendations resulting from the internal audit activities are reported appropriately to the audit committee or supervisory body.

Provision of Litigation Support Services

Section 290.193 defines litigation support services as including activities such as acting as an expert witness, calculating estimated damages or other amounts that might become receivable or payable as the result of litigation or other legal dispute, and assistance with document management and retrieval in relation to a dispute or litigation. Conflicts of interest could arise if the auditor is engaged in both auditing and litigation services because the litigation function requires the auditor to be an advocate for the client. Acting as an advocate for the client is in conflict with the duty of the auditor to practice with professional skepticism.

According to Section 290.194, litigation support services will not be prohibited if the auditor evaluates the significance of threats to independence by examining:

- the materiality of the amounts involved;
- the degree of subjectivity inherent in the matter concerned; and
- the nature of the engagement.

The audit firm is then required to reduce the threat to an acceptable level by including safeguards such as:

- using professionals who are not members of the assurance team to perform the service;
- involving independent experts to assist them.

Provision of Information Technology Systems Services to Financial Statement Audit Clients

Information Technology (IT) systems services are defined as services that involve the design and implementation of financial information technology systems that are used to generate information forming part of a client's financial statements. While this is considered to impair auditor's independence under *self-review* threats, Section 290.188 does allow the provision of such services by an auditor if safeguards are in place. These safeguards require the audit client to:

- designate a competent employee, preferably within senior management, with the responsibility to make all management decisions with respect to the design and implementation of the hardware or software system;
- make all management decisions with respect to the design and implementation process;
- be responsible for the operation of the system (hardware and software) and the data used or generated by the system.

Temporary Staff Assignments to Financial Statement Audit Clients

The lending of staff by an audit firm to its client while potentially creating a self-review threat is allowed if the auditor is not allowed to do the following activities under Section 290.192:

- Making management decisions
- Approving or signing agreements or other similar documents

Further, it is required that:

- the staff providing the assistance should not be given audit responsibility for any function or activity that they performed or supervised during their temporary staff assignment; and
- the audit client should acknowledge its responsibility for directing and supervising the activities of the audit firm.

Provision of Legal Services to Financial Statement Audit Clients

Legal services encompass a wide and diversified range of areas including both corporate and commercial services to clients such as contract support, litigation, mergers and acquisition advice, and support and provision of assistance to clients' internal legal departments. This is allowed provided safeguards are met. Section 290.201 stipulates the following safeguards:

- Members of the assurance team are not involved in providing the service.
- In relation to the advice provided, the audit client makes the ultimate decision, or in relation to the transactions, the service involves the execution of what has been decided by the audit client.

Recruiting Senior Management

The recruitment of senior management for an assurance client may create self-interest, familiarity, and intimidation threats. The severity of the threat may depend on factors such as (a) the role of the person to be recruited and (b) the nature of the assistance sought. Despite this, providing such services by an audit client are allowed under Section 290.203 if adequate safeguards are met. The definition of adequate safeguards is provided in Section 290.163. In summary these safeguards include:

- policies and procedures to prohibit professional staff from making management decisions;
- policies regarding the oversight responsibility with regard to the provision of non-assurance services;
- discussing independence issues related to the provision of non-assurance services with those charged with governance;
- disclosing to those charged with governance, such as the audit committee, the nature and extent of fee charged;
- ensuring that personnel providing non-assurance services do not participate in the assurance engagement.

Corporate Finance and Similar Activities

Corporate finance and similar activities include activities such as promoting, dealing in, or underwriting of a client's shares or consummating a transaction on behalf of the client. Section 290.204 notes that the provision of corporate finance services, advice, or assistance to an assurance client may create advocacy and self-review threats. It is held that the independence threats could be so significant that no safeguards could be applied to reduce the threats to an acceptable level. For example, promoting, dealing in, or underwriting of an assurance client's shares is not compatible with providing assurance services. However, Section 290.205 does provide exceptions to the general rules for certain types of corporate finance activities. The general exceptions noted in the section include:

- policies and procedures to prohibit individuals assisting the assurance client from making managerial decisions on behalf of the client; and
- using professionals who are not members of the assurance team to provide the services.

Developments in the United States

Section 103(a) of the Sarbanes Oxley Act of 2002 directs the PCAOB to establish "ethics standards to be used by registered public accounting firms in the preparation and issuance of audit reports". Moreover Section 103(b) of the Act directs the Board to establish rules on auditor independence "as may be necessary or appropriate in the public interest or for the protection of investors, to implement, or as authorized under Title II of the Act."

In early 2003, the SEC adopted new independence rules in order to implement Title II of the Act. Neither the Act nor the SEC's 2003 independence rules prohibit tax services as long as the services are preapproved by the company's audit committee and do not fall into one of the categories of expressly prohibited services. This is similar to the IFAC rules, which were discussed earlier. However, the major difference between the IFAC Code of Ethics and the ethics standards proposed by the PCAOB relates to the tax services. Since the SEC issued its new rules, two types of tax services have raised serious questions in the United States. First, the IRS and the U.S. Department of Justice have brought a number of cases against accounting firms advising client firms on *tax shelters* for their products. Audit firms have also been criticized for advising senior executives of clients whom they are auditing regarding tax shelters. Although such advice is not considered illegal, it is considered highly unethical because companies and their executives are being advised on how to evade tax by abusing tax shelter laws. Some have questioned whether an auditor's provision of such services could lead to self-interest threats to independence. If the auditor charges contingent fees for such services, this could impair independence. This issue, to date, has not been raised in Europe and by the IFAC.

In order to deal with this, the PCAOB has issued rules on this. (Initially the PCAOB, when it began its work in 2003, adopted all the then existing AICPA rules as interim rules before making changes and amendments (see PCAOB Rule 3500T.)) Relevant PCAOB rules are as follows:

Rule 3521

This treats registered public accounting firms as not independent of their audit clients if they enter into contingent fee arrangements with those clients.

Rule 3522(a)

Rule 3522(a) treats a registered public accounting firm as not independent of an audit client if the firm provides services related to planning or opining on the tax consequences of a transaction that is a listed or confidential transaction under Treasury regulations.

Rule 3522(b)

In addition, Rule 3522(b) included a provision that treats a registered public accounting firm as not independent if the firm provides services related to planning or giving an opinion on a transaction that is based on an aggressive interpretation of applicable tax laws and regulations.

Rule 3523

Rule 3523 sets a new requirement to treat a registered public accounting firm as not independent if the firm provided tax services to officers in a financial reporting oversight role of an audit client.

Rule 3524

Rule 3524 requires a registered public accounting firm to seek pre-approval for tax services and to supply the audit committee with detailed information about tax services provided and discuss with the audit committee the potential effects of the services on the firm's independence and to document the substance of that discussion.

Rule 3502

Rule 3502 codifies the principle that persons associated with a registered public accounting firm should not cause the firm to violate relevant laws, rules, and professional standards due to an act or omission the person knew or should have known would contribute to such violation.

Conclusion

In this chapter, we discussed the ethical standards required by the IFAC. These standards are followed by all countries in the EU and most other industrialized and developing countries. We also discussed the key differences between the ethical standards in the United States, as set by the PCAOB, and in Europe. The main differences in standards relates to the provision of tax services and certain other consulting services. These are seen as more complex in the U.S. relative to other countries. Finally, we comment that the process of establishing ethical principles is complicated. In France and Japan, the ethical code is part of the law. In the United States, Singapore, Mexico and the UK, the standards are developed and regulated by professional bodies. As we noted in Chapter 2, violation of the ethical standards could subject the auditor to sanction by the court in certain instances by professional bodies and may also result in the suspension of the auditor's right to practice before the SEC in the United States.

The key takeaway from this chapter is the general similarity between the ethical standards implemented in the United States and and those enforced by IFAC. However, similar does not mean identical, and therefore, the reader must be careful to relate the relevant ethical code to the geographic area or nation that they are interested in. Also, the reader must be aware that organizations that belong to IFAC must have ethical codes *that are at least as* strict as those set forth by IFAC. Different countries will have different specific restrictions that are relevant to proposed auditor behavior in those nations. They should also be aware of any differences in acceptable auditor behavior for listed as opposed to unlisted clients and adjust their expectations of appropriate auditor behavior accordingly. This overview will help readers to decide where further, if anywhere, they need to go for additional information.

CHAPTER 4

U.S. Auditing Standards and the Role of the PCAOB

Introduction

The purpose of this chapter is to set the foundations for the discussions in the following chapters. In doing so, we:

- Provide important background information on how auditing standards are set for publicly owned companies in the United States;
- Provide a brief summary of the differences between Public Company Accounting Oversight Board (PCAOB) standards and International Standards on Auditing (ISA);
- Provide background information related to the differences between PCAOB and American Institute of CPAs (AICPA) Auditing Standards Board (ASB);
- Discuss potential reasons why there are differences between the PCAOB and ISA.

There are two sources of auditing standards in the United States. One is the American Institute of Certified Public Accountants (AICPA's) ASB, which creates auditing standards for nonpublicly listed companies and other organizations. The second source of these auditing standards is the PCAOB, which sets auditing standards for publicly listed companies. Many of the PCAOB standards originated from ASB since the AICPA ASB was in existence before the PCAOB and PCOAB adopted its first auditing standard, Auditing Standard (AS) 1, on April 16, 2003 from ASB as its interim standard. The interim standards that have not been superseded, modified, or repealed later by PCAOB remain in effect.

Accordingly, these generally accepted auditing standards (GAAS) are under the aegis of the PCAOB. They are titled AS if modified by PCAOB or AU otherwise. AU means that they may be amended and modified or superseded by PCAOB and converted to AS at a later date. In later chapters, we group them together as PCAOB standards (unless otherwise specified) and compare and contrast PCAOB standards with ISA. We show why, from a legal and regulatory standpoint, PCAOB standards could differ from ISA. We provide several examples of differences between PCAOB standards and ISA to illustrate our point. These variations and their importance and implications to auditors and users of the auditors' report are discussed in greater detail in the following chapters.

Brief History of Auditing Standards

Prior to the Sarbanes Oxley Act (SOX) of 2002, the auditing standards in the United States were established by the ASB. This board operated under the supervision of the AICPA, which is a professional association of accountants. The standards developed are popularly referred to as the U.S. GAAS. However, in 2001 and 2002, it was learned that there were major auditing failures involving very large corporations such as Enron and WorldCom. The U.S. Congress concluded that there was a general breakdown of confidence among the public in major economic institutions (e.g., corporations) and in the auditing processes and auditing firms that audited the financial results of these firms. They also concluded that there must be flaws inherent in a system that could allow such massive scandals to take place. The U.S. Congress passed SOX to restore public confidence. SOX in turn created the PCAOB. The purpose of the PCAOB was to oversee the auditing of public companies. Most importantly, section 103 of SOX gave the PCAOB the authority to write auditing standards by itself, or alternatively, to delegate standard setting to the ASB. Even though the former is a more difficult route, the board members of the PCAOB decided to write their own standards rather than rely on the ASB. A member of the PCAOB board, Daniel Goelzer, in a speech on February 12 in 2012 noted that setting its own standards was one of the *foundation stones* of the PCAOB's approach to fulfilling the investor protection mission placed on it by Congress.

PCAOB's authority to set standards was subsequently expanded in 2010 with the enactment of the Dodd-Frank Wall Street Reform and Consumer Protection Act (Dodd Frank Act 2010). This in effect extended the standard setting authority of the PCAOB to auditors of all security broker dealers that file financial statements with the Securities Exchange Commission (SEC). Because the vast majority of these broker dealers are not public companies, the Dodd Frank Act extended the power of the PCAOB to all public and a significant number of nonpublic companies. In essence, today in the United States, the standards that govern audits of all public companies that file reports with the SEC are written by the PCAOB. However, other auditing standards such as those governing private company audits are still written by the ASB. Thus, there are now two sets of auditing standards in the United States. These are the PCAOB standards for public companies and GAAS set by the ASB for nonpublic companies.

How Does the PCAOB Operate and Set Standards?

The PCAOB has set up an open and transparent process allowing a wide range of interested parties to comment. As board member Goelzer notes, there are three major stages in the operation of the PCAOB. These three stages are *conceptualization, proposal,* and *PCAOB and SEC approval.* Each of these is described in turn in the following sections.

Conceptualization

The PCAOB has two consultation or advisory groups. These are called the Standing Advisory Group (SAG) and the Investor Advisory Group (IAG). The SAG comprises individuals with a broad cross section of experience in financial reporting. The SAG could include practicing auditors, preparers of financial statements, investors, and other interested parties. The IAG comprises members who are users of public company financial statements such as financial analysts. The PCAOB may release a *Concept release*. Concept releases describe the problem to be solved or objectives to be accomplished. Ultimately this results in a proposed standard.

Proposal

All proposed standards are published for public comment. This provides an opportunity for all segments of society including, but not limited to, auditors and financial statement preparers to react to a specific proposal with comments and suggestions for improvements. If, based on the feedback, the resulting changes required are significant; the PCAOB may publish a second version for further comment.

Adoption and SEC Approval

Based on the public comments received, the PCAOB formulates the final standard. This has to be approved by the board members of the PCAOB. Once the board has approved the standard, SOX requires the SEC to solicit additional public comment on the standard. Once these additional comments are received, the SEC has the burden of either approving or disapproving the standard. The most important point to note is that PCAOB auditing standards cannot take effect until and unless it is approved by the SEC.

Are There Significant Differences between ISA and PCAOB Standards?

We discuss the differences between the ISA and the PCAOB standards from both a macro and micro perspective. From the macro view point, Goelzer—as a former PCAOB board member responsible for standard setting—noted that, although the fundamental underpinnings are similar, there are some significant differences between the PCAOB and the ISA. This is because of different expectations for audits and the more investor protection-oriented legal framework in the United States compared with the international environment. Some basic differences pointed out by Goelzer are important to note here:

- ISA represent many different countries and cultures. The difference in cultures, in turn, creates differences in the audit environments. Therefore, some latitude must be given in ISA. Thus, ISA have less precision regarding procedures to be followed. PCAOB standards are much more precise about what must be done in an audit. Goelzer notes that, in the United States, because of greater involvement with legal consequences (i.e., there is a greater possibility of being sued) and more intensive regulatory frameworks, there is a greater requirement for precision in an audit. Internationally, there is less possibility of being sued because the British and European system of justice requires that the plaintiff pay the defendant's costs if they lose the case. Therefore, risks associated with filing lawsuits are much greater internationally. Hence, the need for a similar precision in audits has not evolved in the international setting.

- PCAOB standards are constructed with an integrated financial statement and internal control over financial reporting audit in mind. Internationally, most countries do NOT require an opinion on internal control over financial reporting. Accordingly, ISA do not address internal control auditing, whereas PCAOB standards do.

- With the unique legal framework of the United States in mind, PCAOB standards require that the audit be performed with *due professional care*. Goelzer noted that "this requirement underpins much of the US auditor's legal liability. The ISA contains no comparable requirement". The fact that ISA, according to Goelzer, do not have a similar requirement is an important difference. Many PCAOB standards use the words *due professional care*. This wording is largely ignored in ISA. However, our research indicates that Goelzer is *partially* correct. We do not see the words *due professional care* but rather the words *duty of care*.

- Because of SOX, PCAOB considers communications with the audit committee to be of paramount importance. For example, the PCAOB relevant standard requires the auditor to make certain inquiries of the audit committee. The ISA are not aligned with SOX. In fact, internationally the ISA operate in jurisdictions where audit committees play little or no role, or even exist. Hence, although the PCAOB has standards

regarding dealing with communications with the audit committee, the ISA do not have similar requirements or standards.
- The PCAOB is concerned, according to Goelzer, with the
actual existence of items reported in the financial statements,
especially assets. Hence, relative to ISA, there is more focus
across the PCAOB standards on auditing to verify the existence of assets reported. Goelzer adds that he does not mean
to suggest that the PCAOB's standards are *better* than ISA.
Rather, he means that PCAOB standards are better *aligned*
with the legal, regulatory, and business environment in the
United States. One example of this is the requirement in the
relevant PCAOB standard for auditors to require the verification of accounts receivable by sending out confirmations. The
ISA do not place the same emphasis on, and hence no ISA
require confirmation of accounts receivable.

The preceding issues provide the rationale for divergences between
PCAOB standards and ISA standards. From a micro view point, Lindberg
and Seifert wrote in the CPA Journal (2011) that there are five principal
differences between PCAOB standards and ISA. These significant differences are in the areas of:

- Documentation of audit procedures;
- Going concern considerations;
- Assessing and reporting on internal control over financial
reporting;
- Risk assessment and responses to assessed risks; and
- Use of another auditor for part of an audit.

These will be considered in greater depth in the chapters to follow but
are discussed briefly here.

Documentation Procedures

PCAOB standards are more prescriptive than ISA, which rely more on
the professional judgment of the auditor. To illustrate, PCAOB auditing

standards require that an *engagement completion memo* be prepared; there is no such requirement under ISA. Another issue relates to the retention period of audit papers. Here in addition to difference between ISA and PCAOB standards, there is also a rare divergence between PCAOB and the AICPA's GAAS. GAAS, in AU-C Section 230 *Audit Documentation*, requires that audit work papers be retained for a period of at least five years, whereas the PCAOB mandates a retention period of at least seven years. The ISA section 230 entitled *Audit Documentation* requires audit firms "to establish policies and procedures for the retention of engagement documentation. The retention period should be no shorter than five years from the date of the auditor's report, or, if later, the date of the group auditor's report." (Please note that AU numbers were temporarily assigned AU-C with the intention to revert back to AU. However, the AICPA subsequently decided to retain the AU-C references. The interim PCAOB standards are still denoted as AU, not AU-C.)

Going Concern Considerations

Under both PCAOB standards and ISA, the auditor must make a judgment with respect to whether the auditee will likely survive as a *going concern* for a period of time. Going concern means that the entity has the ability to continue as a going concern into the foreseeable future. The PCAOB auditing standards define the foreseeable future as the 12 months following the end of the fiscal period being audited. Under ISA, the foreseeable future is at least, but not limited to, 12 months.

Internal Control over Financial Reporting

When the U.S. Congress passed SOX, it required that management of U.S. public companies assess and report on internal controls over financial reporting. Management is then required to state their assertions about the effectiveness of their company's controls over financial reporting in a report that accompanies the financial statements. Under SOX, the auditor—for the first time in the United States—is required to gain an understanding of, and more significantly test, the effectiveness of the client's internal accounting controls. The standard for doing so was set forth by the PCAOB in its AS 5 (a previous version of standards for auditing internal controls, AS 2, was repealed.) AS 5 requires auditors of public companies to perform an examination of an entity's internal control with respect to the financial reporting process; auditors of U.S. public companies must also express an opinion on the effectiveness of the entity's internal controls over financial reporting as well as express an opinion on the financial statements themselves. The ISA do not require an audit of, or an opinion on, the effectiveness of the client's internal control over financial reporting.

Risk Assessment and Response to Assessed Risks

There are differences between ISA and PCAOB standards, but because we devote a whole chapter (Chapter 7) to this and hence for brevity, these differences will not be elaborated here.

Use of Another Auditor

Under PCAOB standards, the principal auditor refers to the work of another auditor. Under ISA, referring to the work of another auditor is NOT permitted.

Are There Significant Differences between GAAS and PCAOB Standards?

In the previous section, we looked at differences between PCAOB standards and ISA. As mentioned, whereas SOX requires auditors of public companies to follow PCAOB auditing standards, the ASB's GAAS applies to all audits of non-SEC registered entities who are also *not* broker-dealers. John A. Fogarty, former Chairman of the ASB, noted the difference in this way: "The ASB is a body with the authority to promulgate auditing, attestation and quality control standards related to the preparation and issuance of audit reports for non issuers. The PCAOB is a body with the authority to promulgate auditing standards as well as attestation, quality control, ethics, independence and other standards related to the presentation and issuance of audit reports for issuers." The ASB has renumbered its standards to be consistent with the ISA and had each renumbered ASB standard discuss the same topics as the corresponding standard in the ISA. (For example, ISA 240 entitled The Auditor's Responsibility to consider Fraud in an Audit of Financial Statements would be section 240 with the same title in GAAS.) At the same time the ASB renumbered its standards to have numbering consistent with that of the ISA, it also rewrote the standards in a new clarification format, in the process making some previously implicit requirements explicit.

In this section, we discuss whether there are significant differences between GAAS and PCAOB standards. Fogarty notes that the ASB has been very clear in that it "does not intend to create gratuitous differences between its standards and those of the *PCAOB*". Further, in order to help coordinate agendas, the chairs of the ASB and PCAOB and their respective staffs meet at least three times a year to discuss projects. These meetings provide a valuable forum to the ASB for discussing projects, time tables, and goals. Because of this close collaboration, there are hardly any differences between PCAOB and GAAS, according to Fogarty.

Fogarty notes that, in addition to monitoring PCAOB standards very closely (to the extent that even though auditing standards numbers are different, the content and guidelines are very similar), the ASB also collaborates with the International Auditing and Assurance Standards Board (IAASB) to try and harmonize standards. However, despite much overlap, some areas of difference remain. (Please refer, http://www.aicpa.org/research/standards/auditattest/pages/clarifiedsas.aspx.)

The essence of the ASB chairman's remarks can be summarized as follows.

The ASB collaborates with the IAASB to the extent of having the same titles and numbers for all their standards. However, due to differences in cultural, legal, and regulatory frameworks, differences do exist.

Fogarty noted that it is very important for U.S. auditors, especially those from smaller firms, to stay abreast of developments related to ISA. This is because, as international standards in audit and attest services gain worldwide acceptance in cross border operations, U.S. *Certified*

Public Accountants (CPAs), including small firm practitioners, will have to become familiar with ISA in order to perform engagements in accordance with international standards.

The discussion that follows relates to the remaining areas of difference.

Conclusion

This chapter is important because the discussions set the foundations for the further elaborations in the following chapters. Up to now, the PCAOB has published 18 standards. This raises questions about the standards passed by the ASB and not addressed by the PCAOB. As we noted earlier, the AICPA ASB was in existence before the PCAOB and PCOAB adopted its first auditing standard, AS 1, from the ASB as its interim standard. The interim standards that have not been superseded or repealed by later PCAOB standards remain in effect. Hence, these ASB standards can be considered to be under the aegis of the PCAOB. Accordingly, these GAAS are considered as PCAOB standards since the PCAOB now has ultimate responsibility for their use with publicly listed companies and has not yet amended or modified these standards.

We noted earlier that there are differences between PCAOB and the ISA. We also noted that significant differences could arise between ISA and PCAOB for the following reasons:

- Certain items are in different locations in PCAOB compared with ISA;
- There are items in PCAOB not covered in ISA; and
- There are items in ISA not covered in PCAOB.

The reasons why items or requirements may be in one standard but not in another standard are because of variations (such as the legal and regulatory environment) between the United States and other international countries. This is an important takeaway from this discussion. Auditors clearly must be aware of the standard environment within which they operate. It is also helpful to them to be aware of *why* these divergences in standards exist because that may lead the auditor to be even more careful than they otherwise might be in adhering closely to the relevant standard.

Similarly, readers should be aware of the divergences in auditing standards that may impact the audit reports they see. Depending on the differences in particular auditing standards involved, an audit report's conclusion in one environment *may* differ from the report that would be seen in another environment. Although this is an extreme case, it is possible. Other chapters discuss these issues in greater detail.

CHAPTER 5

Planning an Audit and Client Acceptance

Introduction

The purpose of this chapter is twofold:

- Steps an auditor needs to take in audit planning in the United States
- Key differences between International Standards on Auditing (ISA) and Public Corporation Accounting Oversight Board (PCAOB) with respect to planning and what those differences mean to auditors

As mentioned in Chapter 4, the PCAOB is responsible for creating 18 standards so far, (going as Auditing Standards [AS]), many of which superseded pre-existing ASB standards. Another 99 ASB standards have been brought under the PCAOB umbrella and reflect work in progress (going as AU) standards. The PCAOB's statement AS 1 describes these standards as "interim standards". The AU standards may or may not have modifications significant enough to warrant categorization as AS. These will remain as AU standards until amended and accepted by the PCAOB as AS.

Sarbanes Oxley Act (SOX) requires the PCAOB to be responsible for auditing standards relating to publicly listed firms. SOX also addresses the issue of ASB auditing standards published but brought into the PCAOB fold without much amendments (i.e., AU standards). Fogarty, writing in the CPA Journal, notes that these AU standards remain in force as if they had been created by the PCAOB itself. Hence in this and the following chapters we discuss standards first based on the requirements of the ISA, then discuss the differences with respect to related PCAOB standards (AU and AS).

The differences between PCAOB and ISA can be categorized as (a) differences in wording both substantive and less substantive, (b) procedures required by PCAOB but not required by ISA, and (c) procedures required by the ISA but not required by the PCAOB. We adopt this classification based on the categorization in an AICPA website (aicpa.org/FRS). After discussion of the ISA procedures, where applicable, we discuss the differences based on the categories noted earlier and discuss the implications for U.S. auditors. We first talk about issues relating to the engagement process of accepting a client. We then discuss stages in planning an audit. Wherever differences between U.S. and international auditing standards exist, we compare, contrast and discuss the significance of those differences.

Client Acceptance and the Engagement Process

The first stage in planning an audit comprises accepting the client.

Hayes et al. (2005) note that the client acceptance phase of the audit has two objectives. They are:

- Examination of the proposed client to determine if there is any reason to reject the engagement
- Convincing the client to hire the auditor

Procedures in Accepting a New Client

An auditor must exercise care in deciding which clients are acceptable. An accounting firm's legal and professional responsibilities are such that clients who lack integrity can cause serious and expensive problems. Some auditing firms refuse to accept clients in certain high risk industries. For example, Hayes et al. note that in the United States and Northern Europe during the 1990s, many large auditing firms were very careful when accepting audit engagements of financial institutions after the legal judgments and fines resulting from audits of Lincoln Savings, Standard Chartered Bank, and International Bank of Credit and Commerce (BCCI).

At the beginning of the twenty first century, there were great problems in the energy business (Enron, Dynergy, Pacific Gas, and Electric), the telecommunications industry (Worldcom, Global Crossing, Qwest), and healthcare (Health South, ImClone), and even in old line industries such as retailing (K mart, Ahold) and food products (Parmalat).

The procedures potentially leading to acceptance of the client are: acquiring knowledge of the client's business; examination of the audit firm's ethical requirements and technical competence; possible use of other professionals (including outside specialists) in the audit; communication with the predecessor auditor; preparation of client proposal; assignment of staff; and the submission of the terms of the engagement in the form of an engagement letter. Prior to acceptance of a new client, the firm should evaluate the client. The first characteristic that needs to be evaluated is the integrity of the client. With regard to integrity, Hayes et al. state that matters that a firm should consider are:

- the integrity and business reputation of the client's principal owners, key management, related parties, and those charged with its governance;
- the nature of the client's operations including its business practices;
- information concerning the attitude of the client's principal owners, key management, and those charged with its governance towards such matters as aggressive interpretation of accounting standards and the internal control environment;
- whether the client is aggressively concerned with maintaining the firm's fee as low as possible;
- indications that the client might be involved in money laundering or other criminal activities;
- the reasons for the proposed appointment of the firm and non-reappointment of the previous firm.

The firm can obtain this information from the following sources: communications with existing or previous providers of professional accountancy services to the client and discussions with third parties; talking to third parties dealing with the firm such as bankers, legal counsel, and industry peers; and background searches of relevant databases. Acceptance of the client is governed in Section 210 of the ISA (now amended by Section ISA 700). An important element in the steps noted earlier is communication with the predecessor auditor. Here there are differences between the ISA and PCAOB as noted by the AICPA in its website, aicpa.org/FRC. It is noted that paragraph 18 of ISA 210 contains requirements, where laws and financial regulations should take precedence over ISA requirements. However, the PCAOB does not have an equivalent of this. The PCAOB does not prescribe situations where financial laws supersede the PCAOB's rules, perhaps because this situation is atypical in the United States. Hence the implication to a U.S. auditor working in an international environment, following the ISA's rules, is that they should be aware of which local financial laws (if any) supersede or gain precedence over ISA.

There are also requirements in the PCAOB rules that are not in ISAs. The AICPA in its website notes that paragraphs 11 and 12 of Section 210 in the ASB's GAAS initially and the equivalent PCAOB standard (now AU 315) specify how the auditor should communicate with predecessor auditors in initial audit, or even reaudit, engagements should the need arise. As mentioned earlier, the equivalent PCAOB standard is AU 315 *Communication between Predecessor and Successor Auditors*. This requests the successor auditor to communicate either in writing or orally. The successor auditor bears the burden of maintaining confidentiality. AU 315 provides focus for the successor auditor on which areas to cover. AU 315 notes that matters subject to inquiry could include:

- information that could bear on the integrity of the management;
- disagreements with management as to accounting principles, auditing procedures, or other similarly significant matters;
- communications to audit committees or others with equivalent authority and responsibility regarding fraud, illegal acts by clients, and internal control related matters;
- the predecessor's understanding as to the reasons for the change of auditors.

However, there is no equivalent in ISA. Hence, there is more flexibility with respect to communicating with predecessors under ISA. Further, paragraph 13 of PCAOB's AU 315 requires the auditor to remind the client who rehires the auditor of the existing terms of the engagement and to document it. The ISA has no equivalent to AU 315. Rather, paragraphs 11 and 12 of ISA Section 210 merely requires the auditor to assess whether there is a need to remind the client of the terms of the engagement. Does failure to remind the client of the terms of the engagement have any legal consequences? That is, could there be a lawsuit under ISA because the auditor did not remind the clients of the terms of the engagement? Whether the answer is yes or not to these questions depends on each ISA country's law and legal processes. Addressing such questions is beyond the scope of this book.

There are other important requirements in PCAOB rules that are not in the ISA based on our analysis and the European Maastricht report previously mentioned. AU 315 of PCAOB states (refer paragraphs 3 to 11 for entire discussion) that the auditor (when the prior period financial statements were audited by a predecessor auditor) should request and allow management to authorize the predecessor to allow a review of the predecessor auditor's audit documentation and to respond fully to inquiries by the auditor. AU 315 also concerns the auditor's response when management refuses to allow the predecessor auditor to talk to the successor auditor because of disputes between the client and the predecessor auditor (refer paragraphs 3 to 11). The PCAOB believes it is important to address this situation. This is addressed in paragraph 10 of AU 315 of the PCAOB. If the successor auditor receives a limited or unhelpful response, then the implications of that should be considered, and the auditor should seriously consider refusing the engagement. The ISA do not specifically address this and hence there is a grey area where auditors may have to use their professional judgment rather than follow specified guidelines.

This communication between the successor auditor and the predecessor auditor is a requirement of the IFAC* code of ethics. The objective is to determine whether there are technical or ethical issues that the new

---

* Note that the International Federation of Accountants (IFAC) is the parent of the IAASB and the IESBA.

auditor has to be aware of before taking on the new engagement. The objective is to prevent *opinion shopping* by the client. Clients frequently discontinue auditors and attempt to take on new auditors who are willing to be more amenable to their requests. A case serves to illustrate this point. In June 2007 in the United States, a company by the name of Neopharm dropped KPMG Peat Marwick and accepted BDO Seidman as the new auditor. There were a number of *bad news* items that KPMG Peat Marwick wanted to report. These included weaknesses in the existing control systems. The reason ostensibly was to reduce costs according to the news report. The Code of Ethics requires auditors to be honest. When a new auditor requests information, the predecessor auditor is required to inform the existing auditor whether there are any professional reasons why the new auditor should not take on the engagement.

Even with such communication, however, in the case of a new client, ISA 510 (paragraphs 4 to 8) requires the auditor to not accept the word of the predecessor auditor but to actually perform at least one of two or three identified procedures to obtain sufficient audit evidence about whether the closing balances in the prior year (opening balances in the current period) contain material misstatements that could materially affect the current period's financial statements. The procedures required are (a) reviewing the predecessor auditor's audit documentation to obtain evidence regarding opening balances and (b) evaluating whether audit procedures performed in the current audit provide evidence regarding the accuracy of opening balances. The ASB in their website at (http://www.aicpa.org/interestareas/frc/auditattest/downloadabledocuments/clarity/substantive_differences_isa_gass.pdf) notes that they do not believe that either of these procedures on its own provides sufficient evidence regarding opening balances. While under ISA 510, auditors could limit themselves to one procedure, here under the PCAOB AU 315 auditors are required to use more than one procedure. The procedures are identified in AU 315.

The client–auditor (audit firm) relationship is not a one way street where the audit firm evaluates the client and then, judging the client *acceptable*, sends out an engagement letter closing the deal. The market of audit services is competitive, and just as in any other business, there are highly desirable clients with whom any audit firm would like to have an audit relationship. Although not always the case, audit firms prepare and submit engagement proposals to many of their (potential) clients, especially the large ones.

ISA 210 (Appendix 1) emphasizes that the auditor should write an engagement letter before the commencement of the audit and provides an example of a draft engagement letter. The purpose of the engagement letter is to document and confirm (a) the auditor's acceptance of the appointment, (b) the objective and scope of the audit, (c) the extent of the auditor's responsibilities to the client, and (d) the form of any reports. An engagement letter is useful because it helps to avoid mis-understandings with the client during the course of the audit. ISA 210 (paragraph A23 and A24) requires that the engagement letter contain the following:

- The objective of the audit of financial statements
- The management's responsibility with respect to the financial statements
- The scope of the audit, including reference to applicable legis-lation, regulations, or pronouncements of professional bodies to which the auditor adheres
- The form of any reports that the auditor will issue at the end of the engagement (audit)
- A statement that the auditor cannot test every possible transaction or amount, and hence, some material misstate-ments (accidental or intentional) may not be discovered and reported
- The need to obtain unrestricted access to whatever records, documentation, and other information that may be requested during the course of the audit
- The responsibility of the management for establishing and maintaining effective control
- A request for an acknowledgment of the receipt of the engagement letter as client's confirmation of the terms of the engagement

Whereas the preceding issues are expected, paragraph 7 of ISA 210 recommends but does not require the following in the letter:

- Expectation of receiving from management written confirmation concerning representations made in connection with the audit
- Description of any other letters or reports the auditor expects to issue to the client
- Basis on which fee are computed and billing arrangements are made
- Arrangements concerning the involvement of other auditors and experts in some aspects of the audit should the necessity arise
- Any restriction of the auditor's liability when such a possibility exists

An auditor should not accept a client blindly or because of the expected audit fee. International auditing standards require that the auditor obtain an understanding of the client, the environment in which that company operates, and the internal controls of the company. This also enables the auditor to identify the risks associated with the audit. ISA 500 (paragraphs 26 to 35) suggests that the auditor use the following to obtain information about the potential client:

- Inspection of documents (such as business plans and strategies), records, and internal control manuals
- Reading reports prepared by management (such as quarterly management reports and interim financial statements) and those charged with governance (such as minutes of board of directors' meetings)
- Visits to the entity's premises and plant facilities

The standard also suggests that the auditor conduct tests tracing transactions through the information system. These are referred to as *walkthroughs*.

ISA 500 (paragraph 19) requires the auditor to critically analyze the client and its industry and make risk assessments. The standard clearly explains risk assessment procedures that the auditor can use to identify risks associated with a client. It is important that the auditor use information that is current when evaluating a client for acceptance. Hence, ISA 500 in paragraph 19 also recommends that the auditor should determine whether changes that could affect the relevant audit have occurred in the client or its industry. ISA 500 (paragraphs 30 to 34) suggests that the auditor have discussions with the client relating to such issues as changes in management and organizational structure, changes in government regulations that could potentially affect the client, changes in the economic environment, recent or impending changes in technology, types of products or services, and changes in the accounting system and the system of internal control (among others).

Procedures in Continuing With a Current Client

ISA 210 (paragraph A28) provides guidance in the event of a recurring audit. In general, since the auditor has done the audit before, it is suggested that there is no need to send an engagement letter unless the auditor feels circumstances have changed, thus necessitating a new letter. It is suggested by ISA 210 paragraph A28 that the following factors may result in the need for a new letter:

- Any indication in the client's behavior that the client has misunderstood the objective and scope of the audit
- Any revised or special terms of the engagement
- A significant change in ownership
- A significant change in nature or size of the client's business
- Any legal or regulatory requirements

The following discussion is from ISA 210 (paragraphs A27 and A28 in particular). In the case of continuing clients, auditors are advised to perform procedures designed to identify significant changes that have taken place since the last audit. The auditor should then consider if there has been any previous conflicts over issues such as the scope of the audit, fee or management integrity. These factors could determine whether the auditor continues or refuses to audit the client. If the tests appear to indicate that there are significant changes and the auditor concludes that accepting the audit involves more risk than is acceptable to them, they have the freedom to refuse the client. Proving that the risk is unacceptable is sufficient reason to protect auditors from lawsuits from disgruntled clients. If the auditor decides to accept the client, there is no guarantee that the client will, on further deliberation, accept the auditor. This is because it is anticipated that the client will be *auditor shopping* for an auditor that can add value for money. It is contingent on the auditor to make the proposal appear attractive. A new client proposal can include the following:

- Plans for further improvement
- A description of the audit team and any changes in the audit team
- A detailed fee proposal. This involves discussion of the basis on which fees are computed and any billing arrangements

Source: ISA 210 Amended as a Result of ISA 700 in Appendix 2 on Terms of Audit Engagements. Also refer Hayes et al. (page 180) for succinct summary of ISA 210 Amended as a Result of ISA 700 in Appendix 2 on terms of audit engagement.

Prior to client acceptance, other issues that need to be considered are the following:

Independence

The auditor should ensure that the members of the auditor team as well as the entire audit firm meet the relevant independence requirements discussed in Chapter 3.

Competencies

In considering whether the firm has the capabilities, competence, time, and resources to undertake a new engagement from a new or an existing client, the firm must review the specific requirements of the engagement and existing partner and staff profiles. According to paragraph 31 of the International Standard on Quality Control, prior to the engagement, the audit firm must consider the following:

- Do firm personnel have knowledge of the relevant industries or subject matter?
- Do firm personnel have experience with relevant regulatory or reporting requirements or the ability to gain the necessary skills and knowledge effectively?
- Does the firm have sufficient personnel with the necessary capabilities and competence?
- Would additional experts be available if needed?
- Will the firm be able to complete the engagement within the reporting deadline?
- Does the audit team have the technical expertise including expertise or regulations in the company's business?
- Does the auditor have the appropriate information technology at their disposal?
- What type of after-audit services can the auditor provide?

Engagement Letter

The auditor has to send an engagement letter to the client.

An example of an engagement letter obtained from the new ISA 700, which supersedes parts of ISA 210 is shown in Exhibit 5.1. There are no significant differences when comparing the ISA engagement letter with a PCAOB engagement letter.

In this section, we discussed stages in the engagement process. Once the auditor has accepted the client, whether as a new or a continuing client, then the next step involves planning the audit. This is discussed next.

Exhibit 5.1 Example of an engagement letter (Obtained from ISA 700 amendment to ISA 210).

To the Board of Directors or the appropriate representative of senior management

You have requested that we audit the financial statements of X which comprise the balance sheet as at ___, and the income statement, a statement of changes in equity and cash flow statement for the year then ended, and a summary of significant accounting policies and other explanatory notes. We are pleased to confirm our acceptance and our understanding of this engagement by means of this letter. Our audit will be conducted with the objective of our expressing an opinion on the financial statements.

We will conduct our audit in accordance with International Standards on Auditing. Those Standards require that we comply with ethical requirements and plan and perform the audit to obtain reasonable assurance whether the financial statements are free from material misstatement. An audit involves performing procedures to obtain audit evidence about the amounts and disclosures in the financial statements. The procedures selected depend on the auditor's judgment, including the assessment of the risks of material misstatement of the financial statements, whether due to fraud or error. An audit also includes evaluating the appropriateness of accounting polices used and the reasonableness of accounting estimates made by management, as well as evaluating the overall presentation of the financial statements.

Because of the test nature and other inherent limitations of an audit, together with the inherent limitations of any accounting and internal control system, there is an unavoidable risk that even some material misstatements may remain undiscovered.

In making our risk assessments, we consider internal control relevant to the entity's preparation of the financial statements in order to design audit procedures that are appropriate in the circumstances, but not for the purpose of expressing an opinion on the effectiveness of the entity's internal control. However, we expect to provide you with a separate letter concerning any material weaknesses in the design or implementation of internal control over financial reporting that come to our attention during the audit of the financial statements.

We remind you that the responsibility for the preparation of financial statements that present fairly the financial position, financial performance and cash flows of the company in accordance with International Financial Reporting Standards is that of the management of the company. Our auditors' report will explain that management is responsible for the preparation and the fair presentation of the financial statements in accordance with the applicable financial reporting framework and this responsibility includes:

- Designing, implementing and maintaining internal control relevant to the preparation of financial statements that are free from misstatement, whether due to fraud or error;
- Selecting and applying appropriate accounting policies; and
- Making accounting estimates that are appropriate in the circumstances.

As part of our audit process, we will request from management written confirmation concerning representations made to us in connection with the audit.

We look forward to full cooperation from your staff and we trust that they will make available to us whatever records, documentation and other information are requested in connection with our audit.

[Insert additional information here regarding fee arrangements and billings, as appropriate.]

Please sign and return the attached copy of this letter to indicate that it is in accordance with your understanding of the arrangements for our audit of the financial statements.

XYZ & Co
Acknowledged on behalf of ABC Company by
(signed)
Name and Title
Date

Planning an Audit

Objectives in the Planning of an Audit

The objective of planning an audit is to determine the amount and type of evidence and tests required to assure the auditor that there is no material misstatement of the financial statements. ISA 300 *Planning an Audit of Financial Statements* states the auditor should plan the audit so that the engagement is performed in an effective manner. In planning an audit the engagement partner has to decide the extent of involvement of varying skilled professionals.

PCAOB's AU 336 contains requirements regarding the auditor's obligations for determining the extent of involvement of professionals possessing specialized skills. Specialists according to AU 336 can be, but need not limited to, actuaries, appraisers, engineers among others including attorneys. AU 336 provides situations in which specialists should be used. This could be when the specialist is essential in performing substantive tests to evaluate material financial statement assertions. Similar guidance is also provided in AS 9 of the PCAOB. In particular, paragraph 16 of AS 9 states that the auditor should determine whether specialized skill or knowledge is needed to perform appropriate risk assessments, plan or perform audit procedures, or evaluate results. paragraph 17 of AS 9 states that if a person with specialized skill or knowledge employed or engaged by the auditor participates in the audit, the auditor should have sufficient knowledge of the subject matter to be addressed by such a person to enable the auditor to (a) communicate the objectives of that person's work, (b) determine whether that person's procedures meet the auditor's objectives, and (c) evaluate the results of that person's procedures as they relate to the nature, timing, and extent of other planned audit procedures and the effects on the auditor's report. ISA 300 does not contain these requirements.

ISA 315 *Understanding the entity and its environment and assessing the risks of material misstatement* notes to attain the objective the auditor has to (paragraphs 20 to 24):

- Perform audit procedures to understand the entity.
- Perform audit procedures to understand the entity's environment, including the entity's internal control.
- Assess the risks of material misstatements of the financial statements.
- Determine the materiality of the financial statement items to be tested.
- Prepare the planning memorandum and audit program containing the auditor's response to the identified risks.

These are considered individually.

Perform Audit Procedures to Obtain an Understanding of the Entity

Paragraph 7 of ISA 315 states that the auditor should perform risk assessment procedures to obtain an understanding of the entity and its environment. Risk assessment procedures to be performed are described below.

Inquiries of Management and Others Within the Entity   Much information can be obtained by inquiries. Inquiries can be directed towards those charged with governance; internal audit personnel; employees involved in initiating, processing, or recording complex or unusual transactions; in-house legal counsel; and marketing or sales personnel (this is helpful in identifying changes in marketing strategies, sales trends, and contractual arrangements with customers). Overall, the discussions could encompass management objectives such as increasing profit, reducing investment in working capital, and reducing taxes among others. It is noted that although management may be the most effective and efficient information source, it is worthwhile to obtain information from as many sources as possible to reduce the potential for bias.

Analytical Procedures   ISA 315 in paragraph 10 notes that analytical procedures may be helpful in identifying the existence of unusual transactions or events, amounts, ratios, and trends that might indicate matters that have financial statement and audit implications. For example, the ratio of gross profit (sales minus cost of goods sold = gross profit) to sales can be compared from one year to the next to indicate changes in the company's profit generating potential from a consistent product line. Analytical procedures are useful in that they help the auditor develop expectations about plausible relationships; comparison with actual relationships could yield information about unusual or unexpected relationships. In the example, if gross profit ratio (gross profit/sales) increased sharply from one year to the next, other things remaining the same, that would be a signal to the auditor that something may be amiss in the company's inventory count or sales bookings. This could, in turn, identify risks of material misstatement. We discuss this more extensively in a later chapter and will not elaborate further here.

Observation and Inspection   The importance of observation and inspection is that evidence from this could support information previously obtained from inquiries of management. Paragraph 11 of ISA 315 provides examples for auditors including, but not limited to:

- Observation of entity activities and operations;
- Inspection of documents (such as business plans and strategies), records, and internal control manuals;
- Reading reports prepared by management (quarterly management reports) and those charged with governance (minutes of board of directors' meetings);
- Visiting the entity's premises and plant facilities;
- Tracing transactions through the information system relevant to financial reporting (popularly referred to as *walkthroughs*). In discussing transactions, PCAOB's AU 330 includes a requirement to confirm accounts receivable unless certain conditions exist. This is a left over from paragraph 34 of Statements on Auditing Standard (SAS) No. 67, *the Confirmation Process*. This requirement is not in ISA.

ISA 315 paragraph 12 requires a team-wide discussion of the susceptibility of the financial statements to fraud or error. The objective of this discussion is for members of the audit planning team to gain a better understanding of the potential for material misstatements of the financial statements resulting from fraud or error.

Perform Procedures to Understand the Environment of the Entity

This is discussed in paragraph 20 of ISA 315. The auditor is advised to study the following:

Industry, Regulatory and Other External Factors   Paragraph 22 of ISA 315 notes that the auditor should obtain an understanding of the relevant industry, regulatory, and other external factors, including the applicable financial reporting framework. These factors include industry conditions such as the competitive environment, supplier and customer relationships, and technological developments. These factors also include the legal and political environment and environmental requirements affecting the industry and the entity and other external factors such as general economic conditions.

Nature of the Entity   This is covered in paragraph 25 of ISA 315. The auditor should obtain an understanding of the nature of the entity. The nature of the entity refers to the entity's operations, its ownership and governance, the types of investments that it is making and plans to make, the way the entity is structured, and how it is financed. This is important because an understanding of the nature of the entity enables the auditor to understand the classes of transactions, account balances, and disclosures to be expected in the financial statements. An understanding of the ownership and relations between owners and other people or entities is important in determining whether related party transactions (RPTs) have been identified and accounted for appropriately. (Additional guidance is provided in ISA 550, *Related Parties* on this matter.)

Objectives and Strategies and Related Business Risks   Here the entity's objectives are the overall plans for the company as determined by those charged with governance and management. Strategies are the operational approaches by which management intends to achieve its objectives. Business risks result from significant conditions, events, circumstances, actions or inactions that could adversely affect the entity's ability to achieve its objectives and execute its strategies. It is important to understand business risk because most business risk will have a financial consequence that may find their way into financial statements. The purpose of understanding this is to:

- Understand the client's strategic advantage and disadvantages;
- Understand the risks that threaten the client's business objectives;

- Understand and benchmark performance: the evidence that the expected value is being created; and
- Compare reported financial results with expectations and design additional audit test work to address any gaps between expectations.

Measurement and Review of the Entity's Financial Performance   This is covered in paragraph 35 of ISA 315. In order to assess the risk of material misstatements in the financial statements, an auditor should examine internally generated information used by the management and external (third party) evaluations of the company. Internal information may include key performance indicators such as budgets, variance analysis, and divisional, departmental, and other level performance reports. The auditor is also expected to compare the entity's performance with those of its competitors. The auditor is also required to evaluate external information such as analyst's reports and credit rating agency reports. It is important for the auditor because internal or external performance measures may create pressures on management to misstate the financial statements.

Assess Risks of Material Misstatements of Financial Statements

This is addressed in paragraph 100 of ISA 315. The auditor is required to assess the risks of material misstatement at the financial statement level and at the assertion level for classes of transactions account balances and disclosures. paragraph 100 of ISA 315 requests the auditor to do the following:

- Identify risks throughout the process of obtaining an understanding of the entity and its environment, including relevant controls that relate to the risks by considering the classes of transactions, account balances, and disclosures in the financial statements.
- Relate the identified risks to what can go wrong at the assertion level.

- Consider whether the risks are of a magnitude that could result in a material misstatement of the financial statements.

In determining whether these risks exist, there is a difference between the United States and the international auditing standards. In the United States, PCAOB's AU 316 *Consideration of Fraud in a Financial Statement Audit* and also PCAOB's AS 12 *Identifying and Assessing the Risks of Material Misstatement* requires the auditor to consider the risk of misstatement due to fraud. PCAOB's AU 316 contains a specific requirement for the auditor to consider the results of the assessment of the risk of material misstatement due to fraud during planning. However ISA 315 does not. Further, the appendices of PCAOB AU 316 provide examples of how to assess risks of material misstatement due to fraud. This is not so with ISA 315. This is an issue that auditors have to be aware of, namely, the U.S. standards give more prominence to assessing risk of fraud during the planning phase of the audit. Another difference is that PCAOB AU 316 has been expanded to specifically include addressing, when applicable, the issue of whether the person performing the control possesses the necessary authority and competence to perform the control effectively. This is not in ISA 330.

Determine Materiality of Items to Be Tested (ISA 315 Paragraph 48)

In making judgments about materiality the auditor is required to consider the following aspects:

- The events or transactions giving rise to the misstatement
- The size of the entity
- The nature of the entity's business
- The legality, sensitivity, normality, and potential circumstances of the event or transactions
- The nature of the entity's business
- The identity of any other parties involved
- The accounts and disclosure notes affected

There are no differences between the application of ISA 320 and the U.S. equivalent PCAOB's AS 11 entitled *Consideration of Materiality in Planning and Performing an Audit*. The topics and guidance are similar. The identity of any other parties involved, though, may be extremely important in that, if transactions are conducted between related parties, the actual value of the transaction to the organization may never be known. In the next section, we address the differences between the newly adopted PCAOB AS 18 *Related Parties* and the ISA 550.

Related Party Transactions

Introduction

The PCAOB recently requested comment on and then approved AS 18 entitled *Related Parties*. RPTs are a problem because the negotiated price for the exchange of an asset or the price of a service, for example, may reflect the relationship between the decision makers on both sides (e.g., parent–child; husband–wife) and not reflect the fair market value of the asset or service being exchanged. Accordingly, the shareholders or stakeholders of the organization may either receive too few resources for an item or service sold to a related party or pay too much for such an item. AS 18 was adopted by the PCAOB because it was felt that the existing standard, the PCAOB's AU 334 Interim Standard, was insufficient. AS 18 improves upon AU 334 *Related Parties*, the current PCAOB-related party standard, by providing additional guidelines in the form of specific audit procedures for auditors' use in dealing with RPTs. The need to address this is considered especially important because AU 334 has not been substantially updated since it was released in 1983. As a matter of fact, despite such prominent scandals as Enron, Worldcom, and Tyco international, AU 334 has remained virtually unchanged. The PCAOB feels RPTs increase the risk of material misstatement in company financial statements. The issue of RPTs is considered important because, as the PCAOB notes in its release (PCAOB release 2014-002), prominent corporate scandals involving RPTs have undermined investor confidence and resulted in significant losses for investors. The PCAOB's release further noted that existing requirements are inadequate and these weaknesses need to be addressed with special focus on providing greater guidance to auditors.

In particular, the PCAOB felt AU 334 was deficient in that it lacked direction; further, the procedures discussed to tackle and investigate RPT were inadequate. AS 18 provides more procedures for accounting for and disclosure of transactions between a company and related parties relative to ISA 550 and its own AU 334. AS 18 becomes effective on or after December 15, 2014.

Summary Requirements of AS 18

An RPT is a problem because it causes errors in the measurement and the recognition of transactions. These, in turn, cause errors in financial statements that can go undetected by the auditor. In essence RPTs can increase risks of material misstatement. The purpose of AS 18 is to provide greater guidance with respect to identifying, assessing, and responding to risks of material misstatement because of RPTs.

AS 18 requires the auditor to do the following:

a. Perform specific procedures to obtain an understanding of the company's relationships and transactions with related parties. (These new procedures should be performed in conjunction with the auditor's risk assessment procedures provided in PCAOB's AS 12).

b. Evaluate whether the company has properly identified its related parties and relationships and transactions with related parties.

c. Perform procedures to determine if a transaction exists with a related party who is undisclosed to the auditor.

d. Perform specific procedures regarding each RPT that is determined to be a significant risk.

e. Communicate the auditor's evaluation of accounting for and disclosure of RPTS to the audit committee.

A publication by Deloitte Touche notes that AS 18 (forthcoming standard effective December 2014) carries much of the content from the current standards (ISA 550 and AU 334). However, there are important differences.

Given this basic information, we summarize the key differences between PCAOB and ISA with respect to RPT under the following categories:

- Overall content
- Audit procedures associated with RPTs
- Obtaining an understanding of the company's process relative to RPTs
- Performing RPT related inquiries
- Communicating with the audit engagement team and other auditors
- Identifying and assessing risks of material misstatement with RPTs
- Responding to the risks of material misstatement associated with RPTs.
- Evaluating whether the company has properly identified its related parties and RPTs
- Evaluating financial statement accounting and disclosures
- Communications with the audit committee

Overall Content

AS 18 (forthcoming standard) carries forward much of the content from the earlier standards (ISA 550 and AU 334). However, in certain circumstances, the Board made revisions to *clarify and refine various aspects* of the new standard. A Deloitte Touche report (http://www.iasplus.com/en/publications/us/heads-up/2014/pcaob-requirements) notes that the forthcoming AS 18 differs from the currently effective standards in that:

1. It includes additional examples of others in the company to whom an auditor may direct inquiries about related parties.
2. Its wording has been refined to prominently emphasize the auditor's responsibility for the identification of related parties. This includes testing the accuracy and completeness of the company's

identification of its related parties and relationships and transactions with its related parties.

The Deloitte Touche report mentioned earlier provides a comprehensive analysis of the differences between AS 18, on the one hand, and ISA 550 and AU 334 on the other, with respect to identification and handling of RPTs, and we use the findings of this report extensively in our discussion.

Audit Procedures Associated With RPTs

Deloitte Touche report cited earlier also notes that AS 18 adds and expands requirements intended to help auditors achieve the objective of obtaining "sufficient appropriate evidence to determine whether related parties and relationships and transactions with related parties have been properly identified, accounted for and disclosed in the financial statements." The Deloitte Touche report notes that unlike the current ISA 550, the proposed standard specifies the objectives of the auditor's work related to RPTs.

The report also notes that the proposed standard uses a *framework* neutral approach regarding (1) definition of related parties and (2) financial statement disclosure requirements (i.e., the release acknowledges that in preparing financial statements, issuers might use different financial reporting frameworks such as U.S. GAAP or IFRS. This is different from AU 334, which refers auditors only to U.S. GAAP).

The proposed standard retains many of the current standard's requirements related to procedures; however it makes a number of key changes, including adding specific procedures for:

- auditors to respond to risks of material misstatements regarding RPTs;
- auditors to test the accuracy and completeness of RPTs identified by the company;
- improving the auditor's focus on accounting by evaluating the adequacy of the accounting and disclosures of RPTs;
- adding audit committee communications (ISA 550 and AU 334 do not discuss communications to audit committees).

Obtaining an Understanding of the Company's Process with Respect to RPTs

AS 18 requires the auditor to obtain an understanding of the controls that management has established to (1) identify RPTs, (2) authorize and approve transactions with related parties, and (3) account for and disclose relationships and transactions with related parties in the financial statements.

This is more pro-active relative to ISA 550 and AU 334 which state that the auditor should obtain an understanding of the management's responsibilities when determining the work to be performed for possible RPTs. Under AS 18, auditors will need to perform procedures to evaluate the design of such controls and determine that they have been implemented. Examples of specific procedures to evaluate designs of controls are also provided in AS 18. The Deloitte Touche report notes that these provisions differ from those in the current standard, which state that the auditor should obtain an understanding of the management's responsibilities when determining the work to be performed for possible RPTs. Further, the current standard requires the auditor to consider controls over management activities, whereas the new standard requires the auditor to understand the controls for RPTs. Under AS 18 auditors *must* perform procedures to evaluate the design of such controls and determine they have been implemented.

Performing RPT-Related Inquiries

AS 18 *requires* the auditor to make inquiries from management about RPTs and about the company's relationships and transactions with them, including the business purposes of such transactions. AS 18 adds procedures the auditor should perform with respect to inquiries of management and other personnel. The current standards ISA 550 and AU 334 only describe audit procedures that the auditor should consider in determining the existence of related parties. (Examples of audit procedures include requesting from management the names of related parties and whether there were any transactions with these parties during the period under audit.) The key difference is that the current standard only *recommends*, whereas the forthcoming standard AS 18 *requires* the inquiries noted in the preceding lines. In addition ISA 550 and AU 334 do not specify any required communication with the audit committee. AS 18 does specify communication. So, this is a notable difference. AS 18 also includes examples of other individuals in the company to whom it would be appropriate for the auditor to direct such inquiries (e.g., internal auditors, in house legal counsel and human resources director among others). This is not in the current standards ISA 550 and AU 334 and is another difference.

Communicating with the Audit Engagement Team and Other Auditors

AS 18 states that managers should communicate to the engagement team (team conducting the audit) relevant information about related parties, including the names of the related parties and the nature of the company's transactions with those related parties. In audits in which other auditors participate, the auditor should inquire about RPTs from the other auditor. This is another difference between AS 18 and the current standards.

Identifying and Assessing Risks of Material Misstatement Associated With RPTs

AS18 requires the auditor to identify and assess the risks of material misstatements associated with RPTs. Then, use the results as the basis for planning and performing audit procedures.

AS 18 adds requirements for auditors regarding identifying and assessing risks of material misstatements associated with RPTs. The Deloitte Touche report notes that a key difference is that the forthcoming standard is better because the existing standards, ISA 550 and AU 334 do *not* contain specific guidance for auditors in these matters.

Responding to the Risks of Material Misstatement Associated With Related Parties and RPTs

RPTs can increase the risks of material misstatement in financial statements. AS 18 prescribes specific auditing procedures for RPTs that should be disclosed in the financial statements and considered to be of significant risk. The procedures include the following:

a. Read the underlying documentation and evaluate whether the terms and other information are consistent with explanations from inquiries and other methods of getting audit evidence.
b. Determine whether the transaction has been authorized and approved in accordance with the company's established policies and procedures.
c. Determine whether any exceptions to the company's established policies were granted.
d. Evaluate the financial capability of the related parties with respect to significant uncollected balances.

The Deloitte Touche report states that there is no significant difference between AS 18 and existing standards in respect to these procedures.

Evaluating Whether the Company has Properly Identified its Related Parties and RPTs

The forthcoming standard requires the auditor to evaluate whether the company has properly identified its related parties. AS 18 emphasizes that the auditor should not rely solely on representations made by the management about the accuracy and completeness of RPTs. AS 18 notes that, if an auditor determines that RPTs exist, the auditor is required to perform additional procedures. The purpose is to (1) reassess the risk of material misstatement and (2) evaluate the impact of management's nondisclosure and its consideration of fraud.

The above provisions are in a separate section of AS 18. The Deloitte Touche report notes that while the current standards (ISA 550 and AU 334) do cover the issues discussed in theprevious paragraph they provide *limited direction*.

Evaluating Financial Statement Accounting and Disclosures

Under the forthcoming AS 18, the auditor is required to evaluate the company's accounting for and disclosure of relationships and RPTs.

The auditor is specifically required to determine whether the audit evidence supports or contradicts any management assertion that RPTs were conducted on an arm's length basis. If the auditor is unable to obtain sufficient evidence to corroborate the management's assertions or if the management does not agree to any disclosure required by the auditor, the auditor is required to modify the auditor's report and express a qualified or adverse opinion.

The Deloitte Touche report notes that the new standards broaden the requirements of the auditor in terms of the scope of the auditor's responsibility. For example, a preface in a statement that *management believes* or it is the *company's belief* does not change the auditor's responsibility. For example, if the company's belief is that all RPTs have been disclosed, it does not absolve the auditor of his or her responsibility. The auditor has to be proactive and verify. Subject to that, there is little difference between the proposed and existing standards.

Communication with the Audit Committee

AS 18 requires the auditor to communicate the auditor's evaluation of (1) the company's identification of RPT, (2) accounting for RPT, and (3) disclosure of RPTs directly to the audit committee. This is a significant difference to the existing standards ISA 550 and AU 334, which do *not* state that the auditor is required to communicate the above RPT-related information to the audit committee.

Additional Issues

There are three important issues regarding the planning stage of the audit that which have to be addressed. These relate to:

- partner rotation;
- using the work of another auditor; and
- using the work of an expert.

Partner Rotation

Even though the ISA does not mention this specifically, the European Union Guideline requires that to maintain independence, the partners must be rotated every seven years. We previously noted that the auditor must be aware of how national laws affect the audit. Here is an example of local (or European Union-wide) regulation adding rules that the auditor must be familiar with, in addition to being familiar with the ISA rules themselves. In this respect, there is a difference between European regulations and SOX, with the latter requiring that partners be rotated every five years. Given that the ISA is used in over 100 countries, this emphasizes the need for auditors to be aware of additional requirements that national laws or regulations may add to the auditor's burden even in nations that formally use the ISA.

Using the Work of Another Auditor

In certain cases, if the auditor feels they do not have sufficient auditing resources and presence because one part of the business is in another division or country, they have to decide if another auditor with the requisite expertise, (e.g., having audited organizations in that industry before), resources, and independence will be required to audit a part of the business of the client in the other division or country. In this respect, ISA 600 provides guidance to auditors. The guidance under ISA 600 requires the auditor to initially consider whether the auditor can act as principal auditor should they decide to seek the help of another auditor (please refer paragraph 6 for the discussion here). The determination of principal auditor status depends on (a) the extent to which the portion of the financial statements it audits is material and (b) the degree of the auditor's knowledge regarding the business or its components. If the auditor feels that the portion of the financial statements being audited is material and the auditor's knowledge of the business is substantial, then the auditor or she can opt to act as principal auditor. The other party is then referred to as the other auditor.

It is the duty of the principal auditor to ensure that the other auditor is competent and independent. How can the principal auditor determine whether the other auditor is competent? This is difficult to measure. Sources of information include auditors, bankers, and discussions with the other auditor.

The principal auditor is required to advise the other auditor of the independence requirements. If the other auditor feels that its independence could be compromised in any way the other auditor should inform the principal auditor. The principal auditor is required to take an active role in the work of the other auditor. For example, the principal auditor is required to request a written summary of the procedures that the other auditor will apply in the audit and review those procedures. It is suggested that the principal auditor visit the other auditor's premises to review these procedures (refer paragraphs 7 to 11, ISA 600). This is more stringent than PCAOB auditing standards, which do not appear to require visits by the principal to the other auditor's premises nor critical review of the procedures applied by the other auditor. In any event when reading the original ASB and PCAOB standards, one does not see this guidance. (In reality lack of guidance does not preclude an auditor from reviewing procedures applied by the other auditor.) The principal auditor also has the authority to request the other auditor to limit the procedures if the principal auditor feels that the tests are too time consuming and unnecessarily rigorous given the circumstances.

In addition to the issue raised in the previous paragraph, namely, that principal auditors are required to visit the other auditor's premises under ISA but not under PCAOB, there are minor differences pertinent to auditors operating in the U.S. environment vis à vis the international environment. Paragraph 12(b) of ISA 620 requires the auditor to evaluate the significant assumptions and methods of the auditor's selected auditor. The PCAOB uses an expanded wording of this requirement to more clearly articulate the auditor's responsibility in this regard. The ASB believes this does not create a difference between the application of ISA 620 and Section 620 of the original ASB (refer aicpa.org/FRC), which is now PCAOB's AU 336. There are also differences in the ISA not specified in the PCAOB's standards Paragraphs 16 and 17 of ISA 620 contains a conditional requirement regarding the auditor's reference to the specialist or expert (other auditor) hired by the auditor in the auditor's report when such reference is required by law or regulation. Because such reference is not required by law or regulation in the United States, such a requirement is not included in AU 336.

Once the audit is complete the principal auditor is required to document in the audit working papers the components that were audited by the other auditor and their significance to the financial statements. The principal auditor is also required to document the procedures used by the other auditors. If they had requested the other auditors to limit the procedures, however, they do not need to report that nor the reasons for requesting the procedures be limited.

It is required that the other auditor bring to the attention of the principal auditor areas where the other auditor could not conduct work as requested. The other auditor also needs to advise the principal auditor of any matters that came to the attention of the other auditor that may have an important bearing on the principal auditor's work.

There are differences in the requirements in the ISA and PCAOB standards. The AICPA (www.aicpa.org/FRC) notes that ISA 600 does not permit the auditor's report on the client's financial statements to make a reference to a component auditor unless required by law or regulation to include such a reference. PCAOB's AU 543, *Part of Audit Performed by Other Independent Auditor* requires the auditor to make reference to the audit of a component auditor in the auditor's report on the client financial statements. Why? The PCAOB may believe that the ability to make reference to the report of another auditor is appropriate in the United States for two main reasons. This has always been required by GAAS in the United States and there are no compelling new issues or developments to suggest a need to change the approach. In particular, some audits are complex because of factors such as size and diversity of the client operations (auditing of the Federal government is a striking example). In such circumstances, eliminating the option to make reference to a component auditor serves no purpose as it reduces transparency.

If two auditors are involved in the audit, an important issue relates to the responsibility for the audit. This is important, because, for whatever reason, should the client decide to sue, the agreement between the principal auditor and the other auditor will factor into which firm faces damages should the client win the case. This issue is dealt with in paragraph 18 of ISA 600. The paragraph allows auditors to follow the laws of the local country in which the lawsuit occurs. For example, the principal auditor can chose to take full responsibility or apportion responsibility if doing the latter is consistent with, or required by, local law. Paragraph 18 clearly states that, should the principal auditor decide to apportion responsibility, the principal auditor's report should state this fact clearly and should indicate the magnitude of the portion of the financial statements audited by the other auditor. It is important to emphasize that in some countries division of responsibility may not be allowed. Paragraph 11 of the Australian standard AU 600 entitled *Special Considerations-Audits of a Group Financial Report (Including the Work of Component Auditors)* does not allow division of responsibility in Australia. Similarly the Implementation Guidance issued by the Japanese Institute of Certified Public Accountants does not allow this in Japan. SAS 510 (the UK equivalent of ISA 600) does not allow division of responsibility in the UK. That is, the main auditor has to take the full brunt of any legal action. The other auditor is considered as in the employ of the primary auditor, and it is the primary auditor who has to *face the music*. The Canadian standards also do not allow division of responsibility. The United States allows division of responsibility. However, in the audit opinion, the auditor is required to clearly state that the financial statement includes numbers that have been audited by another auditor. Thus, it is vital that auditors in the United States clearly study local legislation when deciding if (and how) to use the work of a local auditor based in a foreign country. As mentioned, in many parts of Europe, unlike the United States, the auditor cannot assign responsibility but bears the full liability. This is an important issue for American auditors to bear in mind.

Using the Work of an Expert

In certain cases, the auditor may have neither the education nor the technical expertise to conduct a component of the audit. Paragraph 6 of ISA 620 provides the following examples where an expert could be called in:

- Valuations of certain types of assets, for example, land and buildings, plant and machinery, works of art and precious stones.
- Determination of quantities or the physical condition of assets, for example, minerals stored in stockpiles, underground mineral and petroleum reserves, and the remaining useful life of plant and machinery.
- Determination of amounts using specialized techniques or methods, for example, in an actuarial valuation.

In such cases, the auditor may contemplate calling in an expert. ISA 620 provides guidance on the use of experts. ISA 620 defines an expert as a person or firm possessing special skills, knowledge, and experience in a particular field other than accounting and auditing. In particular, paragraph 8 of ISA 620 notes that the auditor should evaluate the professional competence of the expert prior to using him/her. This will involve considering the professional certification or licensing by, or membership in, an appropriate professional body. The auditor is also required to assess the experience and reputation in the field in which the auditor is seeking audit evidence. The auditor should also ensure that the expert is independent. (If, for example, the expert has an investment in the entity being audited, that implies that the expert is financially dependent on the entity. This is assumed to impair his or her independence. ISA 620 does not prohibit the auditor from using an expert even assuming impaired independence. Rather, the auditor is required to seek evidence from other experts to corroborate the first expert's evidence. Some countries including the United States do not allow an auditor to use an expert who lacks independence. Thus, the auditor must be careful in choosing an expert and examining the background of the expert.)

The auditor is required to communicate clearly with the expert. The auditor should make clear the scope of the expert's work and intended use of the expert's work by the auditor. The expert should be informed about the extent of his or her access to files and records of the client and also the matters to be covered in the report by the expert to the auditor.

It is also required that the auditor evaluate the work of the expert. Paragraph12 of ISA 620 provides guidance to the auditor. In particular, the auditor is required to examine:

- source data used;
- assumptions and methods used and their consistency with prior periods; and
- results of the expert's work in the light of the auditor's overall knowledge of the business and of the results of other audit procedures.

Paragraph 12 of ISA 620 takes this a step further and even requires an auditor to review and test the data used by the expert and the appropriateness and reasonableness of the assumptions and methods used. If the auditor tests the results and concludes that the results are not consistent with the auditor's results, then the matter has to be resolved. This could involve further discussions with the entity and the expert and applying additional audit procedures even to the extent of engaging another expert. There are differences between ISA 620 and Section PCAOB's AU 336 in the United States. As noted above, ISA 620 requires the auditor to evaluate the significant assumptions and methods of the auditor's specialist (www.aicpa.org/FRC). The PCAOB's AU 336 expanded the wording of this requirement to more clearly articulate the auditor's responsibility in this regard. However, the AICPA notes (www.aicpa.org/FRC) that the ASB then and PCAOB now may believe this does not create a difference between the application of ISA 620 and the application of PCAOB's AU 336. There are also requirements in the ISA not mentioned in GAAS. Paragraph 14 of ISA 620 contains a condition requirement regarding the auditor's reference to the auditor's specialist in the auditor's report when such reference is required by law or regulation. Because such reference is not required by law or regulation in the United States, such requirement is not included in PCAOB's AU 336.

In general it is held that if the auditor issues a clean (unmodified report) to the client, then the work of the expert does not need to be referenced. This is because such a reference might be misunderstood to be a qualification of the auditor's opinion or a division of responsibility, neither of which is intended. If the audit report is qualified, it is recommended that, where appropriate, the auditor refer to the work of the expert and the extent of the expert's involvement. The auditor is also required to clearly name the expert. However, paragraph 17 of ISA 610 requires the auditor to obtain the permission of the expert prior to citing them in the auditor report. If permission is not granted, then a problem arises. This is because ISA 610 does not cover a situation where permission is refused. The assumption is that permission is granted. If permission is refused then the auditor may need to seek legal counsel. This is not an issue under PCAOB where there is no requirement that permission of the expert be required prior to citing them. Hence, U.S. auditors need to be aware that under ISA they must obtain the permission of the expert they used prior to citing them in the auditor's report; otherwise legal issues could arise.

Conclusion

The engagement acceptance process and planning an audit are both very critical, early parts of the auditing process. The engagement process provides the auditor with information that may lead it to accept a potential client and the revenue that accepting the client would provide or reject the client. Earlier in the book we discussed the problem of audit failure—the giving of an inappropriate opinion on the client's financial statements—and auditor legal liability. In order to avoid legal liability as well as to help ensure that the audit firm itself has the right mix of talent and capability to audit a particular client, the auditor is required under both ISA and PCAOB standards to learn about the client. In this chapter, we present a description of how the ISA and PCAOB standards require and suggest that the engagement process be carried out. This information is important because it provides valuable information about how audit firms, in effect, investigate their clients before deciding to accept a potential client.

Next, we describe the process by which the auditor, having accepted the client, begins planning the audit itself. This information is also important to readers because they learn something about the information used to plan the audit, a very important process that impacts how the audit firm's resources will be used during the audit itself. Understanding both the client engagement process and the audit planning process will be very useful in understanding the actual conduct of the audit presented in the following chapters.

CHAPTER 6

Risk Assessment and Tests of Internal Controls

In this chapter we focus on and address the following issues:

- Techniques and guidelines for assessing technological, economic, legal, and other forms of risk both in the United States and internationally
- Special focus on business risk and how the auditor can ascertain and determine substantive tests based on the level of risk
- How assessment of business risk varies between the United States (Public Company Accounting Oversight Board [PCAOB]) and abroad (International Standards on Auditing [ISA])

We then focus on an integrally related aspect, namely, internal controls over financial reporting, with special reference to:

- how auditors should assess internal controls over financial reporting;
- the significant differences, if any, between PCAOB and ISA guidance;
- lessons (if any) auditors should be aware of as a result of these differences.

Introduction

Both topics of risk assessment and tests of internal controls over financial reporting—the only type of internal controls addressed in this book—are intertwined. As mentioned, we first discuss risk assessment and then, based on risk assessment, discuss how the auditors conduct tests of internal controls. The internal control system is the organization's system of checks and balances, a system consisting of review and oversight processes and tools to help ensure that errors or fraudulent entries are not made in the accounting system. The system can also help ensure that assets are not stolen as well. The focus throughout this chapter is oriented to the view point of the auditor in an audit setting.

Why does an auditor need to assess risk? The reason for assessing risk is to help prevent fraud and misstatements in the financial statements. When an auditor audits a company, their main objective is to provide reasonable assurance that the financial statements do not contain material mistakes. This will help ensure better future decisions by the company and its current and future investors and creditors. Understanding overall risk factors that may impact the client firm will help the auditor determine which auditing procedures should be used to test, among others, internal controls to mitigate the probability of fraud and material misstatement of the financial statements. Even apart from internal controls, understanding the overall risk a client firm faces will also help the audit firm assess any other potential sources of financial misstatements in the client's financial statements. For example, some sorts of business risk may lead management to engage in financial statement fraud to help ensure that the firm's financial statements show that the corporation is thriving. These behaviors may not be able to be corrected even by an otherwise excellent internal control system because client management stands atop the internal control system and can make fraudulent accounting entries that the internal control system cannot block because top management controls the internal control system. Accordingly, the auditor must audit both the financial accounting system and the accuracy of its entries and the internal control system that helps—but does not guarantee—the accuracy of its entries. Even apart from fraud, an auditor is required to develop an understanding of the various risks a company faces because doing so helps them appropriately allocate their audit team resources. Knowing, for example, that the technology that a client firm sells is changing rapidly alerts the auditor to obsolete items in the client's merchandise inventory account.

Overall, unlike ISA, PCAOB Auditing Standard (AS) 5 specifically requires an integrated audit. In PCAOB AS 5 paragraph 6, it is noted that "the audit of internal control over financial reporting should be integrated with the audit of the financial statements." Paragraph 6 continues, cautioning that the objectives of the audits are not identical. Therefore, it says, the auditor must plan and perform the work to achieve the objectives of *both audits*. The concept of an integrated audit means that in addition to auditing the financial statements, the auditor must assess whether the test of internal controls show that the internal controls can help ensure financial statements that are not materially misstated. This will be discussed in greater detail at the tail end of this chapter. The differences in overall philosophy between the standards setting bodies with respect to risk assessment and tests of internal controls over financial reporting are significant. We focus on risk and discuss guidelines for auditors assessing the various forms of business risk first and internal control risk second.

It is important to note here that the *general methods* that the auditor could use to evaluate the risk assessment process, the risk the client firm faces, and the design and operation of the internal control system include:

- inquiring of management and client firm personnel about the risk assessment and internal control processes;
- observing how the internal controls operate; and
- inspecting all documentation to gain evidence about the operation of the control system and reperformance.

Techniques and Guidelines for Assessing Technological, Economic, Legal, and Other Forms of Risk Both in the United States and Internationally

ISA 315 *Identifying and Assessing Risks of Material Misstatement through Understanding the Entity and its Environment* (the Auditing Standards Board [ASB] equivalent is Section *315 Understanding the Entity and its Environment and Assessing the Risks of Material Misstatement*) states that the auditor should obtain an understanding of the entity and its environment, including its internal control system. This understanding should be sufficient to identify and assess the risks of material misstatement of the financial statements (whether due to fraud or error). This understanding should also be sufficient to enable auditors to design and perform further audit procedures. The standard notes that obtaining an understanding of the entity and its environment, including its internal control, is a continuous dynamic process of gathering, updating, and analyzing information throughout the audit. Internal control is a vital element that affects the audit process. Everybody in the firm has responsibility for maintaining an adequate system of internal controls. This includes the company's management, board of directors, and other personnel including, most importantly, the internal auditors. Internal auditors are auditors who are direct employees of the client firm itself. Mostly they do not perform financial statement audits. They can, however, be part of the monitoring component of the client's internal controls. They may also evaluate the efficiency and effectiveness of operations, whether corporate policies are being complied with, and so forth.

A company establishes internal controls to achieve its performance goals. Internal controls help ensure that, in the process of attempting to attain those goals, the company has (1) a reliable financial reporting system and (2) is in compliance with relevant laws and regulations. We further discuss and elaborate on internal controls in the last part of this chapter. At this point, the main issue to be aware of is that ISA 315 states that the establishment of effective internal control comprises the following components from the point of view of the auditor. These include understanding the (refer paragraph 20 and onwards):

- industry and its environment;
- nature of the entity;
- objectives and strategies and related business risks; and
- measurement and review of the entity's financial performance.

These are discussed individually.

Understanding the Industry and its Environment

According to ISA 315, the following are the key factors that an auditor should look at for the purpose of risk assessment (obtained from Appendix 1 of ISA 315, with the actual appendix providing greater detail than does our succinct summary):

Industry Conditions

- What is the nature of the market and competition?
- Is demand affected by cyclical and seasonal activity?
- What is the nature of the product technology relating to the company's products? For example, is there a high probability of obsolescence due to the speed of technological development?

Regulatory Environment

- What are the industry specific practices?
- Is there legislation and regulation that could significantly affect the entity's operations that the auditor should be aware of?
- What is the nature of corporate and other taxation for this entity?
- Are there any specific government policies that could affect the entity's business? This includes determining if there are policies that have a positive impact (e.g., financial incentives) and policies that have a negative impact (tariffs and trade restrictions).
- Are there any special environmental regulations that could affect the company's activities?

Other Key Issues

- What is the present general level of economic activity in the industry? (i.e., Is there currently a recession or is the economy in a growth phase?)
- What are the present rates and availability of financing?
- Is there inflation? If so, does it affect the company's ability to expand? Does it harm the company in any way?

A sound illustration is also provided by Hayes et al. (2005). They note that the telecommunications industry has certain risks because it is globally competitive, is characterized by rapid technological changes that render its assets obsolete at a faster rate than assets in other industries and have laws strictly regulating service fee. These factors generate risks that may result in material misstatements of the financial statements of the companies in that industry. Auditors have to adjust their tests accordingly.

Nature of the Entity

The auditor should examine the following issues for the purpose of risk assessment as stated by ISA 315 in Appendix 1:

Business Operations

- What is the nature of revenue sources? (Is the company in manufacturing or in wholesale, import/export, financial services, etc?)
- Who are the major customers? What are the present profit margins? What is the existing market share? Who are the competitors?
- Is the company involved in any alliances, joint ventures and outsourcing activities?
- Is the company involved in any electronic commerce including Internet sales?
- Who are the important suppliers of goods and services? Is there stability of supply? What are the terms of payment and methods of delivery?

Investments

- Is the company planning to acquire another business or enter into a merger? Are there plans to dispose of part of its business segment?
- Are there investments in nonconsolidated entities, including partnerships, joint ventures, and special purpose entities? (This is important because companies like Enron used special

purpose entities for the purpose of illegal off balance sheet financing, according to Schwarcz (2002)). Special purpose entities are a legal entity, usually a limited liability company or limited partnership of some type created to fulfill narrow, specific, or temporary objectives. The main purpose is to isolate the firm from financial risk (refer to International Financial Reporting Standards, IFRS 10).

Financing

- What is the debt structure of the firm? That is, how much debt is short term, needing to be paid back within one year of the balance sheet date, and how much may not have to be paid off for a longer time than that?
- What is the overall group structure? (Major subsidiaries and associated entities if any)
- Are there any related party transactions?
- Does the company use derivative financial instruments in any way? (Derivatives are financial instruments that derive their value in response to changes in interest rates and among others, commodity prices and foreign exchange rates, summarized from the Standard Chartered Bank, Annual Report 2010, p. 56).

Financial Reporting

- What are the industry specific practices for this entity?
- What revenue recognition practices are used?
- Where are the entity's locations and what are the related quantities of the entity's reported inventories?
- Are there any foreign currency transactions? If so, what are the foreign currency assets and liabilities?
- Are there any unusual or complex transactions? (Examples of unusual transactions include emerging areas or areas where the law is not resolved, for example accounting for stock based compensation).

ISA 315 notes that all of the issues mentioned in the preceding list have an impact on the risk of a business which, in turn, affects the financial statements. We define business risk as any risk that could potentially affect the financial statements. For example, the possibility of a company's investment losing its value is an example of business risk. This is because, if investments significantly reduce in value, then it could have an adverse effect on the financial statements, which in turn could potentially create incentives to fraudulently misstate the financial statements.

Financing or finance structure is important in determining business risk. For example, a business could create special purpose entities for the purpose of off balance sheet financing as did Enron. This is not fraud and is legal. However, this could affect business risk because the existence of special purpose entities could create incentives for managers to use it as a device to illegally engage in earnings management. Enron, for example, according to Matthew Benjamin in the U.S. News and World Report (April 8, 2002), overstated profits in1999 by $250 million through the use of special purpose entities. Enron also engaged in related party transactions to double reported earnings in 2000. In the presence of material misstatement, information on debt structure, off balance sheet financing, and related parties can give auditors an insight into the extent of risk of material misstatement. While the PCAOB conforms almost entirely to the ISA with respect to the issues discussed in this paragraph, there are minor differences.

Overall Objectives Strategies and Related Business Risks

According to ISA 315 Appendix 1, examples of issues and matters that the auditor could consider are the following:

- Does the entity have the personnel or expertise to deal with changes in the industry?
- Has the company introduced new products and services? (If so, is there increased product liability?)
- Are there new accounting requirements that the company is required to follow? (Risks could include improper implementation or hidden costs in doing so.)

- Are there regulatory requirements that may increase legal exposure?
- Has the company introduced new information technology (IT)? (A risk here may be that the company's systems and processes may be incompatible or internal controls not implemented.)

All these create pressures on management. Similarly, if there are regulatory requirements that increase legal exposure this also increases business risks. Most business risks eventually have a financial consequence and will find their way into financial statements. Hence, based on the questions in the preceding section, if the auditor feels that business risks are accentuated, then they may have to adjust audit tests accordingly. The differences between ISA and PCAOB would appear to relate only to placement of information. For example, in relation to the guidance discussed above, ISA discusses these issues in ISA 500, whereas in the U.S. the PCAOB discusses the requirements in AS 5. The only difference is placement which does not create a difference between the ISAs as a whole and PCAOB as a whole as the AICPA notes (www.aicpa.org/FRC).

Measurement and Review of the Entity's Financial Performance

Based on Appendix 1 of ISA 315, examples of matters that an auditor could consider for the purpose of risk assessment are the following:

- What are the key ratios and performance indicators that should be used when analyzing the business? What information do these performance indicators tell us?
- What do forecasts and variance analysis reports from budgets tell us?
- What do analyst reports and credit ratings reports tell us?
- What information does period to period comparative analysis (revenue growth/decline, profitability increase/decline, etc) tell us?

Information such as variance analysis based on budgets, and other performance level reports and comparisons of an entity's performance with competitors give the auditor insight into risks. Significant deviations or variations from budgets (e.g., variations of *actual* sales results from the budgeted *expectation* for sales) and significant variations from competitors' reported results may indicate a risk of misstatement of financial information. This is important to the auditor in deciding on audit tests. There are minor differences between the ISA and the PCAOB. Whereas the ISA uses the word *significant* (e.g., *significant* deviations from budget, etc), the PCAOB's AS 5 uses words such as *relevant* and *material*. The AICPA (www.aicpa.org/FRC) believes that this should not create any difference between the application of ISA 330 and the PCAOB's AS 5. However, there is one significant difference. AS 5 specifically addresses the question whether the person performing the control in the client entity possesses the necessary authority and competence to perform the controls discussed here. Under AS 5 of the PCAOB, the auditor has to check the authority and competence of the person performing the different controls. The ISA does not have this.

Now we turn the discussion to internal control tools an organization uses to control risks and the auditor's assessment of the entity's use of those tools. External risks to the entity, such as risks stemming from the nature of its environment, may not be controllable by the entity. Other risks to it, such as those stemming from employee theft and the like, are potentially controllable by it. Both are addressed in the following sections.

Review of Internal Controls

At the outset, we must note the guidance on internal control provided by the Committee of Sponsoring Organizations of the Treadway Commission (COSO), the latest version of which was published in 2013. The COSO 2013 *Internal Control–Integrated Framework* provides additional guidance to organizations. This was felt necessary in the light of changes in the business and operating environments since the original COSO came into effect. The new framework, according to COSO. broadens the application of internal controls in addressing operations and reporting objectives. COSO has also discussed tools for assessing the effectiveness of a system of internal control. We do not delve into this area because that is not the purpose of this book. Rather, we recommend interested readers to check this website for more details: http://www.coso.org/ic.htm.

We now focus on the guidance provided by the ISA with respect to internal controls. ISA 315 states that internal control comprises five inter-related components (based on Appendix 2 of ISA 315):

- The control environment
- The entity's risk assessment process
- The information system, including the related business processes relevant to financial reporting and communication
- Control procedures/activities; and
- Monitoring of controls

These will be discussed individually. A detailed explanation is provided in Appendix 2 of ISA 315.

Control Environment

According to ISA 315 the control environment includes the attitudes, awareness, and actions of management and those charged with governance concerning the entity's internal control and its importance in the entity. According to ISA 315, the control environment encompasses the following elements (refer Appendix 2 of ISA 315):

Communication and Enforcement of Integrity and Ethical Values

If the people administering controls have low integrity and ethical values, the controls cannot be considered to be effective. The controls are only as good as the people who are responsible for administering them. This is the reason that this standard includes integrity and ethical values as essential elements of the control environment. Auditors must check if managers have incentives or temptations to engage in dishonest, illegal, or unethical acts.

Commitment to Competence

Competence is defined as the knowledge and skills necessary to accomplish tasks that define the individual's job. Auditors should check the qualifications and experience of those working in the organization.

Participation by Those Charged With Governance

Those charged with governance should be independent of the management. Auditors should ensure that companies have codes of practice/conduct and other regulations or guidance for those in charge of governance.

Management's Philosophy and Operating Style

These encompass a broad range of characteristics. The auditor can develop an understanding of the management's philosophy and operating style from the managements' attitude in dealing with the auditor. For example if the management is aggressive with respect to selecting accounting principles and it argues with auditors regarding management's choice of accounting principles, then this should send a warning signal to the auditors.

Organizational Structure

Auditors should study the organizational structure including key areas of authority and responsibility and check how operating activities are assigned and how the chain of responsibility for controlling employee behavior is established. The auditor is also required to check the appropriateness of the organizational structure based on the size and nature of the firm's activities. If the organizational structure appears too complicated based on the size of the company and the nature of its activities, then it should be a warning signal to auditors.

Importantly, related to organizational structure is the organization's practices in the assignment of authority and responsibility. Accordingly, the auditor should check how authority and responsibility for operating activities are assigned. Does the firm have policies relating to appropriate business practices? Do the key personnel have adequate knowledge and experience to carry out their tasks? Have all personnel read the manual, and do they understand the company's objectives? Also, if individuals have the authority to carry out an activity but not the responsibility to actually do so or see that it is done, it may not be done. Alternately, if individuals have the responsibility to carry out an activity but not the authority, the activity may also not be carried out.

Human Resources Policies and Practices

This relates to recruitment, training, evaluating, counseling, promoting, compensating, and taking remedial actions against employees. Do the training policies include practices such as adequate training and regular seminars to ensure that employees meet expected levels of performance and behavior? Are promotions driven by periodic performance appraisals? All these provide insight for the auditor about the risk associated with the company.

In summary, elements which indicate a successful environment according to ISA 315 in its Appendix 2 are:

- Communication and enforcement of integrity and ethical values;
- A management committed to competence;
- A management's philosophy and operating style;
- A clear organization structure that fits with the firm's size and operating activities;
- A proper assignment of authority and responsibility; and
- Adequate human resources and policies and practices.

This section addressed the organization's control environment. The control environment establishes key things about the organization that the auditor needs to understand. In the next section, we address the entity's risk assessment process. Organizations need to understand the risks they face in order to prevent avoidable damage to the organization. The auditor, of course, needs to understand how the organization assesses risk. Understanding how the organization assesses risk and the organization's view of what risks it faces helps the auditor in developing its plans for conducting the audit.

The Auditor's Assessment of the Entity's Risk Assessment Process

Appendix 2 of ISA 315 provides clear guidance to the auditor on how to assess risk.

In general, all components of internal control, from the control environment to monitoring, should be assessed for risk. The risk assessment process is the process of identifying business risks and the consequences of those risks to the organization. Whereas our discussion of risk assessment earlier in the chapter was at a more general level, we now focus more narrowly on the organization and on threats to the integrity of the output of its accounting system. From the auditor's perspective, they are required to ask the following questions with regard to the preparation of financial statements:

- How does management identify risk of material misstatement in the financial statements that could distort a *true and fair view*? The terms *true and fair view* and *present fairly in all material respects* are considered equivalent by ISA 200 even though ISA uses *true and fair view* and the PCAOB uses *present fairly*. However this is a subject of controversy. Some auditors argue that the terms *present fairly* and *true and fair view* are not equivalent. Some auditors say *present fairly* means in accordance with laws and regulations. *True and fair view*, they say, includes the possibility of deviating from law and regulation when that deviation provides a *true* view. (Please refer Hayes et al. (2005), chapter one for this discussion). For the purpose of this book, we do not enter into this argument but conform to ISA 200 which still assumes equivalence.
- How does management estimate the significance of events that could jeopardize the presentation of a true and fair view?
- How does management assess the likelihood of their occurrence?
- How does management take action to prevent their occurrence?

An example of events that could cause material misstatement in the financial statements is unrecorded transactions. This is clearly a business risk. The auditor should assess the actions managements take to identify and prevent the possibility of unrecorded transactions. Have they initiated plans, programs, or actions to address the risk of transactions going unrecorded. If the auditor feels that a management is lax in respect to this, then their assessment of risk will be greater relative to a situation where a management appears to be stringent.

ISA 315 notes that the auditor should watch out for the following as they could affect risk or cause change in existing risk. Understanding risks that a client entity faces is vital in understanding potential problem areas for the auditor to scrutinize. Earlier, we described potential areas for risk. For example, we noted that the auditor should ask the following questions of management (please refer Appendix 2 of ISA 315):

- Have there been changes in the operating environment, either technological or competitive?
- Are there new personnel operating in key functions?
- Has the information system been revamped, or has a new information system been introduced?
- Has there been unusually rapid growth in operations?
- Has the company entered into a new business area?
- Has there been corporate restructuring of the business?
- Are there new accounting pronouncements that the company is now required to follow?

All these changes can significantly affect internal control and, hence, influence the tests auditors intend to perform. If any of these events have happened, the auditor is requested to identify the possible problems that may occur. For example, let us take a company such as Walmart. Walmart imports products made in China extensively. Now assume that they intend to import apparel and related products from India. Firm-wide risks that should be considered relate to: quality (e.g., is it of the required quality? Will the products arrive on time?); currency rate fluctuations; potential trade embargoes arising from political instability if the present government is replaced by a socialist regime, and so on.

Paragraphs 8 to 12 of Appendix 2 of ISA 315 also request auditors to examine the information system. In particular, auditors are requested to address the following issues:

- Does the information system identify and record all valid transactions?
- Does the system provide an adequate description of the transactions in sufficient detail to ensure proper classifications of the transactions for financial reporting?
- Are the values of the transactions measured accurately?
- Is the time period of the transactions properly recorded to permit recording in the proper time periods?

If any or all of these issues are not true, it is possible that the financial statements may be materially misstated. In ISA terms, this means that they do not present a *true and fair* view of the entity's underlying economic reality, measured according to IFRS. In PCAOB terms, this means that the financial statements are not *presented fairly* in accordance with generally accepted accounting principles (in the United States).

ISA 315 also makes special provisions for small entities. ISA recognizes that small entities are likely to be less formal than larger entities. Accordingly, small entities are not required to have extensive descriptions of accounting procedures, sophisticated accounting records, or even written policies. ISA 315 also emphasizes special risks arising from technology or changes in technology that management should be aware of.

Significant Risks that Require Special Audit Consideration

As part of the risk assessment, ISA 315 also requires auditors to identify whether there are *significant* risks that warrant the auditor's special attention (paragraphs 108 to 114 and 119). However, ISA 315 does not specify what the term *significant* risk actually means. The auditor is required to use his or her professional judgment. Significant risks are risks that arise from business risks discussed earlier. Significant risks arise from nonroutine, complex transactions, not from routine, simple transactions. Once the auditor determines that a significant risk exists, then the auditor is required (paragraph 109) to ascertain whether:

- The risk relates to fraud; that is, does the existence of this risk create a situation where the entity is vulnerable to fraud by employees or top management?

- The risk is related to recent significant economic, accounting, or other developments.

The probability of the auditor being sued is greater with the existence of fraud. For significant risks, the auditor should specifically examine the entity's related controls over financial reporting and make recommendations. They should then ascertain whether those recommendations have been implemented. By doing this, the auditor can protect themselves from legal liability if an irregularity or fraud is discovered.

The Information System Including Related Business Processes Relevant to Financial Reporting and Communication

ISA 315 says that IT can be used to transfer information automatically from transaction processing systems to the general ledger to financial reporting. It has been noted that the automated processes and controls in such systems may reduce the risk of inadvertent error but create new risk. This is because when IT is used to transfer information automatically, there may be little or no visible evidence that unauthorized intrusion in the information systems occurred. Paragraph 93 of ISA 315 pays special attention to this problem. Hayes et al. summarize the risks that IT poses to an entity's internal control. They state that problems can arise because of the following:

- The managers (and auditor) rely on systems or programs that could be inaccurately processing data or processing inaccurate data or both.
- There could be unauthorized access to data that may result in destruction of data or improper changes to data, including the recording of unauthorized or nonexistent transactions or inaccurate recording of transactions.
- There may be unauthorized changes to data in master files.
- Programmers may fail to make necessary changes to systems or programs.
- Potential loss of data or inability to access data by personnel when required.

(summary of page 249, Hayes et al.)

ISA 315 (paragraph 93) requests the auditor to obtain an understanding of how the entity has responded to risks from IT. The auditor should consider the risks of IT (noted earlier) and examine whether the entity has responded adequately to the risks from IT by establishing effective general IT controls and application controls. General IT controls are defined as those that maintain the integrity of information and security of data and include controls that cover the following (refer paragraph 94 of ISA 315).

- Data center and network operations
- System software acquisition, change, and maintenance
- Access security
- Application system acquisition, development, and maintenance

We now discuss other risks that are highlighted in ISA 315 as requiring special attention.

Control Procedures/Activities

Control procedures are policies and procedures that help ensure that management instructions are carried out. This refers to necessary actions taken to address certain risks that threaten the attainment of the organization's objectives. Paragraph 90 of ISA 315 provides examples of control activities. The following are these control activities:

- Authorization
- Performance reviews
- Information processing
- Physical controls
- Segregation of duties

Authorization

Employees perform tasks and make decisions that affect company assets. Hayes et al. (2005) note that management may not have the time or resources to supervise all activities or approve all related transactions. They establish general policies for employees to follow, and based on the individuals' job descriptions, empower them to perform activities and make decisions. This empowerment is called authorization. Authorization is an important part of an organization's control procedures. Authorizations are often documented by signing, initialing, or entering an authorization code on the document or record representing the transaction. In Europe, most IT systems are now capable of recording a digital signature. This is a means of signing a document with a piece of data that cannot be forged. Auditors are required to review samples of transactions to verify proper authorization. The absence of authorization may indicate that control problems exist. In the case of Parmalat, among the many fraudulent activities subsequently discovered was one in which purchase requisitions authorizing purchases were not authorized by the requisite person in charge but were *personally authorized* by a manager who was not in charge. It must also be noted that certain activities or transactions may be of such importance that management must grant specific authorization for them to occur. For example, in Parmalat, management review and approval was often required for sales in excess of 20,000 Euros, capital expenditures in excess of 10,000 Euros, and uncollectible write-offs in excess of 5,000 Euros. Parmalat was a situation where control requirements were in place but were often violated. Thus the auditor is required to sample transactions to ensure they were properly authorized. They must also check what authorization is required for each transaction type. Examples are shown in the table below. Table 6.1 presents a list of transaction types and related ways to authorize parts of those transactions; for example, when a sale is made, granting credit to the customer must be authorized, then authorization to ship the product must be made, and if any or all of the shipment needs to be returned, there must be an authorization for the sales return or allowance given.

Performance Reviews

Under the PCAOB's AS 5, performance reviews are called independent internal verification. The definitions, however, are basically the same. Performance reviews are independent checks on performance by a third

Table 6.1 Transaction types and authorization examples

Transaction type	Examples of authorization functions
Sales orders	Approval of customer credit
	Approval of shipment
	Approval of sales returns and allowances
	Write offs of uncollectible accounts
Purchases	Authorization to order goods or services
	Authorization of capital expenditures
	Selection of vendors
	Acceptances of delivered products
Production	Approval of products and quantities to be produced
	Approval of raw materials issued for use in production
	Approval of production schedules
	Approval of completed products
Human resources/payroll	Hiring of new employees
	Approval of increases in employee compensation
	Approval of records of time worked
	Approval of payroll withholdings
Cash receipts	Endorsement of checks for deposit in bank
Cash disbursement	Approval of vendor invoices for payment
	Approval of checks written to settle accounts payable

party not directly involved in the activity. An example of an accounting-related performance review is a bank reconciliation. Whereas a general ledger clerk would be responsible for maintaining accounting records and a cashier would be responsible for cash, the bank reconciliation should be done by a third person who handles neither the accounting records nor cash. Another accounting-related example of a performance review relates to reconciliation of accounts receivables. An accounts receivable clerk should maintain the customers' accounts and balances. To determine the accuracy of the balances, a person independent of the accounts receivable clerk and the cashier should open *control accounts*. The total sales for a specified period (monthly, quarterly) and cash received from customers are obtained from the sales clerk and cashier respectively. The accounts receivable totals can be determined by subtracting total cash collected from total credit sales. The total is then checked with the total of the customer balances sent by the accounts receivable clerk. This section is common both for U.S. AS and IAS.

Some performance reviews *are* not accounting-related, but are still important for the auditor to review. For example, in the United States, under the PCAOB standard AS 5 auditors are also required to sample test authorization of nonfinancial controls as well. The importance of doing so was learned from the El Paso Energy Company scandal of 2000. El Paso Energy was accused of illegally withholding power from the state of California during the energy crisis of 2000. Top management was not aware that traders were engaging in such behavior because it did not have an effective monitoring control. The auditors of El Paso Energy Company missed this. The El Paso Energy Company paid a fine of over $1 billion to the state of California because of this behavior. The lesson learnt in the United States was that monitoring should not apply only to financial or reporting controls. Thus auditors in the United States under the PCAOB's AS 5 are required to sample test authorization controls of nonfinancial controls. This appears to be unique to the United States. Sample testing of authorization controls of nonfinancial controls are not emphasized in IAS.

Physical Controls

These are controls to ensure that assets are safeguarded. Cash registers, safes, lockboxes, and safety deposit boxes can be used to limit access to cash, and other paper assets. Restricting access to physical locations, and having locks on doors and guards are also recommended. Computer facilities should also be guarded from unauthorized access. The auditor should test the security arrangements.

Segregation of Duties

Segregation of duties seeks to ensure that no single employee is given too much responsibility. An employee should not be in a position to perpetrate and conceal the fraud. Effective segregation of duty requires that the following functions be separated:

- Authorization: This involves approving transactions and decisions.
- Recording: This involves preparing source documents; maintaining journals, ledgers, or other files; preparing reconciliations; and preparing performance reports.

- Custody: This is the physical control over assets or records. This may be direct, as in the case of handling cash or maintaining an inventory storeroom, or indirect, as in the case of receiving customer checks via mail or writing checks on the organization's bank account.

ISA 315 notes that the separation of these three functions is an essential element of control (based on discussion in paragraph 69 and 90). Individuals who authorize transactions should not be responsible for recording those transactions or be in custody of the assets acquired as a result of the transaction. The same applies under PCAOB standards as well. In the international example involved Barings, a 300 year old British bank, Nicholas Leeson, the manager of the Singapore branch had *custody* of assets and also authority to invest it. Leeson made investments in Nikkei exchange indexed derivatives. The authorization of a transaction and the handling of the related asset by the same person resulted in the situation where Leeson continued to invest after losing money with the hope of recovering his losses.

Information Processing

This refers to the processes of identifying, capturing, and exchanging information in a timely fashion to accomplish the organization's objectives. An effective accounting information processing system should be capable of:

- identifying and recording all valid transactions;
- properly classifying transactions for financial reporting purposes;
- preparing reports showing the current effect of transactions; and
- identifying situations of excessive risk.

Control procedures relating to information processing consist primarily of two control types. These are general controls and application controls. Computer facilities themselves should be safeguarded from intrusion and disaster by taking protective steps, in part similar to steps taken for other assets—such as locks on doors.

General Controls

In the IT environment, ISA 315 recommends that operations responsibility and record keeping and IT duties should be separate (Appendix 2).

Systems Analysis Stage

The analysis and programming functions must be separated from the other functions to prevent unauthorized changes in application programs or data. (If a programmer for a bank were allowed to use actual data to test his/her program, the programmer could erase his or her loan balance while conducting a test).

Programming

Organizations are required to have formal authorizations for program changes. A written description of such changes must be submitted to a supervising manager for approval, and modifications should be thoroughly tested prior to implementation.

Computer Operations

Computer operators should be rotated among jobs and should not have access to program documentation or logic. When possible, two operators should be in the computer room during processing. A processing log should be maintained and reviewed periodically for evidence of irregularities.

Transaction Authorization

User departments should submit a signed form to verify that transactions have been authorized. Data control personnel should verify the signatures and control totals prior to submitting the input for processing. This procedure would prevent a payroll clerk from submitting a form to increase their pay rate.

AIS Library

The AIS librarian maintains custody of data bases, files, and programs in a separate storage area. To separate the custody and operations functions, access to files and programs should be limited to authorized operators at scheduled times or with user authorization. The librarian should keep a record of all data and program file usage but should not have computer access privileges.

Application Controls

Application controls are defined in Appendix 2 of ISA 315 as the application of controls, whether manual or automated, to transaction processing. The primary objective of application controls is to ensure the accuracy of a specific application's inputs, files, programs and outputs, rather than control the system in general. These controls relate to procedures that result in initiating, recording, processing and reporting both financial and other transactions. Use of these controls is intended to ensure that all transactions processed are (a) authorized, (b) complete in themselves, and (c) accurate. ISA 315 notes that there are several tools available to help ensure this accuracy. This could be accomplished by a number of techniques, for example, checking whether a numbered form is missing from a sequence of such forms that has been processed.

Monitoring of Controls

Not only must controls be in place, but the controls must be monitored by the management to help ensure that they are working. ISA 315 paragraph 18 provides guidance on the monitoring of controls. Control monitoring is a process used to assess the quality of internal control performance over time. It involves assessing the design and operation of controls on a timely basis and taking necessary corrective actions. Examples given in paragraph 18 are management's review of whether bank reconciliations are being prepared on a timely basis, internal auditors' evaluation of sales personnel's compliance with the entity's policies on terms of sales contracts and the legal department's oversight of compliance with the entity's ethical or business practice policies among other examples. Ongoing monitoring activities should be built into the normal recurring activities of an entity and include regular management and supervisory activities. For example managers of sales, purchasing, and production at divisional and corporate levels should be in touch with operations and should question reports that differ significantly from their knowledge of operations. The auditor must search for evidence that indicates whether management is actively monitoring the controls put in place. Evidence searches include evidence gathered from making inquiries of management, observing management review of control operation, and inspecting documentation showing that management has reviewed such documents as bank reconciliations.

Other Internal Control Standards

The Sarbanes Oxley Act (SOX) in the United States and the Eighth directive (EU) equivalent, like the ISA, also provide special attention to the design of internal controls. This is because there is now a recognition that sound internal controls are a vital component to enhancing quality of reported earnings in the financial statements. Both SOX and the Eighth directive require the preparation by management of an internal control report. In the internal control report, management is required to (a) state that it is its responsibility to establish and maintain adequate systems of internal control and (b) assess their internal controls and provide an opinion on the effectiveness of the firm's internal controls. The auditor's responsibility is to assess the correctness of management's conclusions about the effectiveness of their internal controls as stated in its internal control report. The process the auditor undertakes under the PCAOB's AS 5 in assessing that correctness is consistent with the internal control assessments required by the ISA. The auditor is required to (partially paragraphs 115 to 118 of ISA 315 but mainly paragraphs 18 to 22 of Appendix 2 of ISA 315):

- study the design of the internal controls, evaluate the extent to which implementation of the controls mitigates risk of material misstatement;

- assess their effectiveness, namely, whether the controls working as effectively as management states and working as intended, taking into account changes in the environment;
- monitor controls to assess the quality of internal control performance over time;
- read management's report; assessing their internal controls; and then;
- provide a report expressing their (the auditor's) opinion on management's assessment report. The auditor has to consider and state clearly and unequivocally whether the controls in their opinion effectively prevents, detects, and corrects material misstatements.

Again, there are significant differences between ISA and PCAOB. These differences range from insignificant to significant. The insignificant ones relate to slight differences in wording or location of information. The significant differences are summarized in Table 6.2 at the end of this chapter.

Finally, the results of the testing may indicate material weakness in internal control, which must be reported to management. ISA 265 (paragraphs 7 to 9) states that, should any weakness or discrepancies be observed, the auditor should communicate to management as soon as possible.

Discussions Relating to Material Weaknesses in Internal Control

In the preceding section, we addressed certain issues relevant to the question of internal control reporting. In this section, we provide more detail on the thinking that underlies the internal control report. For example, we discuss differences between standards-setting bodies (e.g., IAASB and PCAOB) in defining material weakness. We also provide more information about the differences between ISA and PCAOB standards.

If material weaknesses are to be reported, it is important to understand what a material weakness is. For example, even though as noted earlier, ISA 265 recommends communicating material weakness, it does not define the term material weakness. This is because, under ISA, the auditor has to report significant deficiencies. Significant deficiencies *include* material weaknesses. The PCAOB standard on this subject is AS 5, which superseded AU 325. The difference between AS 5 and ISA 265 is that AS 5 defines material weakness whereas ISA 265 does not. Auditors operating in an international arena have more flexibility to define material weakness for the purpose of reporting as opposed to U.S. auditors where AS 5 provides a clear definition. A material weakness is a deficiency or a combination of deficiencies in internal control over financial reporting such that there is a reasonable possibility that a material misstatement of the company's annual or interim financial statements will not be prevented or detected on a timely basis. Paragraph 69 of PCAOB's AS5 also states that a material weakness in internal control over financial reporting *may* exist when financial statements are materially misstated. (However, the paragraph elaborates saying the auditor should be aware that material weakness could exist even if financial statements are not significantly misstated.) Hence, paragraph 6 of PCAOB's AS5 recommends that the audit of internal control over financial reporting should be integrated with the audit of the financial statements.

Even with a definition of material deficiency in hand, there are differences in the requirements of the PCAOB's AS 5 and the ISA 265. These differences arise because there are requirements in PCAOB standards but not in the ISA. PCAOB's AS 5 requires the auditor to evaluate each deficiency to determine, on the basis of the audit work performed, whether, individually or in combination, the deficiencies constitute significant deficiencies or material weaknesses. ISA does not mention the auditor's requirement to evaluate each deficiency in making a determination. However, despite the difference, an AICPA report (aicpa.org/ FRC) notes that the PCAOB may believe that the requirement in AS 5 is consistent with the intent of the ISA. In addition, the PCAOB's AS 5 includes an additional requirement not mentioned in the ISA. The auditor can determine that a deficiency or a combination of deficiencies in internal control is NOT a material weakness if prudent officials having knowledge of the same facts and circumstances would likely reach the same conclusion. This issue is not addressed in the ISA. Auditors have more issues to consider in the U.S. relative to Europe for the following reasons:

- A clear definition of material weakness by PCAOB is provided.
- Auditors are required to evaluate a combination of deficiencies to ascertain if, in combination, there is a material weakness. Significant deficiencies include material weakness.
- Auditors also have to consider whether prudent officials having the same knowledge would likely conclude no weakness exists. They could use this to justify their decision if they felt that despite the deficiencies, it did not amount to a material weakness. In the United States, the auditor can report no material weakness if requested.

In the first part of this chapter, we focused on similarities/differences between ISA and PCAOB standards with focus on risk assessment and internal control assessment. In this part of the chapter we focus specifically on internal control assessment and the purpose of testing internal controls. We focus on similarities and differences between PCAOB and ISA standards with a focus on internal control assessment.

Purpose of Internal Control Assessment

In the United States, AS 5 of the PCAOB establishes requirements and provides direction to the auditor for conducting tests to assess the internal controls. The purpose of internal control assessment is, according to AS 5, to form an opinion on the effectiveness of the company's internal control over financial reporting. Paragraph 3 of AS 5 notes that, because a company's internal controls cannot be considered effective if one or more material weaknesses exist, in order to form a basis for forming an opinion, the auditor must plan and perform tests that are sufficient to form a reasonable assurance about whether material weaknesses exist (as of the date of the assessment). AS 5 requires that tests of internal controls over financial reporting should be integrated with the audit of the financial statements. AS5 provides specific examples of controls that an auditor should test. The following are included in these tests (as per paragraph 14 of AS 5):

- Controls over significant, unusual transactions, particularly those that result in late or unusual journal entries
- Controls over journal entries and adjustments made in the period-end financial reporting process
- Controls over related party transactions
- Controls related to significant management estimates
- Controls that mitigate incentives for, and pressures on, management to falsify or inappropriately manage financial results

In this respect, there is a significant difference between AS 5 and ISA 315 because ISA 315, although exhaustive, does not have a section that provides examples as shown earlier regarding which specific internal controls to test. Those mentioned in the preceding list particularly relate to fraud detection. This shows an overall philosophical difference between AS 5 and ISA 315. The focus of the PCAOB appears to be somewhat more oriented towards shareholder accountability. This could be a function of the fact that the PCAOB was created by the SOX Act. SOX is concerned with, among others, corporate governance. Corporate governance has a fundamental tenet; organizations are accountable to shareholders. SOX imposed additional duties on boards of directors and tightened the rules of enforcement. Legislation recommends procedures for the audit committee of boards, increases penalties for noncompliance with securities laws among others. Whereas PCAOB has this as a fundamental tenet, this is not the orientation of the ISA. This may be the reason for the differences between the two institutions.

Tests of Internal Controls and Communication of the Results of Those Tests

We find that, with respect to tests of internal controls, there are differences between the ISA and the PCAOB standards. One difference relates to definitions. The other relates to communication of results.

Difference in Definition

Both PCAOB and the ISA require that the purpose of internal control testing should be to identify material weaknesses and significant deficiencies. However, the relevant ISA (ISA 265) does not provide definitions. Unlike ISA 265, the PCAOB's AS 5 (dealing with communications about control deficiencies in an audit of financial statements) makes a distinction between material weaknesses and significant deficiencies. The following definition is in the PCAOB's AU 5 but not in ISA: *Material weaknesses are deficiencies such that there is a reasonable possibility that a material misstatement of the company's annual or interim financial statements will not be prevented or detected on a timely basis.* A significant deficiency is defined by the PCAOB as a *deficiency, or combination of deficiencies in internal control over financial reporting that is less severe than a material weakness, yet important to merit the attention by those responsible for oversight of the company's financial reporting.* (PCAOB's AS 5).

Communication of Results of Internal Control Tests

In this section, we compare and contrast the responsibility of the auditor with respect to communicating internal control weaknesses to management and audit committees.

- Must an auditor communicate all significant deficiencies and material weaknesses in writing to management and audit committees?
  - PCAOB's AS 5: Yes.
  - ISA 265: Only if these were not communicated to the management by other parties.
- Must the auditor evaluate the appropriateness of communicating internal control problems to the management directly?
  - PCAOB's AS 5: Paragraph 81 states that the auditor should communicate to the management all internal control over financial reporting deficiencies of which the auditor becomes aware, deficiencies that have not previously been communicated to the management. In this process, the auditor is required to inform the audit committee of its communication of internal control over financial reporting deficiencies.

- ISA 265: If deemed inappropriate, the auditor does not have to communicate internal control problems directly to management.
- Does the auditor receive direction on the timeliness of such communication to management?
    - PCAOB's AS 5: The communication must occur before release of the audit report.
    - ISA 265: The auditor is required to communicate on a timely basis, but nothing further is specified.
- What are the restrictions, if any, on who can receive the auditors' communication of internal control test results?
    - PCAOB's AS5 does not restrict the audience that can receive the auditor's communication of internal control test results.
    - ISA 265 does not restrict the audience that can receive the auditor's communication of internal control test results.
- What can the auditor report in writing if no significant internal control test deficiencies are found?
    - PCAOB's AS 5 explicitly states that the auditor should not report in writing that no significant internal control test result deficiencies were discovered during an audit of the financial statements.
    - ISA265 requires the auditor to state the results, whether negative or positive.
- When should the auditor communicate about material internal control weaknesses discovered during the audit?
    - PCAOB's AS 5 requires that when timely communication is important, the auditor should communicate issues regarding material internal control weaknesses during the audit.
    - ISA 265 states that the auditor should report material internal control weaknesses at the end of the audit and has no reference to timing.

- Is the auditor required to repeat information about deficiencies previously reported to the client?
  - ○ PCAOB's AS 5 paragraph 81 states that it is not necessary for the auditor to repeat information about the deficiencies that have been included in previously issued written communications, whether by the auditor, the internal auditor, or others. However, if a deficiency reappears in subsequent audit periods, the auditor retains an obligation to report the deficiency.
  - ○ ISA 265 requires the auditor to repeat information about internal control deficiencies irrespective of whether this information had been previously disclosed.

An important key difference between the PCAOB and ISA audits is that the PCAOB requires the auditor to make an assessment of the effectiveness of internal controls and to integrate that with the audit of the financial statements. AS 5 paragraph 6 clearly states that tests of internal controls should be integrated with the audit of financial statements. This is referred to as an integrated audit. More important, there is an established direction (guidelines) for integrated audits. Such guidelines are not found in ISAs. Hence, the basic difference is that there is no comparable direction on integrated audits in ISAs.

In summary, in the ISA, reporting on internal controls tests is incidental to the audit of the financial statements and mainly carried out for the purpose of assessing the risk of material misstatement (reasons follow). The PCAOB appears to have a different philosophy. This philosophy holds that reports on internal controls are integral and not incidental. As mentioned, the PCAOB's AS5 paragraph 9 provides direction with respect to planning integrated audits. Under AS 5 paragraphs 93 to 98, the auditor is also required to inquire about changes in internal control that could affect financial reporting, which may have occurred after the balance sheet date but before the auditor's report date. If there are changes in internal control, the auditor is required to evaluate their impact on the audit report. This requirement is not in the ISA. AS5 also provides direction on using internal auditor's work on integrated audits of the financial statements and internal control over financial report. This is not mentioned in the ISA.

A summary of this discussion is provided in Table 6.2.

Table 6.2 Comparison of internal control test results requirements

Question	PCAOB's AS 5	ISA 265
Must an auditor communicate all significant deficiencies and material weaknesses in writing to the management and the audit committees?	Yes	Only if not communicated to the management by other parties.
Must the auditor evaluate the appropriateness of communicating internal control problems to the management directly?	The auditor need not address the issue of appropriateness.	If deemed inappropriate, the auditor does not have to communicate internal control problems directly to the management.
Is the auditor given direction on the timeliness of such communication to management?	PCAOBAS 5: The communication must occur before release of the audit report.	Only says that the auditor should communicate on a timely basis, but nothing further is specified.
What are the restrictions, if any, on who can receive the auditors' communication of the internal control test results?	PCAOB AS 5 paragraph 6 states that the communication is intended solely for the use of the board of directors, the audit committee, the management, and others within the organization.	Does not restrict the audience that can receive the auditor's communication of internal control test results.
What can the auditor report in writing if no significant internal control test deficiencies are found?	PCAOB AS 5 paragraph 8 states that the auditor should not report in writing that no significant internal control test result deficiencies were discovered during the financial statement audit.	ISA 265 requires the auditor to state the results, whether negative or positive.
When should the auditor communicate about material internal control weaknesses discovered during the audit?	PCAOB AS 5 paragraph 9 requires that, when timely communication is important, the auditor communicates issues regarding material internal control weaknesses during the audit.	ISA 265 states that the auditor should report material internal control weaknesses at the end of the audit and makes no reference to timing.
Is the auditor required to repeat information about deficiencies previously reported to the client?	PCAOB AS 5 states that it is not necessary for the auditor to repeat information about the deficiencies that have been included in previously issued written communications. However, if the same deficiency appears from one audited period to the next, the auditor retains the obligation to report the deficiency.	ISA 265 requires the auditor to repeat information about internal control deficiencies irrespective of whether this information has been previously disclosed.

Conclusions

The responsibilities of the auditor to help assure the integrity of the client's financial statements are complex. In order to achieve this goal, the auditor must acquire an enormous amount of information about the client entity, the risks it faces and the mechanisms it has in place to address those risks. This chapter discusses the auditor's assessment of risks that the client faces from outside the client firm (e.g., changing technologies) and the risk that the client faces from internal threats (e.g., incompetent or dishonest employees). In doing so, the chapter compares the guidance provided by standards issued by the ISA and the PCAOB. Understanding the nature of internal and external risks facing the client firm and the adequacy of the methods and mechanisms that the firm uses to deal with those risks is clearly important for the client firm. It is also important for the auditor. Unless the auditor understands how risk assessment works and how assessment of internal controls over financial reporting works, it will be difficult for the auditor to do a professionally competent job. Readers of this book also benefit from understanding the sources of risk to an organization and tools available for assessing those risks. Importantly also, readers should understand how auditors examine the internal controls over financial reporting in order for the reader to gain a better grasp of the meaning of both ISA and PCAOB-governed audit reports and the differences between them.

CHAPTER 7

Analytical Procedures

The purpose of this chapter is to examine the guidance the International Standards on Auditing (ISA) and Public Corporation Accounting Oversight Board (PCAOB) provide on the use of analytical procedures and compare key differences between the ISA and PCAOB and discuss the implications of these differences on auditors operating in these two regimes. In this chapter in particular we focus on the following issues:

- The nature of analytical procedures used in auditing
- Guidance provided by the ISA versus PCAOB on the use of analytical procedures
- Examine key differences between the ISA and PCAOB
- Discuss the implications of these differences on auditors operating in these two regimes

Introduction

Guidance regarding the use of analytical procedures is provided in ISA 520 entitled *Analytical Procedures*. The corresponding standard in the United States is AU 329 of the PCAOB also entitled *Substantive Analytical Procedures*. We first discuss the key requirements provided by ISA 520 and then compare and contrast those requirements with AU 329. ISA 520 states that analytical procedures may help identify the existence of unusual transactions or events, amounts, ratio, and trends that might indicate matters that have audit implications. Unusual or unexpected relationships that are identified may assist the auditor in identifying risks of material misstatements, especially risks of material misstatement due to fraud. ISA 520 notes that the auditor should apply analytical procedures as risk assessment procedures to obtain an understanding of the entity and its environment and in the review at the end of the audit. In ISA 520, analytical procedures are defined as techniques for evaluation of financial information made by a study of plausible relationships among both financial and nonfinancial data. Analytical procedures also cover the investigation of identified fluctuations and relationships that are inconsistent with other relevant information or deviate significantly from predicted amounts. Overall, the procedures covered in analytical procedures allow the auditor to look at things overall and answer the question: Do the numbers make sense?

Analytical procedures are noted in the PCAOB's AU 329 as an important part of the audit process. The analytical procedures consist of evaluations of financial information made by a study of plausible relationships among the financial and nonfinancial data. So the definition is identical to ISA 520. The PCAOB's AU 329 states that analytical procedures should be used to assist the auditor in planning the nature, timing, and extent of other auditing procedures during the initial stage of the audit, as a substantive test to obtain evidential matter about particular assertions and finally in the final review stage of an audit for overall review purposes.

PCAOB's AU 329 has an additional requirement not in ISA 520. It mentions that there could always be a possibility of management overriding controls. It requires auditors to use analytical procedures to evaluate this risk. Thus under the PCAOB's AU 329, analytical procedures have a specific fraud detection role, which it does not have under ISA. This is a significant difference.

Examples of Analytical Procedures

Analytical procedures range from simple comparisons to the use of complex models involving many relationships. Paragraph 5 of PCAOB's AU 329 states that analytical procedures involve comparisons of recorded amounts or ratios developed from recorded amounts to expectations developed by the auditor. The auditor should develop expectations by identifying and using plausible relationships that are reasonably expected to exist based on the auditor's understanding of the client and of the industry in which the client operates. The following are examples of sources for the auditor expectations (based on paragraph 5 of AU 329):

- Financial information for comparable prior periods giving
  consideration to known changes—by "known" changes it

is meant changes anticipated by the auditors as a result of changes in circumstances or the environment that the auditor is aware of

- Anticipated results—for example, client budgets or forecasts including extrapolations from interim or annual data
- Relationships among elements of financial information within the period
- Information regarding the industry in which the client operates—for example, gross margin information
- Relationships of financial information with relevant nonfinancial information

Nature and Purpose of Analytical Procedures

A basic premise of using analytical procedures in ISA is that there exist plausible relationships among data and these relationships can be reasonably expected to continue. This is echoed in paragraph 2 of PCAOB's AU 329. It notes that a basic premise underlying the application of analytical procedures is that plausible relationships among data may reasonably be expected to exist and continue in the absence of known conditions to the contrary. In essence, paragraph 4 of ISA 520 note that analytical procedures include comparing the entity's financial information with the following, which are the sources of auditor expectations for the client referenced above:

- Comparable information for prior periods
- Anticipated results of the entity (using budgets or forecasts or expectations of the auditor)
- Similar industry information. This could include, for example, comparison of the entity's ratio of sales to accounts receivable with industry averages or with other entities of comparable size in the same industry
- ISA 520 also advises that analytical procedures should include consideration of the following relationships:
  - Among elements of financial information that would be expected to conform to a predictable pattern, based on the

entity's experience, such as gross profit percentage changes
from one year to the next

○ Between financial information and relevant nonfinancial
information such as payroll costs to number of employees.

As mentioned before, paragraph 7 of ISA 520 states that analytical
procedures should be used for the following purposes:

- As risk assessment procedures to obtain an understanding of
  the entity and its environment
- As substantive procedures when their use can be more effective or efficient than tests of details, which include procedures
  that aid in reducing the risk of material misstatement at
  the assertion level to an acceptably low level. (For example,
  the PCAOB's AU 329 gives examples of uses of analytical
  procedures as tests for determining the extent of substantive
  tests to be conducted. For example a comparison of aggregate
  salaries with number of personnel may indicate unauthorized
  payments that may not be apparent from routine tests of
  controls.)
- As an overall review of the financial statements at the end of
  the audit

These will be considered individually.

Analytical Procedures as Risk Assessment Procedures to Obtain an Understanding of the Entity and its Environment

This may indicate aspects of the entity of which the auditor was unaware
and should assist in assessing the risks of material misstatement in order
to determine the nature and level of further audit procedures.

Analytical procedures used as risk assessment procedures can use both
financial and nonfinancial information. Examples included in paragraph
9 of ISA 520 could be the relationship between sales and square footage of
selling space or volume of goods sold. It would be expected, for example,
that if sales increase, then the volume of goods sold should have increased
as well, changes in price of items sold being held constant.

Analytical Procedures as Substantive Procedures

Analytical procedures in their role as substantive procedures discussed in the previous paragraph can be used to assess risk, subject to certain provisos discussed later in this chapter. ISA 520 cautions auditors to, where possible, use analytical data prepared by the auditor, provided the auditor is satisfied that such data has been properly prepared by the client.

Analytical Procedures in the Overall Review at the End of the Audit

ISA 520, paragraph 13 recommends that the auditor apply analytical procedures at or near the end of the audit when forming an overall conclusion as to whether the financial statements as a whole are consistent with the auditor's understanding of the entity. The conclusions drawn from the results of such audit procedures are intended to corroborate conclusions formed during the audit of individual components or elements of the financial statements and assist in arriving at the overall conclusions as to the reasonableness of the financial statements. However, they could also potentially identify a previously unrecognized risk of material misstatements. In such circumstances, the auditor may need to re-evaluate the planned audit procedures, based on the revised consideration of assessed risks for all or some of the classes of transactions, account balances or disclosures, and related transactions.

When to Use Analytical Procedures

When the auditor has determined that an assessed risk of material misstatement is a significant risk, the auditor should perform analytical procedures that are specifically targeted at assessing risk. Overall, ISA 520 notes that analytical procedures should also be used when the auditor feels that there are significant risks of material misstatement. In such a situation the auditor could use the analytical procedure results to *help* identify the existence of unusual transactions or events, amounts, and trends. These unusual or unexpected relationships may help the auditor in corroborating the existence of material misstatements.

The PCAOB's AU 329 states that analytical procedures should be used for the following purposes (condensed from AU 329, paragraphs 4, 5, and 10):

- To assist the auditor in planning the nature, timing, and extent of other audit procedures, AS 12 notes that analytical procedures can be used as substantive tests. The decision about which procedure or procedures to use to achieve a particular audit objective should be, in part, based on the auditor's judgment after considering the results of the substantive analytical procedures. If they determine risks of material misstatement to be significant, the nature and extent of other audit procedures should be amended. In particular, AS 12 notes (paragraph 46) that analytical procedures in this regard have two main objectives; namely to (a) enhance the auditor's understanding of the client's business and the significant transactions and events that have occurred since the previous year-end and (b) identify areas that might represent specific risks relevant to the audit. These include the existence of unusual transactions and events, amounts, ratios, and trends that warrant investigation.
- As an overall review of the financial information in the final review stage of the audit (e.g., AS 14, paragraph 4a).

These are the same requirements set forth in ISA 520. ISA 520 states that analytical procedures can also be applied as a tool in addition to substantive testing if the assessed risk of material misstatement is high and further tests are required. The purpose of analytical procedures is to further highlight risk areas, alerting the auditor of the need to devote additional attention to those areas. The PCAOB has a different focus. AS 12, which replaced AU 329 paragraphs 4 and 5, states that analytical procedures should be used as a primary test to assist the auditor in planning the audit based on risk assessment. The auditor is required to assess risk by performing risk assessment tests. Hence, the difference appears to be that ISA is of the notion that analytical procedures should be used as a tool in addition to substantive testing procedures if assessed risk of material misstatement is high. The PCAOB appears to believe that analytical procedures should be used as a primary test to assist the auditor in planning other audit procedures based on our reading of AS 12. So, as we understand it, there is a philosophical difference: The ISA feels analytical procedures should be used to complement substantive testing procedures, whereas the PCAOB provides a more prominent focus to analytical procedures as a primary test assertion about account balances or classes or transactions.

According to the PCAOB's AS 12, analytical procedures should be used to see the big picture, that is, to obtain evidence to identify misstatements in account balances and thus to reduce the risk of misstatements. Analytical procedures should be done to enhance the auditor's understanding of the client's business and identifying unusual events, amounts, ratios, and trends.

The PCAOB's AS 14 paragraph 4a notes that in the overall review stage (the final stage of the audit), analytical procedures should be used in the evaluation of the overall audit results, an evaluation that necessarily includes assessing the conclusions reached about the overall financial statement presentation. It may be used to detect material misstatements that other tests can overlook, such as those due to fraud or understatement.

Types of Analytical Procedures

General analytical procedures include trend analysis, ratio analysis, statistical and data mining analysis, and reasonableness tests. ISA 520 and the PCAOB's AS 12 provide the following examples.

Trend Analysis

This is the analysis of changes in an account balance over time. For example, has the gross profit percentage increased from one year to the next?

Ratio Analysis

This is the comparison of relationships between different parameters in the financial statements or accounts, the investigation of relationships between financial and nonfinancial data, or the comparison of data across firms in an industry. For example, is the client entity's gross profit percentage markedly different than its competitors?

Data Mining

This is a set of computer assisted techniques that use sophisticated statistical analysis, including artificial intelligence techniques, to examine large volumes of data with the objective of indicating hidden or unexpected information or patterns. For these tests auditors generally use computer aided software.

Reasonableness Testing

This is the analysis of account balances or changes in account balances within an accounting period in terms of their *reasonableness* in the light of expected relationships between accounts. For example, if the gross profit percentage increases sharply but the product mix being sold remains the same, this might be seen as unreasonable pending acquisition of further information about pricing and cost of inventory to the entity.

ISA 520 recommends that the auditor use any of the techniques mentioned to test the operating effectiveness of controls. The extent of testing would be contingent on the auditor's perception of assessed risks.

PCAOB's AU 329 notes that, when designing substantive analytical procedures (using any of the techniques above), the auditor should also evaluate the risk of management override of controls. The auditor should also test the design and effectiveness of controls using the techniques mentioned. Overall, despite the differences in wording, it would appear that the responsibility to identify and detect fraud is the same under ISA and PCAOB. Both require effective controls. These controls, in turn, support more accurate information generation.

Stages in the Analytical Process

Hayes et al. uses a practitioner four stage approach. This approach is most common in the literature. The following are the four stages of this approach:

Stage one: Formulate expectations (expectations).

Stage two: Compare the expected value to the recorded amount (identification).

Stage three: Investigate possible explanations for a difference between expected and recorded values (investigation).

Stage four: Evaluate the impact of differences between expectation and recorded amounts on the audit and financial statements (evaluation).

Stage One: Develop Expectations

The PCAOB's AU 329 paragraph 17 notes that the expectation should be precise enough to provide the desired level of assurance that differences may be potential material misstatements, individually or when aggregated with other misstatements. PCAOB AU 329 does not elaborate further. However, ISA 520 provides more guidance. The auditor should assess whether the expectation can be developed to be sufficiently precise to identify a material misstatement at the desired level of assurance. The key issue is whether the expectation can be developed to be sufficiently precise. In this respect paragraph 12e of ISA 520 recommends considering the following in determining whether a sufficiently precise expectation can be developed:

- The accuracy with which the expected results of substantive analytical procedures can be predicted. For example, the auditor should ordinarily expect greater consistency in comparing gross profit margins from one period to another than in comparing discretionary expenses such as research on advertising.
- The degree to which information can be disaggregated. For example, substantive analytical procedures may be more effective for disaggregated components of an entity than when applied to entities as a whole.

The PCAOB's AU 329 provides the following guidance, guidance which overlaps with that given in ISA 520. This topic is covered in paragraph 19. The guidance is as follows: (1) expectations developed at a detailed level generally have a greater chance of detecting misstatement of a given amount than do broad comparisons. Further, (2) monthly amounts will generally be more effective than annual amounts and comparisons by location or line of business usually will be more effective than company-wide comparisons. And (3) the level of detail that is appropriate will be influenced by the nature of the client, its size, and its complexity. The risk that material misstatement could be obscured by offsetting factors increases as a client's operations become more complex and more diversified. Disaggregation helps reduce the risk. This is similar to ISA 520. Whereas ISA 520 mentions the availability of information, the PCAOB's AU 329 assumes it.

Stage Two: Compare the Expected Value to the Recorded Amount (Identification)

ISA 520 notes that this comparison should be influenced primarily by materiality and the consistency with the desired level of assurance. The auditor increases the desired level of assurance as the risk of material misstatement increases by reducing the amount of difference from the expectation that can be found without further investigation. There is more in terms of guidance. PCAOB's AU 329 in paragraph 18 provides similar guidance.

Stage Three: Investigate Possible Explanations for a Difference between Expected and Recorded Values (Investigation)

This is covered in paragraphs 17 and 18 of ISA 520. These note that when analytical procedures identify significant fluctuations or relationships that are inconsistent with other relevant information or that deviate from predicted amounts, the auditor should investigate and obtain adequate explanations and appropriate audit evidence. The investigation of unusual fluctuations and relationships ordinarily begin with inquiries to management followed by:

- corroboration of management's responses, for example, by comparing them with the auditor's understanding of the entity and other audit evidence obtained during the course of the audit; and

- consideration of the need to apply other audit procedures based on the results of such inquiries if management is unable to provide an explanation or if the explanation is not considered adequate.

In this respect the PCAOB's AU 329 provides guidance with a different slant. Paragraph 21 particularly notes that the auditor should evaluate significant unexpected differences. Reconsidering the methods and factors used in developing the expectation and inquiry of management may assist the auditor in this regard. Thus, there is an additional step in PCAOB AU 329, which involves reconsidering the methods used to derive expectations and checking whether the results are consistent. After this, management's explanations should be requested. Both ISA 520 and the PCAOB's AU 329 require that management responses should be corroborated with other evidential matter. In those cases when an explanation for the difference cannot be obtained, ISA520 and PCAOB AU 329 require that the auditor should obtain sufficient data about the assertion by performing other audit procedures to satisfy themselves as to whether the difference is a misstatement. In designing such procedures, the auditor should consider whether unexplained differences may indicate an increased risk of material misstatement due to fraud. The differences, it would appear to us, are subtle particularly with respect to evaluating significant unexpected differences by reconsidering methods and factors used in generating expectations.

Stage Four: Evaluate the Impact of Differences between Expectation and Recorded Amounts on the Audit and Financial Statements (Evaluation)

This stage as mentioned in ISA 520 involves evaluating the impact on the financial statements of the difference between the auditor's expected value and the recorded amount. It is usually not practical to identify factors that explain the exact amount of a difference investigated. The auditor should attempt to quantify that portion of the difference for which plausible explanations can be obtained and, where appropriate, corroborated. If the amount that cannot be explained is sufficiently small, the auditor may conclude that there is no material misstatement.

Differences between PCAOB and ISA

Based on the above discussion, one can see some significant differences. PCAOB's AU 329 covers the same ground as ISA 520 with respect to substantive analytical procedures. However, there is an additional purpose. Unlike ISA 520, the PCAOB's AS 12 states that analytical procedures should also be used to assist the auditor in planning the nature, timing, and extent of other audit procedures. Another difference relates to the use of analytical procedures. The PCAOB's AS 12 discusses analytical procedures as a primary test. Unlike the PCAOB's AS 12, ISA 520 discusses the use of substantive tests (i.e., analytical procedures and tests of details) as a response to assessed risk of material misstatement.

The PCAOB's AU 329 stipulates two additional requirements from the auditor relative to ISA 520 when performing analytical procedures as substantive tests. These are:

- Evaluate the risk of management overriding controls
- Test the design and operating effectiveness of controls over financial reporting (unless the auditor has performed other procedures to support the completeness and accuracy of the underlying information).

Whereas the PCAOB's AU 329 paragraph 16 states that the auditor should test the operating effectiveness of controls, a testing which helps ensure the reliability of the information used in the analytical procedures, testing controls is not the primary purpose of AU 329. ISA 520 suggests that the auditor may consider testing the operating effectiveness of controls. The ISA approach is similar to that of the AICPA's ASB approach.

Conclusions

Analytical procedures serve a very important function for the auditor in that inspection of different analytical procedure results (e.g., changes in gross margins as a percentage of sales from one year to the next) directs the auditor's attention to potential problem areas. For example, if the gross margin as a percentage of sales increases sharply and the client cannot respond meaningfully to auditor inquiry, the auditor will now be alert to the need to investigate this area more fully. Understanding the differences between the ISA and the PCAOB approaches will help all readers of this book better understand steps taken in the audit process and the importance of the underlying information used by the auditors. Given that better organizational governance is vital, understanding the role of analytical procedures provides all with tools to employ in their own investigations of the creditworthiness or investment worthiness of company equity or liabilities. The following table, Table 7.1, summarizes some differences between the ISA and PCAOB analytical procedures discussions.

Table 7.1 Comparison of some Analytical Procedure (AP) requirements

Question	ISA 520 coverage	PCAOB AU 329
Detect management control override?	Not mentioned	Yes. Useful in designing audit procedures to detect management control override
AP focus?	As addition to substantive tests	Primary test measure
Significant unexpected differences?	Same as PCAOB AU 329 except for reconsideration of the way in which expectations were formulated	Same as ISA 520 except for one additional step required: reconsideration of the way in which expectations were formulated

CHAPTER 8

Substantive Testing

In this chapter we focus on and address the following issues:

- Guidelines given to auditors on how to evaluate audit evidence (in the United States and internationally)
- Substantive procedures that should be used to find audit evidence
- Use of substantive audit procedures for obtaining audit evidence in the United States (as required by the Public Company Accounting Oversight Board [PCAOB]) and internationally (as required by the International Standards on Auditing [ISA])
- Implications for researchers, practitioners, and students with respect to the differences in these procedures

Introduction

The work of an auditor entails using audit tests to find appropriate audit evidence regarding the assessed risks of material misstatements. This is done by designing and implementing appropriate audit tests for those risks. The appropriate audit tests are referred to as substantive procedures. Substantive procedures are important audit tests. ISA 330 entitled *The Auditor's Procedures in Response to Assessed Risks* defines substantive procedures as "audit procedures designed to detect material misstatements at the assertion level" (paragraph 3, ISA 330). ISA 330 categorizes substantive procedures into two broad groups. These are:

- Tests of details (classes of transactions, account balances, and disclosures)
- Analytical procedures.

The purpose of substantive procedures is to obtain audit evidence to detect material misstatements in the financial statements.

As mentioned, audit evidence is the information used by the auditor in arriving at the conclusions on which the audit opinion is based. Audit evidence can be obtained from source documents and accounting records underlying financial statements. The steps to be taken by the auditor are broken down into four steps based on ISA 330 (paragraph 2). The steps are as follows:

- *Step 1—Overall Responses.* The auditor is required to take a *global approach* and determine overall responses to address potential risks of material misstatement at the financial statement level. How should the auditor formulate an *overall* response? This section provides guidance on the nature of the auditor's responses.
- *Step 2—Audit Procedures to Identify Risks of Material Misstatement.* This section guides the auditor on how to design and perform additional audit procedures. These additional tests could include tests of whether controls are working. This section also gives guidance on the nature, timing, and extent of substantive procedures. The nature of a substantive procedure refers to the type of procedure used. The timing of a procedure refers, for example, to how close to the balance sheet date the procedure should be conducted. The extent of a procedure refers to the extent to which a procedure is used, for example, how much evidence should be collected. These will be elaborated on later in the chapter.
- *Step 3—Evaluating the Sufficiency and Appropriateness of Audit Evidence Obtained.* This section helps the auditor to evaluate whether previously determined risk assessments remain appropriate. This section also guides auditors by helping them to determine whether sufficient appropriate audit evidence has been obtained.
- *Step 4—Documentation of Working Papers.* This section guides the auditor on what gets documented in the working papers.

Next, we further elaborate on these four steps. We begin our discussion with the relevant international standards (internationally predominantly ISA 330) and bring in the PCAOB equivalent for comparison purposes noting relevant differences where applicable. As noted earlier, the PCAOB standards, unless revised by the PCAOB, are based on the AICPA ASB standards, which came under the aegis of the PCAOB on the latter's formation. The four issues noted earlier will now be elaborated on.

Overall Responses

ISA 330 paragraph 4 requires that the auditor determine overall responses needed to address the risks of material misstatement at the financial statement level. What is meant by overall responses? Overall responses could include the following:

- Emphasizing to the audit team the need to maintain professional skepticism in gathering and evaluating audit evidence
- Assigning more experienced staff or those with special skills or using experts to conduct specific tests and help determine whether further audit tests should be performed

Paragraph 4 advises that the auditor's understanding of the control environment should be contingent on the assessment of the risks of material misstatement at the financial statement level. If the control environment is sound then it will allow the auditor to have more confidence in the effectiveness of internal controls. This will also increase confidence in the reliability of audit evidence generated inside the client firm. Overall responses could include assessing weaknesses (if any) in the control environment; conducting more audit procedures as of the period end; seeking more extensive audit evidence from substantive procedures; modifying audit procedures to obtain more persuasive audit evidence; and increasing the number of areas to be included in the audit scope.

Audit Procedures Responsive to Risks of Material Misstatement at the Assertion Level

Audit procedures could include:

- tests of material misstatements at the assertion level (an example of an assertion, for example, is that assets shown on the balance sheet exist);
- type and extent of substantive tests;
- factors to consider in designing substantive procedures;
- tests of operating effectiveness of controls;
- guidance on responses to risk assessment; and
- issues related to timing with focus on interim dates.

The audit procedures will now be elaborated on individually.

Tests of Material Misstatements at the Assertion Level

Paragraph 49 of ISA 330 requires that the auditor should design and perform substantive procedures for each material class of transactions, account balances, and disclosure. This requirement, it is noted, takes into account that the auditor's assessment of risk is judgmental and may not be sufficiently precise to identify all risks of material misstatement. ISA 330 also notes that the auditor should design and implement responses to address the assessed risks of material misstatement at the financial statement level. Further, the auditor should design and perform further audit procedures whose nature, timing, and extent are based on and are responsive to the assessed risks of material misstatement at the assertion level.

We reviewed the PCAOB standards and noted that the equivalent discussions are found in the PCAOB's AS 8, AS 13, and AU 329. AS 13 notes that whenever the auditor has concluded that there are significant risks of material misstatement of the financial statements, the auditor should consider this in determining the nature, timing, and extent of procedures as well as in assigning staff or requiring appropriate levels of supervision. AS 8 and AS 13 and AU 329 (hereafter referred to as PCAOB equivalent standards since parts of these standards relate to material covered by ISA 330, which is the basis of our discussion) note that the knowledge, skill, and ability of personnel assigned significant engagement responsibilities should be commensurate with the auditor's assessment of the level of risk for the engagement. Ordinarily, higher risk requires the auditor to use more experienced personnel or alternatively, should necessitate more extensive supervision by the senior auditor with final responsibility for the engagement during both the planning and the conduct of the engagement. Higher risk may cause the auditor to expand the extent of procedures applied, apply procedures closer to or as of the year end, particularly in critical audit areas, or modify the nature of procedures to obtain more persuasive evidence.

Further, under PCAOB standards the auditor is required to consider audit risk at the individual account balance or class of transactions level because such consideration directly assists in determining the scope of auditing procedures for the balance or class and related assertions. The auditor is also required to restrict audit risk at the individual balance or class level in such a way that at the completion of the audit, the auditor will be able to express an opinion on the financial statements as a whole at an appropriately low level of audit risk. In general, PCAOB standards appear to be more comprehensive in addressing how the auditor responds to identified risks than ISA 330. ISA 330 requires the auditor to determine the overall response at the financial statement level as well as responses to assessed risk at the assertion level. For example, ISA 330 notes that the auditor shall design and implement overall responses to address the assessed risks of material misstatement at the financial statement level (paragraph 49) whereas PCAOB standards do not require (at least explicitly) an overall response but focuses on providing direction on responses at the assertion level.

Type and Extent of Substantive Tests

ISA 330 notes that there are inherent limitations to internal controls. Such limitations include management's ability to override controls. Hence, it is recommended that even if the auditor determines the risk of material misstatement to be reduced to an acceptably low level (by performing only tests of controls for a particular assertion, account balance, or disclosure), the auditor should not be satisfied. The auditor should perform substantive tests for each material class of transactions, account balances, and disclosures. Paragraph 49 provides examples of substantive audit procedures to be used. This includes, but is not limited to, the following:

- Agreeing or reconciling the financial statements with the underlying accounting records
- Examining material journal entries and other adjustments made during the course of preparing the financial statements

The nature and extent of the auditor's examination of journal entries and other adjustments will depend on the nature and complexity of the entity's financial reporting process and the associated risks of material misstatement.

ISA 330 refers the auditor to paragraph 108 of ISA 315 entitled *Understanding the Entity and its Environment and Assessing the Risks of Material Misstatement.* This paragraph provides guidance on assessing risk of material misstatement at the assertion level. Paragraph 51 of ISA 330 states that, if the auditor has determined that an assessed risk of material misstatement at the assertion level is a significant risk, then the auditor should perform substantive procedures that are specifically responsive to that risk. For example, if the auditor identifies that management is under pressure to meet earnings expectations, there may be a risk that management is inflating sales by improperly recognizing revenue related to sales agreements with terms that are inconsistent with current revenue recognition principles, whether these principles were set forth by the U.S. generally accepted accounting principles (GAAP) or International Accounting Standards (now called International Financial Reporting Standards or IFRS). Invoicing sales before shipment would be an example of improper revenue recognition. In these circumstances, the auditor may, for example, design external confirmations not only to confirm outstanding amounts owed to the client firm but also to confirm the details of the sales agreements, including date, any rights of return and delivery terms. Confirmations could also include inquiries made of nonfinancial personnel of the entity being audited regarding any changes in sales agreements and delivery terms.

Factors to Consider in Designing Substantive Procedures

The auditor is asked in ISA 330 to specifically consider the guidance in paragraphs 53 and 64 in designing the (a) nature, (b) timing, and (c) extent of substantive procedures for significant risks. In order to obtain sufficient appropriate audit evidence, the substantive procedures related to significant risks should be designed to obtain audit evidence with high reliability.

Paragraph 53 of ISA 330 advises when substantive procedures should be used relative to tests of details. In designing substantive analytical procedures, the auditor should consider such matters as the following (paragraph 55):

- The suitability of using substantive analytical procedures given the assertions
- The reliability of the data, whether internal or external, from which the expectation of recorded amounts or ratios is developed
- Whether the expectation is sufficiently precise to identify a material misstatement at the desired level of assurance
- The amount that is acceptable in respect of any difference in recorded amounts from expected values

Paragraph 55 notes that substantive analytical procedures are generally more applicable to large volumes of transactions that tend to be predictable over time. Tests of details, it is noted, are ordinarily more appropriate to obtain audit evidence regarding certain assertions about account balances, including existence and valuation. In some situations, the auditor may determine that performing only substantive analytical procedures may be sufficient to reduce the risk of material misstatement to an acceptably low level. For example, the auditor may determine that performing only substantive analytical procedures is appropriate based on the assessed risk of material misstatement for a class of transactions. This could be a class of transactions where the auditor's assessment of risk is supported by audit evidence from performance of tests of the operating effectiveness of controls.

Substantive Tests as Tools to Reduce the Risks of Material Misstatements

ISA 330 refers the reader to paragraph 115 of ISA 315. This paragraph notes that sometimes it may not be possible (or even practical) to reduce the risks of material misstatement to an acceptably low level using substantive procedures alone. In this case, the auditor should perform tests of relevant controls to test their operating effectiveness. Paragraph 26 of ISA 330 notes that when performing tests of operating effectiveness of controls, the objective of the auditor should be to obtain evidence that the controls operate effectively. This includes answering such questions as:

- How were the controls applied at relevant times during the period under audit?
- Were controls applied consistently?
- By whom were the controls applied and by what means?

ISA 330 (paragraph 26) states that if findings reveal that substantially different controls were applied during the period under audit, the auditor should consider each separately. When considering each, the auditor could use tests that are not specifically designed as tests of controls. However, these can also provide audit evidence about the operating effectiveness of controls and consequently serve as tests of controls. For example, the auditor may have made inquiries about management's use of budgets, observed management's comparison of monthly budgeted and actual expenses, and inspected reports pertaining to the investigation of variances between budgeted and actual sales volumes. These are not tests of controls. However, these audit procedures provide knowledge about the design of the entity's budgeting policies and whether they have been implemented. They may also provide audit evidence about the effectiveness of the operation of budgeting policies in preventing or detecting material misstatements in the classification of expenses. In such circumstances, the auditor should also consider whether the audit evidence provided by those audit procedures is sufficient.

Paragraph 29, ISA 330 notes that the auditor should use inquiry techniques together with performing other audit procedures to test the operating effectiveness of controls. Although different from obtaining an understanding of the design and implementation of controls, tests of operating effectiveness of controls ordinarily include the same types of audit procedures used to evaluate the design and implementation of controls. Tests could also include *reperformance*. This means retest the performance of a control. The standard emphasizes that inquiry and observation alone is not sufficient. Hence, it is recommended that the auditor use inquiry combined with audit procedures to obtain sufficient audit evidence regarding the effectiveness of controls. The combination of inquiry and observation combined with reperformance control tests could provide more assurance than not using a combination of controls. For example, an auditor may inquire about and observe the entity's procedures for opening the mail and processing cash receipts to test the operating effectiveness of controls over cash receipts. Because an observation is pertinent only at the point in time at which it is made, the auditor should supplement the observation with inquiries of entity personnel. The auditor could also inspect documentation about the operation of such controls in order to obtain evidence.

The nature of the particular control influences the type of audit procedure required to obtain audit evidence. We are talking about audit evidence to support whether the control was operating effectively at relevant times during the period of the audit. For some controls, operating effectiveness can be evidenced by documentation. In such circumstances the auditor may decide to inspect the documentation to obtain audit evidence about operating effectiveness. For other controls, however, such documentation may not be available or relevant. For example, documentation of operations may not exist for some factors in the control environment. Examples where there is lack of documentation could include assignment of authority and responsibility and related control activities. This could also include control activities performed by a computer. In such circumstances, audit evidence about operating effectiveness may be obtained through inquiry in combination with other audit procedures such as observation or the use of Computer Assisted Audit Techniques (CAATs).

Paragraph 31 of ISA 330 notes that in designing tests of controls, the auditor should consider the need to obtain audit evidence supporting the effective operation of controls directly related to the assertions as well as other indirect controls on which these controls depend. For example, the auditor may identify a user review of an exception (problem) report of credit sales over a customer's authorized credit limit as a direct control related to an assertion. In such cases, the auditor considers the effectiveness of the user review as a direct control related to an assertion. In such cases, the auditor should also consider in addition to the effectiveness of the user review as a direct control the controls related to the accuracy of the information in the report.

Guidance on Responses to Risk Assessment

Paragraph 33 of ISA 330 notes that when responding to a risk assessment, the auditor may design a test of controls to be performed concurrently with a test of details on the same transaction. The objective of tests of controls is to evaluate whether a control operated effectively. The objective of tests of details is to detect material misstatements at the assertion level. Although these objectives are different, both may be accomplished concurrently through performance of a test of controls and test of details on the same transaction also known as a dual purpose test. For example, the auditor may examine an invoice to determine whether it has been approved and to provide substantive audit evidence of a transaction. The auditor has to carefully consider the design and evaluation of such tests to accomplish both objectives.

The auditor is cautioned that absence of misstatements detected by a substantive procedure does not provide evidence that controls related to the assertion being tested are effective. However, misstatements that the auditor detects by performing substantive procedures are considered by the auditor when assessing the operating effectiveness of related controls. A material misstatement detected by the auditor's procedures and that was not identified by the entity ordinarily is indicative of the existence of a material weakness in internal control and is communicated to management and those charged with governance.

Issues Related to Timing With Focus on Interim Dates

When the auditor obtains audit evidence about the operating effectiveness of controls during an interim period, the auditor should determine what additional audit evidence should be obtained for the remaining period.

ISA 330 notes that performing substantive procedures at an interim date without undertaking additional procedures at a later date increases the risk that the auditor will not detect misstatements that may exist at the period end. This risk increases as the remaining period is lengthened since additional problems may occur during the intervening period. Factors such as the following may influence whether or not to perform substantive procedures at an interim date (paragraphs 16 and 17):

- The control environment and other relevant controls
- The availability at a later date of information necessary for the auditor's procedures
- The purpose of the substantive procedures
- The assessed risk of material misstatement
- The nature of the class of transactions or account balance and related assertions
- The ability of the auditor to perform appropriate substantive procedures or substantive procedures combined with tests of controls to cover the remaining period in order to reduce the risk that misstatements will remain undetected at period end.

ISA 330 paragraph 29 states that factors such as those mentioned in the following sections may determine whether to perform substantive analytical procedures with respect to the period between the interim date and the period end:

- Whether the period end balances of the particular classes of transactions or account balances are reasonably predictable with respect to amount, relative significance, and composition
- Whether the entity's procedures for analyzing and adjusting such classes of transactions or account balances at interim dates and for establishing proper accounting cutoffs are appropriate
- Whether the information system relevant to financial reporting will provide sufficient information concerning the balances at the period end and the transactions in the remaining period to permit investigation of the following

- ○ Significant unusual transactions or entries (including those at or near the period end)
- ○ Other causes of significant fluctuations or expected fluctuations that did not occur
- ○ Changes in the composition of the classes of transactions or account balances

Paragraph 31 to 34 and 37 of ISA 330 note that in making that determination, the auditor should consider the significance of the assessed risks of material misstatement at the assertion level, the specific controls that were tested during the interim period, the degree to which audit evidence about the operating effectiveness of those controls was obtained, the length of the remaining period, and the extent to which the auditor intends to reduce further substantive procedures based on the reliance of the control and the control environment. The auditor should obtain audit evidence about the nature and extent of any significant changes in internal control, including changes in the information system, processes, and personnel that occur subsequent to the interim period.

If the auditor plans to use audit evidence about the operating effectiveness of controls obtained in prior audits, the auditor should obtain audit evidence about whether changes in those specific controls have occurred subsequent to the prior audit. The auditor should obtain audit evidence about whether such changes have occurred by performing inquiry in combination with observation or inspection to confirm the understanding of those specific controls.

Paragraph 23 of ISA 500 entitled *Audit Evidence* states that the auditor should perform audit procedures to establish the continuing relevance of audit evidence obtained in prior periods when the auditor plans to use the audit evidence in the current period. For example, in performing the prior audit, the auditor may have determined that an automated control was functioning as intended. The auditor obtains audit evidence to determine whether changes to the automated control that affect its continued effective functioning have been made, for example, through inquiries of management and the inspection of logs to indicate what controls have been changed. Logs keep a record of activities on the system and, therefore, serve a useful purpose in allowing inspection of the record of such activities. Consideration of audit evidence about these changes may support either increasing or decreasing the expected audit evidence to be obtained in the current period about the operating effectiveness of the controls.

When we compare the ISA with the PCAOB equivalent standards, we find they cover the issues as follows: PCAOB equivalent standards note that before applying principal substantive tests to the details of asset or liability accounts at an interim date, the auditor should assess the difficulty in controlling the incremental audit risk. In addition, the auditor should consider the cost of the substantive tests that are necessary to cover the remaining period in a way that will provide the appropriate audit assurance at the balance sheet date. Applying principal substantive tests to the details of asset and liability accounts at an interim date may not be cost effective if substantive tests to cover the remaining period cannot be restricted due to the assessed level of control risk.

PCAOB equivalent standards also note that assessing control risk at below the maximum is not required in order to have a reasonable basis for extending audit conclusions from an interim date to the balance sheet date; however, if the auditor assesses control risk at the maximum during the remaining period, the auditor should consider whether the effectiveness of certain of the substantive tests to cover that period will be impaired. The auditor should consider whether there are rapidly changing business conditions or circumstances that might predispose management to misstate financial statements in the remaining period.

PCAOB equivalent standards further note that the auditor should consider whether the year-end balances of the particular asset or liability accounts that might be selected for interim examination are reasonably predictable. They should also consider whether the entity's proposed procedures for analyzing and adjusting such accounts at interim dates and for establishing proper accounting cutoffs are appropriate. In addition, the auditor should consider whether the accounting system will provide information concerning the balances at the balance sheet and the transactions in the remaining period that is sufficient to permit investigation of (a) significant unusual transactions or entries (including those at or near year end, (b) other causes of significant fluctuations or expected fluctuations that did not occur, and (c) changes in the composition of the account balances. If the auditor concludes that evidential matter related to the above would not be sufficient for purpose of controlling audit risk, the account should be examined as of the balance sheet date.

The application and other explanatory material of ISA 330 (paragraph 52 and 53) lists factors that may influence the decision to perform substantive procedures at an interim date similar to the PCAOB's equivalent standards. The factors listed in the application and other explanatory material of ISA 330 differ to some extent from the factors listed in the PCAOB equivalent standards. For example, the PCAOB equivalent standards explicitly mention that the auditor should consider rapidly changing business conditions or circumstances that might predispose management to misstate financial statements in the remaining period. This appears not to be mentioned in ISA 330.

Evaluating the Sufficiency and Appropriateness of Audit Evidence

Paragraph 6 of ISA 330 notes that, based on the audit procedures performed and the audit evidence obtained, the auditor should evaluate whether the assessments of the risks of material misstatement at the assertion level remains appropriate. It is noted that information that differs significantly from the information on which the risk assessment was based may come to the auditor's attention. For example, the extent of misstatements that the auditor detects by performing substantive procedures may alter the auditor's judgment about the risk assessments and may indicate a material weakness in internal control. In addition, analytical procedures performed at the overall review stage of the audit may indicate a previously unrecognized risk of material misstatement. In such circumstances the auditor may need to reevaluate the planned audit procedures based on the revised consideration of assessed risks for all or some of the classes of transactions, account balances, or disclosures and related assertions. Detailed explanations are given in paragraph 119 of ISA 315.

In evaluating the effectiveness of operating controls, paragraph 68 of ISA 330 notes that the auditor should expect some deviations in the way controls are applied by the entity. Deviations from prescribed controls may be caused by such factors as changes in key personnel, significant seasonal fluctuations in volume of transactions, and human error. When such deviations are detected during the performance of tests of controls, the auditor should make specific inquiries to understand these matters and their potential consequences. For example, a specific inquiry would be to inquire about the timing of personnel changes in key internal control functions. The auditor determines whether additional tests of controls are necessary or whether the potential risks of misstatement need to be addressed using substantive procedures.

The sufficiency and appropriateness of audit evidence to support the auditor's conclusions throughout the audit are a matter of professional judgment. The auditor's judgment as to what constitutes sufficient appropriate audit evidence is influenced by such factors as the following (refer paragraph 71):

- Significance of the potential misstatement in the assertion and the likelihood of its having a material effect, individually or aggregated with other potential misstatements, on the financial statements
- Effectiveness of management's responses and controls to address the risks
- Experience gained during previous audits with respect to similar potential misstatements
- Results of audit procedures performed, including whether such audit procedures identified specific instances of fraud or error
- Source and reliability of the available information
- Persuasiveness of the audit evidence
- Understanding of the entity and its environment including its internal control

In conclusion ISA 330 refers the reader to ISA 701 entitled *Modifications to the Independent Auditor's Report* for further guidance. This states that if the auditor has not obtained sufficient appropriate audit evidence as to a material financial statement assertion, the auditor should attempt to obtain further evidence. If the auditor is unable to obtain sufficient appropriate evidence, the auditor should express a qualified opinion or a disclaimer of opinion (paragraphs 12 and 13 of ISA 701).

Finally, by way of comparison, in considering the sufficiency of evidence, the PCAOB equivalent standards state that the auditor should consider the cost of the substantive tests that are necessary to cover the remaining period in a way that will provide the appropriate audit assurance at the balance sheet date. A report by the Maastricht Accounting Auditing and Information Management Research Center notes that applying principal substantive tests to the details of asset and liability accounts at an interim date may not be cost effective if substantive tests to cover the remaining period cannot be restricted due to the assessed level of control risk. Careful review of ISA 330 shows that the issue of cost/benefit analysis with respect to using substantive tests has not been addressed. The ISA do not have a requirement comparable to the PCAOB equivalent standards. Unlike the requirements under ISA 330, the PCAOB equivalent standards require the auditor to consider the cost of performing substantive tests to cover the remaining period (i.e., the period between the interim date and the balance sheet date). The relevant explanatory material of ISA 330 does not address the principle of cost versus benefit in the application of substantive tests, and this is a significant difference.

Documentation

The PCAOB's AS 3 (paragraph 12), which focuses on audit documentation, notes that the auditor should document the overall conclusions to address the assessed risks of material misstatement at the financial statement level and the nature, timing and extent of the further audit procedures, the linkages of those procedures with the assessed risks at the assertion level, and the results of the audit procedures. In addition, if the auditor plans to use audit evidence about the operating effectiveness of controls obtained in prior audits, the auditor should document the conclusions reached with regard to relying on such controls that were tested in a prior audit. The auditors' documentation should demonstrate that the financial statements agree or reconcile with the underlying accounting records.

Paragraph 10 of ISA 230 entitled *Audit Documentation,* which also covers this area to a certain extent, requires the auditor to include abstracts or agreements in order to document the auditing procedures undertaken related to inspection of those significant contracts or agreements. ISA 230 paragraph 3 of ISA 230 states the auditor *may* include abstracts or copies of the entity's records (for example, significant and specific contracts and agreements) as part of audit documentation. This is substantially different from PCAOB's AS 3 that includes a requirement that documentation of auditing procedures related to the inspection of significant contracts or agreements *should* (note *not may*) include abstracts or copies of the documents. The documentation allows the reviewer to reperform the audit procedures.

Finally, we note that ISA 230 requires the auditor to assemble the audit documentation in an audit file and complete the administrative process of assembling the final audit file on a timely basis after the date of the auditor's report, and the related application and other explanatory material indicates that an appropriate time limit within which to complete the assembly of the final audit file is not more than 60 days following the report release date. The auditor is required by paragraph 15 of ISA 230 to document the report release date in the audit documentation. PCAOB's AS 3, paragraph 15, requires a 45 day period, and hence there is a difference here as well (www.aicpa.org/FRC). Other related important issues, such as subsequent events, are discussed in Chapter 11 and will not be elaborated on here.

Conclusions

In this chapter, we discussed the ISA and PCAOB standards as they apply to substantive testing. Substantive testing enables an auditor to discover errors at a detailed level, whereas tests of controls (discussed in a previous chapter) reveal flaws in the controls, which, in turn, provide clues to what may be wrong but provide no details. Understanding the differences between ISA and PCAOB standards, therefore, would be of great assistance to readers in understanding the testing undertaken that led to the opinions rendered in the audit reports. We will detail the differences between the ISA and PCAOB audit reports in a subsequent chapter.

CHAPTER 9

Audit Sampling

The purpose of this chapter is to discuss the following issues:

- Selecting items for sampling
- Determining appropriate sample size
- Determining whether and when to use statistical sampling techniques
- Differences between auditing techniques required by International Standards on Auditing (ISA) and the Public Corporation Accounting Oversight Board (PCAOB)
- Implications of these differences in required techniques for auditors

Evolution of the PCAOB Standards on Audit Sampling

The focus of this chapter is audit sampling. Internationally, sampling guidelines are provided by ISA 530 entitled *Audit Sampling*. The purpose of ISA 530 is to establish standards and provide guidance on the use of audit sampling procedures and other means of selecting items for testing to gather audit evidence. ISA 530 provides key definitions for auditors. In the United States, the original standard in this area was the American Institute of Certified Public Accountants' (AICPA's) SAS 39 entitled *Audit Sampling*. The AICPA subsequently modified this standard and reissued it under the title SAS 39 *Audit Sampling Redrafted*. Subsequently the Auditing Standards Board (ASB) used this to develop a section (AICPA refers to ASB standards as *sections,* and we will use the same terminology) entitled *Audit Sampling*. Subsequently, PCAOB brought *Audit Sampling* under its aegis as AU 350.

It may be easier to summarize the steps as follows:

- The original standard on Audit sampling was SAS No. 39 by the AICPA, effective beginning in February 1982.
- The AICPA subsequently redrafted SAS No. 39. The new standard was referred to as SAS No. 39 *Audit sampling (Redrafted)*.
- The ASB came up with a section that was numbered 530. ASB section 530 incorporates all the fundamental guidance offered in SAS No. 39 Redrafted and guidance provided by ISA 530. The number was intended to be consistent with the ISA standard on Audit sampling entitled ISA 530 Audit sampling. We note this was part of the clarified standards effort. AU 350 was amended by the PCAOB risk standards, Nos. 8 to 15.
- The PCAOB subsequently took the ASB section 350 under its aegis. It is called AU 350 Audit sampling by the PCAOB. This standard governs issues relating to audit sampling now as conducted for SEC-registrant entities.

Techniques for Audit Sampling and Whole Population Selection

When deciding on audit procedures, the auditor is required to determine appropriate means of selecting items for testing. The means that an auditor can:

- select all items (100 percent examination);
- select specific items; or
- audit a sampling.

These techniques will now be discussed in brief.

Selecting All Items (Whole Population Selection)

The auditor could potentially decide to examine all the items that make up a population. This type of 100 percent examination, as noted in paragraph 24 ISA 530 entitled *Audit Sampling and Other Testing Procedures,* is unlikely in the case of tests of controls. However, it is more common for tests of details. A 100 percent examination is appropriate when (a) the population constitutes a small number of large value items, (b) when there is a significant risk and other means do not provide sufficient audit evidence, or (c) when the repetitive nature of a calculation or other processes performed automatically by an information system makes a 100 percent examination cost effective. Selecting the *whole population* does not constitute audit sampling.

Selecting Specific Items

Paragraph 25 of ISA 530 states that the auditor may decide to select items from a population based on such factors as (a) the auditor's understanding of the entity, (b) the assessed risk of material misstatement, and (c) the characteristics of the population being tested. However, we are warned that the judgmental selection of specific items is subject to nonsampling risk. (Nonsampling risk is discussed later in this chapter.) Specific selected items could include the following:

- *High value or key items.* The auditor may decide to select specific items from within a population because they are of high value or exhibit some other characteristic of interest. Other characteristics include being suspicious, unusual, or particularly risk prone.
- *All items over a certain amount.* The auditor may decide to examine items whose values exceed a certain amount. In doing so, the auditor may be able to verify a large proportion of the total amount of a class of transactions or an account balance. For example, an entity may have one or two accounts receivable customers who owe extremely large balances that together constitute a large proportion of the total accounts receivable balance.
- *Items to obtain information.* The auditor may examine items to obtain information about matters such as the nature of the entity, the nature of transactions, and the quality of the internal control system's design and operations.
- *Items to test control activities.* The auditor may use judgment to select and examine specific items to determine whether or not a particular control activity is being performed.

Audit Sampling

This is discussed in separate sections below. The auditor may decide to apply audit sampling to a class of transactions or account balance. Audit sampling can be applied using either nonstatistical or statistical sampling methods. Statistical sampling involves the use of statistical methodology to determine sample size. Nonstatistical sampling basically involves the auditor's judgment. A key difference between the two methods is that with statistical sampling, the results of a test of, say, 5 percent of the total population, can be projected to the account balance as a whole. That is, if the total difference between the book value and the sample's actual value is $1,000 for that 5 percent of the total population, then the auditor can estimate that the entire population for that account is off by $20,000. With nonstatistical sampling, the auditor cannot project an error from the nonstatistical sample chosen to the population of the account as a whole. In essence, the difference between statistical and nonstatistical sampling is the ability to project sampling error, not the ability to conclude about the population. Both methods allow the auditor to conclude about the population as a whole.

Audit Sampling: Key Differences between ISA and PCAOB

The differences are quite marginal. The key issues are discussed below.

Definition

Paragraph 3 of ISA 530 defines audit sampling as involving the application of audit procedures to less than 100 percent of items within a class of transactions or account balances such that all sampling units have an equal probability of being selected. This will enable the auditor to obtain and evaluate audit evidence about some characteristic of the items selected in order to assist the auditor in forming a conclusion about the population from which the sample was drawn. For example, in a sample of sales invoices, if the comparison of sales invoices to recorded values in the entity's accounts show that the accounting entries recording sales transactions in the accounting records are, on average, overstated by 1 percent compared to the actual sales invoices, the auditor may conclude that the population of recorded sales may be overstated by 1 percent as well. This is an example of extrapolating from the sample's results (involving, say, 100 invoices and related accounting entries) to the population as a whole (involving, say 1,500 invoices and related accounting entries). Auditors can use either a statistical or nonstatistical approach.

The difference between ISA 530 and PCAOB's AU 350 is marginal in our opinion. A report by the AICPA (www.aicpa.org/FRC) states that the PCAOB believed that the ISA wording in its definition was too imprecise to be meaningful. The wording of ISA 530 requires the auditor to select items such that *all items have a chance of selection*. This was noted in the AICPA report as too imprecise to be meaningful. The PCAOB, although adhering to a somewhat similar definition, refers the reader to Auditing Standard (AS) 15 of the PCAOB, which also discusses the fundamental concept of representativeness. These are subtle changes, and we are not sure how it would affect a practicing auditor in their sampling decision.

Sample Selection

As mentioned above, there appears to be a very marginal difference in guidance for sample selection. ISA 530's paragraph 42 notes that the auditor should select items for the sample with the expectation that all sampling units in the population have an equal chance of selection. Guidance with respect to the principle methods of sample selection is then provided. This includes discussion of haphazard and random-based selection methods. (Haphazard selection is a case where the auditor selects the sample without following a structured technique. Random-based methods include the use of computerized random number generator through a system referred to as Computer Assisted Audit Techniques (CAATs) or random number tables. Whereas the same ground is covered in PCAOB's AU 350, the PCAOB's AU 350 (paragraph 24) states that sample items should be selected in such a way that the sample can be expected to be representative of the population. ISA 530 notes that the auditor should select items for the sample with the expectation that all sampling units have an equal chance of selection. Hence, there is a marginal difference in wording. (But we note that it really is a difference without a distinction.)

Another wording difference is that AU 350 provides a detailed explanation of how an auditor should adopt a selection method that will increase the likelihood of selecting items from the entire period under audit. This is important because failing to do so may increase the likelihood that the sample will not be representative of all the transactions that occurred during the period. Thus, the auditor may draw incorrect conclusions from the testing of the sample drawn.

In the PCAOB's AU 350, the auditor is also referred to paragraphs 44 through 46 of the PCAOB's AS No. 13 entitled *The auditor's responses to the risks of material misstatement* for further guidance. These paragraphs focus on performing certain substantive procedures on the audit samples selected. It is noted that interim testing of sample (i.e., tests of data collected before the end of the financial statement period) to assess the risks of material misstatement could permit early consideration of matters affecting the year-end financial statements. This (i.e., performing substantive procedures on the selected samples) decreases the risk of an undetected material misstatement in the year-end financial statements. In contrast, there is no reference in ISA 530 to other standards that could help the auditor to identify risks of material misstatement. Hence there is a clear difference between PCAOB's AU 350 and ISA 530. On the other hand, International Auditing Assurance Standards Board (IAASB) has also issued ISA 240, which is a fraud standard equivalent to the PCAOB standard.

Issues with Respect to "Representative" Sampling

It is noted in ISA 530 that the audit sampling process should adopt some form of random sampling for the selected sample with the goal of having the sample representative of the population. Such sampling could include random sampling, stratified random sampling with probability proportional to size, and systematic sampling (paragraphs 36 to 38 provide a more detailed description). Random sampling means choosing the sample based, for example, on a random number chart. In doing this, for example, each selected number in the random number chart would be matched with all or part of an invoice number. If the random number matched all or part of a specific invoice number that invoice would be selected for testing. This procedure gives each item in the population an equal, random, chance of being selected to be part of the sample. Stratified random sampling occurs when some subsets of the sample differ greatly from other subsets of the sample. For example, there could be some very large dollar balance accounts receivable accounts and a lot of small dollar balance accounts receivable accounts. Stratifying the sample, in this context, means treating the accounts receivable account *as if* it consisted of two separate accounts. All or 100 percent of the high balance accounts could be examined completely. On the other hand, with the small balance accounts, only a small percentage of them may be chosen to be examined. Sampling with probability proportional to size means that if, each dollar in an account is considered as a single sample item, then an account with a balance of $100 is 10 times more likely to be examined than would an account balance totaling $10.

In this respect, the PCAOB's AU 350 provides a more detailed explanation and greater selection of tools. Accordingly, it provides guidance more capable of helping an auditor select a *more representative sample* as opposed to the *more likely less representative sample* selected following ISA 530 guidance. Whereas the ISA discusses stratification, the discussion relates to the objective of stratification, which is to increase the level of uniformity of items within each stratum and, therefore, allow sample size to be reduced without causing a proportional increase in sampling risk. Sampling risk, of course, is the risk that the sample chosen will not be representative, that is reflect the characteristics of the whole population of items. If that is true, then any conclusions drawn from the sample will not be valid for the entire population. The PCAOB's AU 350, in addition, focuses on a variety of techniques such as sampling with probability proportional to size, which is not mentioned in ISA 530. The main difference in our opinion is that ISA 530 focuses on rationale while the PCAOB's AU 350 appears to be more practically oriented and focuses on methods to achieve representativeness.

Issues Relating to "Dual Purpose" Sampling

Another key difference in our opinion relates to the issue of dual purpose samples. This was added to AU 350 by the PCAOB (that is the PCAOB added a paragraph on this in AU 350, which was not there when the auditing standard was brought under its aegis) and is applicable for audits for fiscal years beginning on or after December 15, 2010. A dual purpose test exists when a sample can be used both as a test of controls *and* as a substantive test. It is discussed in paragraph 44 of AU 350. One example of a dual purpose sample would be if the auditor is selecting credit memos, memos issued by the credit manager of an entity to authorize a reduction in the accounts receivable balance of a customer's account. Such memos should be signed by the credit manager to indicate that the authorized person approves of the customer accounts receivable balance reduction. If the auditor selects a sample of credit memos, a test of controls would be to see whether the credit memo had upon it the authorized signature. That would answer one of the dual purposes of the sample. A second purpose achieved by the sample is when the auditor notes whether the credit memo was correctly entered into the customer's accounts receivable balance. This is a substantive test, not a test of controls. It therefore serves the second purpose of the dual purpose testing procedure. This additional information provided by the PCAOB serves to enable the auditors to increase the efficiency of the audit. There are conditions in which the use of a dual purpose sample is more helpful than in others. For example, it is advised that an auditor planning to use a dual purpose sample should make a preliminary assessment that there is an acceptably low risk that the error rate would exceed the level acceptable to the auditor.

The size of a sample designed for dual purposes should be the larger of the samples that would otherwise have been designed for the two separate purposes. In evaluating such tests, deviations from the control that was tested and monetary misstatements should be evaluated separately using the risk levels applicable for the respective purposes. This is further elaborated on by the PCAOB in paragraph 14 of AS No. 13 entitled *The auditor's responses to the risks of material misstatement* with paragraph 44 providing reference to this. This discussion, namely the design of dual purpose samples, is not present in ISA 530. There is a discussion in ISA 530 (paragraphs 31 to 34) of sample design providing guidance, but there is no discussion of the issue of the design of dual purpose samples.

It is unclear why the ISA does not refer to the use of dual purpose sampling. The failure to reference it, however, does not mean that it cannot be used by auditors following ISA because the use of dual purpose sampling should increase both (a) the efficiency of the auditing process and (b) the effectiveness of the auditing process in detecting fraud.

Issues Relating to Statistical and Nonstatistical Sampling Techniques

In this section, we discuss any differences that may exist between the PCAOB's AU 350 and ISA 530 with reference to guidance regarding the use of statistical techniques versus nonstatistical techniques and the implications thereon if differences do exist. We have already observed that statistical sampling is an objective approach using probability to make an inference about a population. The method will determine the sample size and the selection criteria of the sample. Nonstatistical sampling, on the other hand, relies on judgment to determine the sampling method, the sample size, and the selection items in the sample. We have also observed that the difference between statistical and nonstatistical sampling relates to the ability to project sampling error, not the ability to conclude about the population. The issue of projecting errors will be discussed more fully later.

Paragraph 28 of ISA 530 states that the choice between statistical versus nonstatistical sampling is a matter that the auditor has to decide on when the auditor considers which of the two would most efficiently allow them to obtain sufficient appropriate audit evidence in the particular circumstances. For example, in the case of tests of controls, the auditor's analysis of the nature and cause of errors will often be more important than the statistical analysis of the mere presence or absence of errors. In such a situation non-statistical sampling may be more appropriate. Statistical sampling may be more suitable for tests of controls and tests of details. ISA 530 also provides advice on how to determine sample size using statistical and nonstatistical approaches.

The differences between ISA 530 and the PCAOB's AU 350 are as follows. First, the AU 350 definition is more thorough as it also includes discussion of how statistical sampling can help the auditor, whereas ISA 530 appears to take this for granted. AU 350 in paragraph 46 notes that statistical sampling can help the auditor to (a) design an efficient sample, (b) measure the sufficiency of the evidential matter obtained, and (c) evaluate the sample results. These elements are not discussed in ISA 530. More importantly, AU 350 discusses the costs and benefits of using statistical sampling. It clearly notes that statistical sampling involves additional costs in the form of costs of training auditors, designing individual samples to meet statistical requirements, and selecting the items to be examined. The auditor should choose the appropriate sampling technique after considering the relative costs and benefits. ISA 530 does not have a discussion of costs and benefits.

PCAOB's AU 350 also introduces and provides guidance on statistical and nonstatistical approaches. But the significant difference is that PCAOB's AU 350 takes a broad brush approach and notes that the auditor should use professional judgment in planning, performing, and evaluating a sample and in relating the evidential matter produced by the sample to other evidential matter when forming a conclusion about the related account balance or class of transactions. What is lacking in ISA 530 is the emphasis on the *use of professional judgment* in choosing between statistical versus nonstatistical approaches and the emphasis on the use of *professional judgment* in all activities in the planning, performing, and evaluation of a sample. On the other hand, AU 350 gives the auditor greater flexibility by emphasizing the use of professional judgment in all activities relative to sampling, an emphasis.

Issues Relating to Audit Opinion Formulation

PCAOB's AU 350 links audit sampling to opinion formulation. Paragraph 7 notes that some degree of uncertainty is implicit in the concept of a *reasonable basis for an opinion*. Auditors can be justified in accepting some uncertainty. The justification for accepting some uncertainty arises from the relationship between such factors as the cost and time required to examine all of the data and the adverse consequences of possible erroneous decisions based on conclusions resulting from examining only a sample of the data. If these factors do not justify the acceptance of some uncertainty, the only alternative is to examine all of the data. This was introduced by the PCAOB as a separate paragraph and is unique to PCAOB. The broad-based concept of linking the auditor's opinion to sampling is not considered in ISA 530.

Issues Relating to Error and Anomalous Error

Paragraph 4 of ISA 530 defines error as involving control deviations when performing tests of controls or misstatements when performing tests of details. Referring back to our previous example of dual purpose testing, a control deviation would exist when a credit memo does not have the signature of the authorized person, the credit manager, upon it. A misstatement would exist when the sales invoice does not match the recorded amount of the sale seen in the sales account. Anomalous error is an error that arises from an isolated event that has not recurred other than on specifically identifiable occasions and is, therefore, not representative of errors in the population. There are several differences here. First, there is a clear definition of the term anomaly and its treatment in ISA 530. AU 350 does not have an equivalent wording for *anomaly*. The requirement in paragraph 13 of ISA 530 that addresses the issue of anomalies is not included in AU 350 of the PCAOB. The issue of anomalies is also not discussed in section 530 of the ASB. The PCAOB may believe that the deletion of the option to consider a misstatement an anomaly will enhance the quality of the audit. The justifications for the differences are made by the ASB (refer aicpa.org). ASB justifies this because, otherwise, the auditor may focus on anomalies and not misstatements, thus missing out on a lot of potential misstatements. The ASB also expresses concerns about terms used in ISA 530, which uses words such as *in the extremely rare circumstance* and a *high degree of uncertainty*. For example, it is stated "in the extremely rare circumstance that an error arises from an isolated event" the auditor could decide to "identify all items in the population that possess the common feature". Similarly, the guidance states that, to be considered an anomalous error, the auditor has to have a high degree of certainty that such error is not representative of the population. These terms are not used in section 530 of the ASB because the ASB believes that these terms are subjective and would not be consistently interpreted in practice. Because ASB's section 530 is now under the aegis of the PCOAB, (although under a different title, that of AU 350) and the PCAOB has not made any amendments, we hold this is the view of the PCAOB as well.

Issues Relating to Sampling Risk

Paragraph 7 ISA 530 notes that sampling risk arises from the possibility that the auditor's conclusions based on a sample may be different from the conclusion reached if the entire population were subjected to the same audit procedure. ISA 530 defines sampling risk as follows:

- The risk that the auditor will conclude in the case of a test of controls that controls are more effective than they actually are or, in the case of a test of details, that a material error does not exist when in fact it does. This type of risk affects audit effectiveness and is more likely to lead to an inappropriate audit opinion.
- The risk the auditor will conclude in the case of test of controls, that controls are less effective than they actually are or, in the case of a test of details, that a material error exists when in fact it does not. This type of risk affects audit efficiency as it would usually lead to additional work to establish that initial conclusions are incorrect.

Paragraph 10 of the PCAOB's AU 350 notes that sampling risk arises from the possibility that when a test of controls or a substantive test is restricted to a sample, the auditor's conclusions may be different from the conclusions the auditor would reach if the test were applied in the same way to all items in the account balance or class of transactions. That is, a particular sample may contain proportionately more or less monetary misstatements or deviations from prescribed controls than exist in the balance or class as a whole. Paragraph 12 of AU 350 notes that the auditor should apply professional judgment in assessing sampling risk. In performing substantive tests of details the auditor is concerned with two aspects of sampling risk:

- The risk of incorrect acceptance is the risk that the sample supports the conclusion that the recorded account balance is not materially misstated when it is materially misstated.
- The risk of incorrect rejection is the risk that the sample supports the conclusion that the recorded account balance is materially misstated when it is not materially misstated.

Hence, in this respect, it is very similar to the guidance provided by ISA 530. Paragraph 12 of AU 350 also states that the auditor should be concerned with two aspects of sampling risk in performing tests of controls when sampling is used. These risks are the same risks mentioned earlier for ISA 530.

The preceding discussion has as its heart issues relating to the operating effectiveness of a control. But we conclude PCAOB's AU 350 potentially provides a marginally broader perspective on the use of statistical sampling with regard to internal controls to auditors relative to that provided by ISA 530. But here the *differences* are not significant.

There are requirements in ISA 530 not in AU 350. ISA 530 requires, for test of details, the projection of misstatements found in a sample to the population (www.aicpa.org/FRC). The PCAOB believes that projection of misstatements *is also relevant to tests of controls and tests of compliance*. Tests of compliance are undertaken to confirm whether a firm is following the rules and regulations applicable to an activity. The PCAOB, accordingly broadened the requirement in paragraph 14 of ASB section 530 to project the results of audit sampling to also include tests of controls and tests of compliance, not just tests of details. This was subsequently carried forward to PCAOB's AU 350.

Issues Relating to Nonsampling Risk

This arises from factors that cause the auditor to reach an erroneous conclusion for any reason not related to the size of the sample. For example, ordinarily the auditor finds it necessary to rely on audit evidence that is persuasive rather than conclusive. The auditor might use inappropriate audit procedures, or the auditor might misinterpret audit procedures, or the auditor might misinterpret audit evidence and fail to recognize an error. We do not notice any significant differences between ISA 530 and PCAOB's AU 350 with respect to issues relating to the measurement and handling of nonsampling risk and hence will not engage in further discussion with respect to nonsampling risk.

Once the auditor has decided on the sample size, selected a representative sample and decided on the method (statistical versus nonstatistical sampling) to use, and examined the selected items, the next step is to project errors based on the sampling technique used. The auditor is then required to evaluate performance. This is discussed next.

Projecting Errors

ISA 530 requires that, for tests of details, the auditor should project monetary errors found in the sample to the population and should consider the effect of the projected error on the particular audit objective and on other areas of the audit (refer paragraphs 51 to 53 and 54 to 56 for a more elaborate discussion). The auditor is required to project the total error for the population to obtain a broad view of the scale of errors and to compare this to the tolerable error. For tests of details, tolerable error (now called performance materiality under ISA) is the tolerable misstatement and will be an amount less than or equal to the auditor's materiality used for the individual class of transactions or account balances being audited. (Please note that performance materiality replaced tolerable error under both ISA and AICPA standards.) When an error has been established as an anomalous error it may be excluded when projecting sample errors to the population. If a class of transactions or account balance has been divided into strata, the error is projected for each stratum separately. Projected errors plus anomalous errors for each stratum are then combined when considering the possible effect of errors on the total class of transactions or the account balance. For tests of controls, no explicit projection of errors is necessary since the sample rate is also the projected rate of error for the population as a whole.

With respect to the PCAOB, there are differences. The PCAOB does cover the issue related above. Hence, that will not be repeated here. However, when reading this section, PCAOB's AU 350 refers the reader to AS No. 11 entitled *Consideration of materiality in planning and performing an audit.* The PCAOB links projecting errors to materiality in the context of an audit. AS 11 cites the Supreme Court. In interpreting federal securities laws, the Supreme Court of the United States has held that a fact is material if there is a substantial likelihood that the fact would have been viewed by a reasonable investor as having significantly altered his or her decision to invest. While ISA 530 does not cite other auditing standards or view projecting error from a materiality point of view, the PCAOB does encourage auditors to do this. In particular, PCAOB considers materiality of the monetary errors and their projection to the population. This includes, but is not limited to, projections by stratum and then combined to the total class of transactions. It appears that the PCAOB in AU 350, by incorporating a paragraph requiring auditors to read AS No. 11, also wants auditors to use the results to establish materiality levels for the financial statements as a whole. The auditor now (based on our reading of AS 11) is required to establish materiality levels for projected errors from the sampling results to the financial statements. The auditor should determine the amount of tolerable misstatement (tolerable errors) for the purposes of assessing risks of material misstatement at the financial statement level. This is a much more broad-based view than ISA 530 (and ISA 240, which deals with the auditor's responsibility to consider fraud in an audit of financial statements). Further a detailed description is given in paragraph 26 of AU 350 on how to project errors. This is discussed in the appendix. Such detailed description is not available under ISA (a reflection of the fact that ISAs are principles-based). But the differences are marginal.

Performance and Evaluation of Results

The sample results have to be evaluated. Paragraph 54 of ISA 530 provides guidance on how the auditor should evaluate results. It notes the auditor should evaluate the sample results to determine whether the assessment of a relevant characteristic of the population is confirmed or needs to be revised. In the case of tests of controls, an unexpectedly high sample error rate may lead to an increase in the assessed risk of material misstatement, unless further audit evidence substantiating the initial assessment is obtained. In the case of tests of details, an unexpectedly high error amount in a sample may cause the auditor to believe that a class of transactions or an account balance is materially misstated in the absence of further audit evidence that no material misstatement exists. If the total amount of projected error plus anomalous error is less than, but close to, that which the auditor deems tolerable, the auditor should consider the persuasiveness of the sample results in the light of other audit procedures, and may consider it appropriate to obtain additional audit evidence. If the evaluation of sample results indicates that the assessment of the relevant characteristic of the population needs to be revised, the auditor may, according to paragraph 56, do all or any of the following:

- Request management to investigate identified errors and the potential for further efforts, and to make any necessary adjustments

- Modify the nature, timing, and extent of further audit procedures. For example, in the case of tests of controls, the auditor might extend the sample size, test an alternative control, or modify related substantive procedures
- Consider the effect on the audit report

AU 350 covers the area above. However, there is a difference between PCAOB's AU 350 and ISA 530. The following paragraph was added by the PCAOB to AU 350 and is effective for the months beginning on or after December 15, 2010. This is not in ISA. The paragraph, paragraph 25, notes that auditing procedures that are appropriate to the particular audit objective should be applied to each sample item. In some circumstances the auditor may not be able to apply the planned audit procedures to selected sample items because, for example, supporting documentation may be missing. The auditor's treatment of unexamined items will depend on their effect on the evaluation of the sample. If the auditor's evaluation of the sample results would not be altered by considering those unexamined items to be misstated, it is not necessary to examine the items. However, if considering those unexamined items to be misstated would lead to a conclusion that the balance or class of transactions contains a material misstatement, the auditor should consider alternative procedures that would provide them with sufficient evidence to form a conclusion. The auditor should also evaluate whether the reasons for their inability to examine the items have (a) implications in relation to their risk assessments (including the assessment of fraud risk), (b) implications regarding the integrity of management or employees, and (c) possible effects on other aspects of the audit.

Hence this paragraph, which was added by PCAOB to AU 350, has fraud implications by discussing tying issues related to unexamined items, possible misstatements of identified items, alternative procedures to examine misstatement, and the implications of these on the risk of fraud. However, we note that a critical reading of ISA 240, which is to a certain extent the ISA equivalent dealing with the auditor's responsibility to consider fraud in an audit of financial statements, shows that the differences between PCAOB and ISA with respect to the issues covered above is marginal at the best

Conclusions

Auditors, as part of the audit, may have to digest enormous amounts of data, whether in the form of transactions or even account balances. Trying to verify the existence of a huge multitude of transactions may be extremely time-consuming and expensive. The auditing standards discussed in this chapter provide an alternative to engaging in a brute force attack on mountains of transactions, for example, that a client entity might have. Instead, the professional standards of the ISA and the PCAOB allow the auditor to use statistical sampling techniques. By use of statistical sampling techniques the auditor can choose a representative subset of all the transactions and infer the condition of the accounts as whole from the results of this representative sample.

The information in this chapter relevant to the ISA and PCAOB standards is important information to readers learning about the differences between the standards in that they will better be able to appreciate what one set of standards requires or emphasizes, and another does not. We find that there is more guidance provided to the auditor in PCAOB auditing standards with respect to audit sampling than is present in the ISA standard. This finding is consistent with our earlier discussion that the PCAOB provides more of a rules-based framework for conducting an audit, whereas the ISA standard is more principles-based. Greater levels of guidance may force the auditor to do more work than it would otherwise, or it may provide the auditor with a feeling of comfort in only doing the explicitly mentioned amount of work using techniques mentioned in the PCAOB standard. In a principles-based auditing framework like the ISA, in contrast, the auditor must use a greater level of professional judgment in deciding how much sampling work to do and which methods to use. In reviewing auditors' reports from auditors operating under the different sets of rules, therefore, the reader can bring the information covered here to mind in evaluating the worth of the report. Different inclusions or exclusions between the sets of standards may be believed to have implications for the audit report's quality. We make no conclusions of our own on this point. Be that as it may, this chapter presents an important view of a key consideration in the auditing process: How much evidence should be collected, using which methods (statistical, nonstatistical), and how much judgment was permissible in allowing the auditor to arrive at the auditor's conclusions?

Appendix: Description of How to Project Misstatement Results as per the PCAOB's AU 350

Paragraph 26 of the PCAOB's AU 350 provides a detailed description of how to project misstatement results of the sample to the items from which the sample was selected. We follow this description closely here. There are several acceptable ways to project misstatements from a sample. For example, an auditor may have selected a sample of every twentieth item from a population containing one thousand items. Therefore the sample includes 5 percent of the population. If the auditor discovered overstatements of $3,000 in that sample, the auditor could project a $60,000 overstatement by dividing the amount of misstatement in the sample by the fraction (5 percent) of total items from the population included in the sample. The auditor should add that projection of the misstatements to those discovered in any items examined 100 percent. This total projected misstatement should be compared with the tolerable misstatement for the account balance or class of transactions and appropriate consideration should be given to sampling risk. If the total projected misstatement is less than tolerable misstatement for the account balance or class of transactions, the auditor should consider the risk that such a result might be obtained even though the true monetary misstatement for the population exceeds tolerable misstatement. For example, if the tolerable misstatement in an account balance of $1 million is $50,000 and the total projected misstatement based on an appropriate sample is $10,000, the auditor may be reasonably assured that there is an acceptably low sampling risk that the true monetary misstatement for the population exceeds tolerable misstatement. On the other hand, if the total projected misstatement is close to the tolerable misstatement, the auditor may conclude that there is an unacceptably high risk that the actual misstatements in the population exceed the tolerable misstatement. An auditor should use professional judgment in making evaluations.

Please note that this type of detailed instruction is not available in ISA and as mentioned earlier, this illustrates the importance given by the PCAOB to detecting material misstatements. However a critical reading of ISA 240 shows that the ISA standard appears to have the same focus with respect to detecting material misstatements. Our conclusion is that there are no significant differences between PCAOB and ISA in this regard.

CHAPTER 10

Audit Documentation and Working Papers

The purpose of this chapter is to discuss the following issues:

- What should be the content of the working papers?
- What information should be kept in the permanent and current files?
- How long should documents be retained?
- How are International Standards on Auditing (ISA) different than Public Company Accounting Oversight Board (PCAOB) Auditing Standards (AS) and AU standard?

Introduction

The relevant ISA standard on documentation is ISA 230 entitled *Audit Documentation*. This provides the basic principles underlying documentation. The purpose of ISA 230 is to establish standards and provide guidance on documentation. ISA 230 advises that the auditor should document matters which are important in providing evidence to support the audit opinion. ISA 230 in particular (paragraph 2) notes that the auditor should prepare, on a timely basis, audit documentation that provides:

- a sufficient and appropriate record of the basis for the auditor's report and
- evidence that the audit was performed in accordance with ISAs and applicable legal and regulatory requirements.

Audit documentation is also referred to as working papers. To aid the auditor in planning the audit, all necessary information should be available in the working papers. PCAOB's AS 3 in paragraph 2 notes that working papers should be used as the:

- written record of the basis for the auditor's conclusions and the support for the auditor's representations, whether contained in the auditor's report or otherwise;
- basis for facilitating the planning, performing, and supervision of the engagement;
- as the basis for the review of the quality of the work because it provides the reviewer with written documentation of the evidence supporting the auditor's significant conclusions; and
- the records of the planning and performance of the work.

Once the audit opinion is provided in the published final report, the working papers are the physical proof that the audit was conducted adequately. Auditors work with original documents and accounting records that are required to be left behind on completion of the audit. The working papers act as an index to those documents. This is especially important if the auditor is called upon to prove that the audit was completed in accordance with ISAs should there be a lawsuit or regulatory inquiry.

Paragraph 9 of ISA 230 advises that the auditor should prepare the audit documentation in such a manner as to enable an experienced auditor, having no previous connection with the audit to understand:

- the nature, timing, and extent of the audit procedures performed to comply with the ISA and applicable legal and regulatory requirements;
- the results of the audit procedures and the audit evidence obtained; and
- significant matters arising during the audit and the conclusion reached thereon.

As paragraph 3 of ISA 230 notes, preparing sufficient and appropriate audit documentation on a timely basis helps to enhance the quality of the audit. It also facilitates the effective review and evaluation of the audit evidence obtained and conclusions reached before the auditor's report is finalized.

Purpose of Audit Documentation

Audit documentation serves a number of purposes some of which have already been discussed in the prior section. However, some issues raised are important enough to bear repeating. Paragraph 5 of ISA 230 states that the purposes of documentation should include:

- assisting the audit team to plan and perform the audit;
- assisting members of the audit team responsible for supervision to direct and supervise the audit work *and* to discharge their review responsibilities in accordance with ISA 220 entitled *Quality Control for Audits of Historical Financial Information;*
- enabling the audit team to be accountable for its work;
- retaining a record of matters of continuing significance for future audits;
- enabling an experienced auditor to conduct quality control reviews and inspections in accordance with International Standards on Quality Control (ISQC) 1 entitled *Quality control for firms that perform audits and review of historical financial information and other assurance and related services engagements*; and
- enabling an experienced auditor to conduct external inspection in accordance with applicable legal, regulatory, or other requirements.

Nature of the Audit Documentation

Paragraph 7 of ISA 230 notes that audit documents may be recorded on paper or on electronic or other media. The components of the working papers should include audit programs, the auditor's analysis, summaries of significant matters and copies of the entity's records (e.g., significant documents including specific contracts and agreements). However, paragraph 7 cautions that audit documentation is not a substitute for the entity's accounting records.

This means they cannot be equated with the entity's accounting records. The latter are the primary documents in an audit.

Content of Working Papers

When discussing what the content of working papers should be, it has to be noted that there are differences between ISA 230 and PCAOB (this issue is covered in AS 3, entitled *Audit Documentation*) with respect to the form and content of working papers, which is noted in a report published by the Maastricht Accounting, Auditing and Information Management Research Center (available at http://ec.europa.eu/internal_market/auditing/docs/ias/evalstudy2009/appendix_en.pdf). (We had mentioned this center in Chapter 1). To recapitulate, ISA 230 notes that the content of the working papers should be sufficiently complete and detailed to provide an overall understanding of the audit. As mentioned, the working papers are required to contain information on planning the audit work; the nature, timing, and extent of the audit procedures performed; the results of the audit procedures; and the conclusions drawn that led to the audit opinion. Paragraph 23 of ISA 230 notes that in documenting the nature, timing, and extent of audit procedures performed, the auditor should record (a) who performed the audit work and the date such work was completed and (b) who reviewed the audit work and the date and extent of such review.

In summary, ISA 230 notes that the extent of audit documentation depends on factors such as (refer paragraph 230.A2):

- the nature of the audit procedures to be performed;
- the identified risks of material misstatements;
- the extent of judgment required in performing the work and evaluating the results;
- the significance of the audit evidence obtained;
- the nature and extent of exceptions identified; and
- the audit methodology and tools used.

Types of Audit Documentation

In practice, auditors provide two types of documentation. They are:

- permanent and
- temporary files

However, in the standards ISA 230 and PCAOB's AU 339A entitled *Working Papers*, there is no recommendation that auditors should categorize and retain documents based on whether the information in the working papers can be categorized as permanent or temporary. Our statement is based on our audit work experience and information in auditing text books (Hayes et al. 2005 as an example).

The permanent file is expected to include audit working papers containing all the data that are of continuing interest from year to year (Hayes et al. 2005). An example of a permanent file used in practice is shown in Table 10.1.

Table 10.1 Sample work papers: permanent file contents

Index	Page numbers (not shown)	Client description
I		**General client and engagement information**
		Engagement letter
		Client information form
II		**Statutory and legal information**
		Articles of association or incorporation
		Special legal, statutory, or contractual definitions
		Minutes of continuing relevance from management
		Insurance summary
		Borrowing, lease agreements
		Title deeds
		Details of any other important agreements
III		**Accounting system and internal control**
		Documentation of accounting system and internal control
		Chart of accounts
		Authorization limits, initials and signature list
		Accounting procedures
IV		**Audit**
		Correspondence of continuing relevance
		Documentation: Computer programs
V		**Financial statement information**
		Financial statement analysis/previous year's summary
		Details: Property, plant, and equipment
		Details: Other tangible fixed assets
VI		**Personnel, employment conditions**
		Overview of personnel
		Standard employment contracts, salary scales
		Pension/early retirement rules and regulations
		Sick pay rules and regulations
		Expense allowance rules and regulations
		Other employment conditions
VII		**Taxation**

Source: Adapted from Hayes et al. 2005, 479

Table 10.2 Sample work papers: current file contents

Index	Page numbers (not shown)	Contents
I		**Reports**
		Financial statements
		Auditor's report
II		**Consolidated financial statements**
		Trial balance
		Consolidated financial statements
III		**Consolidation schedules**
		Interoffice memoranda and reports from other offices
IV		**Engagement planning**
		Strategy document
		Planning memorandum and audit plan
		Memos of instruction from other offices
		Audit program
		Audit progress reports
		Budget
		Detailed audit planning and work allocation
V		**Engagement completion**
		Completion memorandum
		Accounting disclosure checklist
		Subsequent events review
		Notes for partner/manager
VI		**Engagement administration**
		Time sheets
		Hours and fee analysis
VII		**Control overview document**
VIII		**Representations**
		Letter of representation
		Major points discussed with management
		Client lawyer's letter
IX		**Planning analysis**
		Budget
		Interim financial statements
X		**Correspondence in respect of current year's audit**
XI		**Prior work papers from permanent file**

Source: Adapted from Hayes et al. 2005, 481

An example of a current file is shown in Table 10.2.

The tables are not meant to be all inclusive. The next important issue relates to the time period for preparation of the documentation and the duration for which the working papers should be retained? These issues will be discussed next.

Time Periods for Preparation of Documentation

ISA 230 in paragraph 7 states that the auditor shall prepare audit documentation on a timely basis. Paragraph 14 builds on this. The paragraph notes that the auditor should assemble the audit documentation in an audit file and complete the administrative process of assembling the final audit file on a timely basis after the date of the auditor's report. Paragraph 21 states that an appropriate time limit should ordinarily be not more than 60 days after the report release date.

PCAOB's AS 3 (paragraph 5) discusses the same topic. It notes that prior to the report release date, the auditor must complete all necessary auditing procedures and obtain sufficient evidence to support the representations in the auditor's report. (This is discussed in detail in the Maastricht Accounting, Auditing and Information Management Research Center report mentioned previously in this chapter.) The PCAOB standard notes that a complete and final set of audit documents should be assembled for retention as of a date not more than 45 days after the report release date. If a report is not issued in connection with an engagement, then the documentation completion date should not be more than 45 days from the date that the fieldwork was substantially completed. If the auditor was unable to complete the engagement, then the documentation completion date should not be more than 45 days from the date the engagement ceased.

Hence, there is a difference. The PCAOB's AS 3 (in paragraph 15) puts more pressure on the auditor in that AS 3 requires the auditor to assemble a complete and final set of audit documentation not more than 45 days after the report release date, whereas under ISA 230, it is 60 days. Another difference is that AS 3 entitled *Audit Documentation* (paragraph 15) contains specific requirements on documentation completion dates in case a report is not issued in connection with an engagement or if the auditor was unable to complete the engagement. This issue is not mentioned in ISA. Rather, it would appear that this is left to the judgment of the auditor.

Document Retention

ISA 230 states that the auditor should adopt appropriate procedures for maintaining the confidentiality and the safe custody of the working papers and for retaining them for a period sufficient to meet the needs of the practice and in accordance with legal and professional requirements of record retention. The standard provides no further guidance on documentation retention.

In the United States, the Securities and Exchange Commission (SEC) introduced detailed regulations (rule 210-06) regarding document retention as mandated by the Sarbanes Oxley Act (SOX). The regulation sets forth detailed requirements regarding the types of document (e.g., working papers, memos and the like that contain conclusions, opinions, analyses, etc) that should be retained and the specific period of time they should be retained. This is regardless of whether such documents support, or are inconsistent with, the final audit conclusions.

Hayes et al. (2005) noted that under SOX section 103, each registered public accounting firm is required to prepare and maintain audit working papers and other information related to any audit report for a period of not less than seven years. This same issue is covered in PCAOB's AS 3. It states audit documentation must be retained for seven years from the date of completion of the engagement as indicated by the date of the auditor's report unless a longer period of time is required by law (refer paragraph 15).

Under SOX section 105, the PCAOB may also require:

- the testimony of the firm or any person associated with a registered public accounting firm and
- the production of audit work papers and any other document or information in the possession of a registered public accounting firm or any associated person and may inspect the books and records of such a firm or associated person to verify the accuracy of any documents or information supplied.

The above discussion in SOX provides guidance to the PCAOB. The PCAOB in AS 3 does not cover this as it is already covered in SOX, section 105. ISA 230 does not have an equivalent discussion similar to that required in SOX section 105, and hence, there is a difference. ISA 230 states that the auditor "should adopt appropriate procedures for maintaining the confidentiality and safe custody of the working papers and for retaining them for a period sufficient to meet the needs of the practice and in accordance with legal and professional requirements of record retention". We reviewed ISA 230 carefully and found no other guidance on document retention.

There is a significant difference between ISA 230 and PCAOB AS 3 with respect to document retention, where, for AS 3, there is a specified clear guidance of seven years. However, the time period issue is addressed in ISQC. It requires firms to establish policies and procedures for the retention of engagement documentation. The retention period for audit engagement documentation is ordinarily required under ISQC 1 to be no shorter than five years from the date of the auditor's report or, if later, the date of the group auditors report. Hence, by default, auditors in the international arena would follow this guideline. ISQC 1 and ISA 230 also do not address the possibility of retention periods in case the auditor, for whatever reason, does not complete an audit.

In the case of PCAOB, AS 3 is very clear. There is no default here. AS 3 states that the auditor must retain documentation for seven years from the "date the auditor grants permission to use the auditor's report in connection with the issuance of the company's financial statements" (by this is meant the report release date). The main difference is that, unlike ISA 230, AS 3 paragraph 14 explicitly requires that the documentation be retained for seven years from the date the auditor grants permission to use the auditor's report unless a longer period is required by law. Further, unlike ISA 230, AS 3 contains specific requirements about retention in case no report is issued in connection with an engagement or if the auditor is unable to complete the assignment.

Another related important issue relates to the necessity to make alterations to the working papers.

Alterations of Working Papers after Completion of the Audit

The PCAOB's AS 3 paragraph 16 notes that circumstances may require subsequent additions to audit documentation. An example would be when evidence is obtained after completion of the audit or if work performed before engagement was finished and was documented only after completion. The PCAOB notes that the documentation added must indicate the date the information was added, by whom it was added and the reason for adding it (paragraph 16).

SOX specifically notes that audit documentation must not be deleted or discarded. Further, SOX provides criminal penalties for altering documents. The requirements of SOX are echoed by the PCAOB. Thus, there is a difference with ISA 230 since the latter does not discuss the issue of deleted or discarded or altered documents or legal penalties for doing so. This may be attributed to the fact that the PCAOB was instituted in the wake of Arthur Andersen's destruction of documents in the wake of the problems with the Enron entity and its audits coming to light. Accordingly, preventing another wholesale destruction of audit documents by the auditor became a U.S. and, therefore, PCAOB priority. It is not similarly a priority for the International Auditing Assurance Standards Board (IAASB) in its writing of the ISA. Next, we discuss additional important issues relating to audit documentation.

Custodial Issues Related to Audit Documentation

The PCAOB's AS 3 notes that matters specific to a particular engagement should be included in the audit documentation of the pertinent engagement (more elaborate discussion is provided in paragraphs 4 to 10). In particular issues such as level of auditor independence with respect to conducting the engagement, extent of staff training and proficiency of client (or lack thereof), and issues relating to client acceptance and retention may be documented in a central repository of the public accounting firm or in the particular office participating in the engagement (paragraph 11). If such matters are documented in a central repository, the audit documentation of the engagement should include a reference to the central repository. There is no mention of this in ISA 230. This is a significant difference between ISA 230 and AS 3 of PCAOB. Unlike AS 3, ISA does not mention that some items can be documented in a central repository, whereas others should be included in the documentation of the pertinent engagement.

Significant Matters and Issues Relating Thereto

Now, we discuss the issue of significant matters. ISA 230 does not define significant matters. It notes that judging the significance of a matter requires an objective analysis of the facts and circumstances. Examples of significant matters are provided. ISA 230 states that the auditor may consider it helpful to prepare and retain, as part of the audit documentation, a summary that describes the significant matters identified during the audit and how they were addressed. ISA 230 notes that judging the significance of a matter requires an objective analysis of the facts and circumstances. Paragraph 14 states that significant items could include:

- matters that give rise to significant risks as defined in ISA 315 *Understanding the Entity and its Environment and Assessing the Risks of Material Misstatement*;
- results of audit procedures indicating (a) that the financial information could be materially misstated or (b) a need to revise the auditor's previous assessment of the risks of material misstatement and the auditor's responses to those risks;
- circumstances that cause the auditor significant difficulty in applying necessary audit procedures; and
- findings that could result in a modification of the auditor's report.

Hayes et al. 2005 provides further examples of significant matters. Hayes et al.'s list (page 74) includes, but is not limited to, the following:

- The selection, application, and consistency of accounting principles including related disclosures (examples of significant matters in this category include accounting for complex or unusual transactions, accounting estimates, and uncertainties as well as related management assumptions)
- Results of auditing procedures that indicate a need for significant modification of planned auditing procedures
- The existence of material misstatements
- Omissions in the financial statements
- The existence of significant deficiencies in internal control over reporting
- Audit adjustments and the ultimate resolution of these items (ISA 230 describes an audit adjustment as a proposed correction of a misstatement of the financial statements that could, in the auditor's judgment, either individually or in the aggregate have a material effect on the company's financial reporting process.)

- Disagreements among members of the engagement team or with others consulted on the engagement about conclusions reached on significant accounting or auditing estimates
- Circumstances that cause significant difficulty in applying audit procedures
- Significant changes in the assessed level of audit risk for particular audit areas.

Significant Differences between the Auditor and the Client

AS 3, on the other hand, provides a definition of significant matters (paragraph 12 of AS 3). AS 3 states that the auditor must identify all significant findings, findings that *may or may not* create differences or issues with the client, depending on whether the client is amenable to the auditor's proposed resolution or not, and document these significant matters in a document referred to as an Engagement Completion Memorandum. The concept of the Engagement Completion Memorandum is unique to AS 3. The Engagement Completion Memorandum is required to include all information necessary to understand the significant findings of the audit. These significant findings are required to be cross referenced to other available supporting audit documentation. It is required that (paragraph 11) the document along, with any documents cross referenced, should collectively be as specific as necessary in the circumstances for a reviewer to gain a thorough understanding of the significant findings or issues.

There are differences between ISA 230 and PCAOB's AS 3. Unlike ISA 230, PCAOB's AS 3 (paragraph 13) requires that an engagement completion memorandum be prepared and maintained in the audit documentation. AS 3 requires that the office of the firm issuing the auditor's report be responsible for ensuring that all audit documentation (specified in paragraphs 4 to 13 of AS 3) be prepared and retained. The PCAOB's AS 3 also notes that relevant audit documentation supporting the auditor's work performed by other auditors—including auditors associated with other offices of the firm, affiliated firms, or nonaffiliated firms—must be retained by or be accessible to the office issuing the auditor's report. In addition, the office issuing the auditor's report must obtain, review, and retain, prior to the report release date, documentation related to the work performed by other auditors including auditors associated with other offices of the firm, affiliated firms or nonaffiliated firms.

Here, there are significant differences between PCAOB standards and ISA. Unlike ISA 230, PCAOB's AS 3 in paragraph 18 states very clearly that the office of the firm issuing the auditor's report is responsible for ensuring that audit documentation is retained. Also documentation supporting the work of other auditors must be retained or accessible to the office issuing the auditor's report. Moreover, PCAOB's AS 3 paragraph 19 requires the office that issues the report to obtain, review, and retain specific documentation related to the work performed by other auditors, unless the auditor decides to make reference in the report to the audit performed by the other auditor. After careful review, we note that these issues are not addressed in ISA 230.

In summary, in ISA 230, there appears to be a presumption that the auditor would know what a significant matter is. However, PCAOB is different in that a definition of significant matters is provided. It notes that significant matters relate to significant findings or issues and is all embracing in that it should include actions taken to address them (including additional evidence obtained and the basis for the conclusions reached).

Conclusions

Earlier chapters described the audit process, a process that results in collecting a great deal of information about the client's financial statements and internal controls systems through the application of auditing standards. The information obtained in the audit, as well as the particular audit procedures employed, is required to be documented. This chapter describes the information that needs to be retained in order to comply with ISA and PCAOB standards. The importance of this chapter to the readers is that it provides a description of the information to be retained and presents the differences between the ISA and PCAOB audits. However diligently an auditor works, the failure to appropriately document that work may cause the auditor severe problems should the auditor be challenged in a legal forum later, whether that legal forum is in the United States or abroad. Maintaining documentation helps the auditor document that the appropriate evidence was gathered in sufficient quantity.

Plus, maintaining records on how the audit was conducted provides valuable information to the auditors in the following year as to what problems and strengths characterized the client earlier. While the auditor must always update that information to fully account for circumstances that confront the auditor during the new audit, having access to appropriate information from prior years remains valuable.

CHAPTER 11

Audit Reports and Communication

Introduction

In this chapter we focus on the following with particular emphasis on differences (when differences exist) between International Standards on Auditing (ISA) and the standards set by Public Company Accounting Oversight Board (PCAOB):

- What is the purpose of an auditor's report?
- What items should go into an auditor's report?
- What uncertainties should lead to a qualification of audit opinions?
- When should the auditor issue a modified opinion as opposed to an unmodified opinion?
- If and when should auditors communicate with those charged with corporate governance?
- What criteria go into deciding on whether an audit report should be modified (by the United States) or qualified (internationally)?
- What are subsequent events and how are auditors in the United States and internationally required to deal with them? Are there fundamental differences, and are these differences significant?
- In the presence of going concern uncertainties, what are the requirements of ISA for testing and reporting and how does this differ from the PCAOB standards?

In this chapter, wherever differences between the ISA on the one hand and PCAOB on the other exist, we discuss those differences and the implications of these differences for auditors and regulators. Please note that, whereas ISA discusses this in ISA 570 *Going Concern* and the main relevant discussion for the PCAOB is in AU 341 entitled *The Auditor's Consideration of an Entity's Ability to Continue as a Going Concern,* other relevant PCAOB AUs are discussed for comparison at appropriate junctures of this chapter.

Background

The audit report is the final product of the audit. ISA 200 states that the objective of an audit of financial statements is to enable the auditor to express an opinion as to whether the financial statements are prepared, in all material respects, in accordance with the applicable financial reporting framework. The wording of the auditor's report is standard unless required by law or regulation to use different wording. The key words require that the financial statements *give a true and fair view* or *are presented fairly, in all material respects.* ISA 200 (paragraphs 37 and 38) describes the auditor's responsibility to determine whether the financial reporting framework adopted by the management in preparing the financial statements is acceptable.

We now focus on the United States. Marden, Edwards, and Stout (2003) note that until 2002 corporate officers of publicly traded companies in the United States were not penalized for misstated financial statements unless fraud could be proven. This is because, prior to 2002, the law had no teeth. By fraud it is meant that the officers deliberately misstated. The U.S. Congress enacted the Sarbanes Oxley Act of 2002 (SOX) in response to a number of highly publicized business failures and allegations of corporate improprieties. Now corporate financial officers can face significant penalties if they certify that the company's books are accurate when they are not. The executives could face up to a five-year prison sentence, fines, and other disciplinary action such as civil and criminal litigation. SOX (section 404) requires the management to acknowledge its responsibility for establishing and maintaining adequate internal controls, including asserting their effectiveness in writing. The auditor, in turn, must report on the management's assertion about the effectiveness of its internal controls as of the company's year end. SOX (section 302) requires that the chief executive officer or the equivalent and the principal financial officer or the equivalent certify, in each quarterly and annual report submitted to the U.S. Securities and Exchange Commission, the following (section 302 of SOX):

- The signing officer has reviewed the report;
- The report does not contain any untrue statement of a material fact or omit to state a material fact;
- The financial statements, and other financial information, fairly present, in all material respects the financial condition of the company;
- The signing officers are (1) responsible for establishing and maintaining internal controls, (2) have evaluated the effectiveness of the company's internal controls, and (3) have presented in their report their conclusions about the effectiveness of their internal controls based on the evaluation of the controls that they are required to make under SOX;
- The signing officers have disclosed to the company's auditors and the audit committee of the board of directors, the following: (1) all significant deficiencies in the design or operation of internal controls which could adversely affect the company's ability to record, process, summarize and report financial data, (2) have identified for the company's auditors any material weaknesses in internal controls, and (3) any fraud, whether or not material, that involves the management or employees who have a significant role in the company's internal controls;
- The signing officers have indicated in the report whether or not there were significant changes in internal controls or in other factors that could significantly affect internal controls subsequent to the date of their internal control evaluation.

In essence, SOX has caused big changes for both auditors and the companies they audit. We note that auditors of public companies are now required to certify a company's internal controls. From the management's point of view, a key result involves much greater auditing costs. Under the American Institute of Certified Public Accountants (AICPA) auditing standards, however, the auditors are not required to report on internal controls. They are, however, required to understand the internal control system—as discussed in an earlier chapter—and use that understanding in developing and implementing the audit program for nonpublic company clients.

Key Elements in an Auditor's Report

The audit report is the key outcome of the audit process, described earlier in this book. The report provides information as to the responsibility for the underlying financial reporting process and the statements and provides very general information of use in understanding the auditor's procedures in generating the evidence that results in a particular type of report. The audit reports described here are those currently required by the ISA and the PCAOB. We present these but note that the AICPA, the IAASB, and the PCAOB are all looking at changing the auditor's report to be more explanatory.

We now discuss the basic elements of an auditor's report.

Paragraphs 18 to 60 of ISA 700 *The Independent Auditor's Report on a Complete Set of Financial Statements* contains the basic elements of the auditor's report, which include the following:

- Title
- Addressee
- Introductory paragraph
  - Management's responsibility for the financial statements
  - Auditor's responsibility
- Scope paragraph
- Auditor's opinion
- Other matters
- Other reporting responsibilities
- Auditor's signature
- Date of the auditor's report
- Auditor's address

These will be considered individually.

Title

Paragraph 18 of ISA 700 notes that the auditor's report should have a title that clearly indicates that it is the report of an independent auditor. The most frequently used title is "Independent auditor" or "Auditor's Report" in the title to distinguish the auditor's report from reports that might be issued by others.

Addressee

Paragraph 20 of ISA 700 states that the auditor's report should be addressed to those charged with governance of the entity whose financial statements are being audited. Hence, the report is addressed to either the shareholders or the supervisory board or the board of directors of the entity whose financial statements are being audited. The PCAOB has a similar requirement (paragraph 8), based on typical U.S. corporate governance setups. With respect to the ISA, such corporate governance setups will vary by country, as will the legal requirements for including an addressee as well. In some countries, such as the Netherlands, auditor's reports are not addressed at all because the reports are meant to be used by (the anonymous) public at large.

Next we delve further into the auditor's opinion. First we discuss the structure of the audit opinion, paragraph-by-required-paragraph. Then we expand on certain critical matters relevant to these individual paragraphs.

Introductory Paragraph

Paragraph 22 of ISA 700 states that the introductory paragraph in the auditor's report should identify the entity whose financial statements have been audited and should state that the financial statements have been audited. The introductory paragraph should also:

- identify the title of each of the financial statements that comprise the complete set of financial statements;
- refer to the summary of significant accounting policies and other explanatory notes; and

- specify the date and period covered by the financial statements.

There are certain requirements in the ISA that are not in the PCAOB's AU 341. ISA 700 states that financial statements should be prepared in a compliance framework (also known as rules-based framework). The PCAOB standards require that financial reporting frameworks used in the United States should be prepared in accordance with a fair presentation framework. What is the difference and why is it important?

A compliance framework requires compliance with the provisions of the framework. That is, *strict obedience* to the instructions is required. The preparers of financial statements have no choice but to follow the requirements of the framework. The compliance framework does not allow any room for flexibility. PCAOB standards do not include any references to compliance frameworks because the PCAOB believes that all financial reporting frameworks used in the United States should be fair presentation frameworks. Hence AU 508 (paragraphs 3 and 4) requires preparation in accordance with a fair presentation framework. A fair presentation framework is based on a different philosophy.

A fair presentation framework requires compliance but it allows for alternatives if such alternatives help achieve better presentation of financial statements, that is financial statements that are more relevant and reliable. (This holds even if the management has to make additions or go against the requirements of the framework.) Accordingly, under PCAOB AU 341 and U.S. financial accounting rules (called in the U.S. Generally Accepted Accounting Principles [GAAP]), the management has to provide more relevant financial information but allows for alternatives if the management can justify such alternatives. Having more heavily judgmental accounting principles, such as those that prevail in the European Union, may provide a greater shield against legal liability than more thoroughly detailed accounting standards such as those which apply in the United States. For the interested reader, we provide a full discussion of fair presentation and compliance frameworks in the appendix.

We note that paragraph 7 of ISA 700 provides definitions of compliance frameworks and also of fair presentation frameworks. The reader has to be alert to notice the difference; otherwise there is an assumption that the PCAOB does not have a definition.

The introductory paragraph should include a statement that the financial statements are the responsibility of the entity's management. The preparation of these statements requires the management to make significant accounting estimates and judgments as well as to determine the appropriate accounting principles and methods used when preparing the statements. The introductory paragraph is also required to refer to the summary of significant accounting policies and other explanatory information. The introductory paragraph should also have a statement that the responsibility of the auditor is to express an opinion on the financial statements based on the audit.

We now provide an illustration of an ISA opening (introductory) paragraph:

We have audited the accompanying balance sheet of XYZ Company as of December 31, 2013, and the related statements of income and cash flows for the year then ended. These financial statements are the responsibility of the Company's management. Our responsibility is to express an opinion on these financial statements based on our audit.

At this juncture, we discuss other paragraphs that are important.

Scope Paragraph

Scope refers to the auditor's ability to perform audit procedures deemed necessary in the circumstances. The scope paragraph is a factual statement of what an auditor did in the audit. Basically, the purpose of the scope paragraph is to provide the reader assurance that the audit has been carried out in accordance with established standards or practices for such engagements. It is required that the scope paragraph include a statement that the audit was planned and performed to obtain reasonable assurance about whether the financial statements are free of material misstatement and that the audit provides a reasonable basis for the opinions. Hayes et al. (2005) notes that the use of the above phrases serves to convey a signal that while the audit provides a high level of assurance, it is not a guarantee.

We provide an illustration of an ISA scope paragraph.

> We conducted our audit in accordance with International Standards on Auditing (or refer to relevant national standards or practices). Those Standards require that we plan and perform the audit to obtain reasonable assurance about whether the financial statements are free of material misstatement. An audit includes examining, on a test basis, evidence supporting the amounts and disclosures in the financial statements. An audit also includes assessing the accounting principles used and significant estimates made by management as well as evaluating the overall financial statement presentation. We believe that our audit provides a reasonable basis for our opinion.

If the company is traded on a U.S. stock exchange, there is another difference between PCAOB standards and ISA. PCAOB's Auditing Standard (AS) No 1 *References in Auditors' Reports to the Standards of the Public Company Accounting Oversight Board* requires that the audit report must refer to the standards of the PCAOB instead of United States generally accepted accounting standards or standards generally accepted in the United States wherever AS 1 has expressed views. This is emphasized in paragraph 1 of AS No. 1. This states that the SOX authorized the PCAOB to establish auditing and related professional standards to be used by registered public accounting firms.

Opinion Paragraph

The opinion paragraph of the auditor's report should clearly indicate the financial reporting framework used to prepare the financial statements. It should state the auditor's opinion as to whether the financial statements give a true and fair view (or are presented fairly, in all material respects) in accordance with the financial reporting framework and where appropriate, whether the financial statements comply with statutory requirements. The special terms used—*give a true and fair view* or *present fairly, in all material respects*—are considered equivalent by many. Both terms indicate, amongst others, that the auditor considers only those matters that are material to the financial statements. The ISA 200, for example, considers the terms equivalent and the PCAOB uses the term *present fairly*. For our purposes, we will consider them equivalent. An illustration of an opinion paragraph is as follows:

> In our opinion, the financial statements give a true and fair view of (or present fairly, in all material respects) the financial position of the Company as of "December 31, 2015," and of the results of its operations and its cash flows for the year then ended in accordance with International Financial Reporting Standards (or title of a financial reporting framework with reference to the country of origin).

Here we note some differences between the ISA and the PCAOB standards. ISA 700 discusses the preparation of financial statements that give a *true and fair view* (or present fairly in all material respects) in the auditor's opinion. The Auditing Standards Board (ASB) originally and now the PCAOB (in AU 508) do not include any references to a *true and fair view*. The AICPA, in a report it published on the differences in wording (aicpa.org/FRC), notes that this could be because such wording has not historically been used in the United States.

The PCAOB recommends a continuation of using the words *present fairly in all material respects* in the auditor's opinion. The ASB, according to the AICPA report, believes that this difference in wording does not result in a difference in the application of ISAs (internationally) or PCAOB (United States).

Finally, we note that we did not note any differences between the wordings of qualified and adverse opinions in the ISA and the PCAOB and, hence, do not discuss these here.

Other Matters Paragraph

This does not appear to be in ISA. It is unique to PCAOB and, prior to that, to AICPA standards. Hence, it is an important difference. What happens when a company is issued audit opinions in previous period(s) by predecessor auditors with which the current auditor does not agree? PCAOB's AU 508 provides requirements on how to approach this. It is basically guidance on how to address the situation when an auditor's opinion on prior period financial statements differs from an audit opinion previously expressed by a predecessor auditor. PCAOB's AU 508 requires this be included in an *other matter* paragraph. A similar situation could arise if the prior period financial statements were not audited. Paragraphs 56 and 57 basically provide guidance to the auditor by requiring the auditor to disclose this also in an *other matter* paragraph. There appears to be no reference to this situation in the ISA based on our reading of ISA 700. ISA 710 entitled *Comparatives* also does not discuss this issue or any requirements the auditor should adhere to. PCAOB feels this is appropriate for the U.S. environment, and the relevant PCAOB standard is AU 508. Having described the order of paragraphs within the audit report, we next go further into discussing important issues that affect the responsibility for the financial statements themselves and the auditor's responsibility with respect to, but not for, the financial statements.

Manager's Responsibility for the Financial Statements Paragraph

Paragraph 26 of ISA 700 requires the auditor's report to state that management is responsible for the preparation and fair presentation of financial statements in accordance with the applicable financial reporting framework. The management is also responsible for implementing such internal controls as it determines are necessary to enable the preparation of financial statements that are free from material misstatement (whether due to fraud or error). However section 700 of ASB requires the auditor's report to state that the management's responsibility includes the design, implementation, and maintenance of internal control relevant to the preparation and fair presentation of the financial statements. The PCAOB, following SOX, also holds the management responsible for the financial statements and for maintaining and performing annual evaluations of its own internal control system. In the earlier chapter on internal controls, we noted that *internal control audits* and, therefore, *internal control reports* are required for PCAOB audits (as per AS 5) but not for audits conducted under AICPA or ISA standards. Under these latter two sets of standards, the auditor is required to gain an understanding of internal controls but need not test the controls and issue a report on them.

Paragraph 24 of ISA 700 requires the report to use a term that is "appropriate in the context of the legal framework in the relevant jurisdiction" when the auditor's report discusses the management's responsibilities. Here there is a difference. The PCAOB's AU 508 does not include this requirement. The ASB may have proceeded on the basis that this paragraph related to jurisdictions where the corporate law is different relative to the United States as per an AICPA report (refer aicpa.org). We assume this view is also held by the PCAOB, as they brought this under their aegis without change.

There are other issues that we feel should be addressed. These relate to requirements in PCAOB standards and not in the ISA. PCAOB AU 508 adds a requirement that the description in the auditor's report of the management's responsibilities for the financial statements should not be referenced to a separate statement by the management about such responsibilities (Appendix footnotes section, footnote 4). This is not in the ISA standard. PCAOB's AS 3 states that the term *sufficient appropriate audit evidence* implies that the audit documentation has been reviewed and that it is possible to come to an appropriate opinion on the financial statements (or, for an internal control audit, the internal controls). ISA 700 does not contain these requirements. The PCAOB standard, and the related ASB standard, make explicit the responsibility of the auditor to both collect and come to a decision on the audit outcomes. Making this explicit may result in less chance of auditor error or oversight. The ISA 700, however, does not make these responsibilities explicit, perhaps on the assumption that auditors would naturally both collect enough evidence and carefully evaluate it. We refrain from drawing other conclusions as to why the sets of standards differ on what seems to us to be a key part of the audit.

Auditor's Responsibility

Auditor's Responsibility With Respect to Compliance With Ethical Requirements.   Paragraph 32 of ISA 700 requires the auditor's report to state that the responsibility of the auditor is to express an opinion on the financial statements based on the audit. The auditor's report should state that the auditor's report was conducted in accordance with international (or PCAOB if applicable in the United States) standards on auditing. The auditor's report should say that the standards require that the auditor comply with ethical requirements (paragraph 30) and that the auditor plans and performs the audit to obtain reasonable assurance whether the financial statements are free from material misstatement.

There is a difference here. While paragraph 30 of ISA 700 requires the auditor's report to include in the *Auditor's Responsibilities* section a statement that the auditing standards require that the auditor should comply with ethical requirements, PCAOB's AU 508 does not contain this requirement. This could be because, in the United States, auditors must comply with the ethical standards contained in the AICPA Code of Professional Conduct. The PCAOB may have proceeded on the basis that the title indicating that it is the report of an independent auditor affirms that the auditor has met the ethical requirements, and, therefore need not make an additional reference in the auditor's report.

Auditor's Responsibility With Respect to Supplementary Information.   Paragraph 46 of ISA 700 contains requirements when supplementary information that is not required by the applicable financial reporting framework is presented with the audited financial statements. If such supplementary information is not clearly differentiated from the audited financial statements, ISA 700 requires the auditor to ask the management to change how the unaudited supplementary information is presented, and if the management refuses to do so, the auditor should explain in the auditor's report that such supplementary information has not been audited. An example of supplementary information that may be required in certain jurisdictions is adequacy of accounting records. The auditor should express an opinion in a different paragraph following the auditor's opinion. The auditor is required to differentiate and address these separately to clearly distinguish them from the auditor's responsibilities for, and opinion on, the financial statements. In the United States, PCAOB AU 558 entitled *Required Supplementary Information* (paragraph 6) addresses the auditor's responsibility when engaged to report on supplementary information, which is in addition to the regular audit report. (Required supplementary information differs from other types of information because, according to paragraph 6 of AU 558, the Financial Accounting Standards Board [FASB] considers the information an essential part of the financial reporting of certain entities. Accordingly, the auditor should apply certain limited procedures to required supplementary information and report deficiencies in the information or omission of such information. We do not notice this discussion in the ISA.) In conducting the financial statement audit, the auditor also has the responsibility of ascertaining whether any of the information in the annual report contradicts the audited financial information. At the present time, no ISA exist that correspond to AU 558. The PCAOB's AU 558 does not include the requirement for the auditor to ask the management to change how the unaudited supplementary information is presented when the supplementary information is not clearly differentiated from the audited financial statements.

Auditor's Responsibility With Respect to Audit Description.   The auditor's responsibility is also to describe the audit by stating in the audit opinion that:

- an audit involves performing procedures to obtain audit evidence about the amounts and disclosures in the financial statements;
- the procedures selected depend on the auditor's judgment including the assessment of risks of material misstatement of the financial statements, whether due to fraud or error; and
- an audit also includes evaluating the appropriateness of the accounting policies used, the reasonableness of accounting estimates made by the management as well as the overall presentation of the financial statements.

There does not appear to be any difference with respect to ISA versus PCAOB, hence there is no further discussion here.

Auditor's Opinion

An auditor can give different types of opinions. Paragraph 39 of ISA 700 states that an auditor can express an unqualified opinion if the auditor concludes that the financial statements give a true and fair view or are presented fairly, in all material respects, in accordance with the applicable financial reporting framework. There does not appear to be any difference between ISA and PCAOB here. We will discuss the types of auditor opinion possible further below.

Other Reporting Responsibilities

In some international jurisdictions, the auditor may have additional responsibilities to report. For example, the auditor may be asked to report certain matters if they come to the auditor's attention during the course of an audit. Alternatively, the auditor may be asked to perform and report on additional specified procedures or to express an opinion on specific matters such as the adequacy of accounting books and records. Auditing standards in the specific jurisdiction or country often provide guidance on the auditor's responsibilities with respect to specific additional reporting responsibilities in the jurisdiction or country. This has been stated before but is worth repeating. Paragraph 24 of ISA 700 requires the report to use a term that is "appropriate in the context of the legal framework in the relevant jurisdiction" when the auditor's report discusses management's responsibilities. Here there is a difference. PCAOB AU 534 *Reporting on Financial Statements Prepared for Use in Other Countries* does not include this requirement. The ISAs have been adopted by over 100 nations and have been customized by different nations to fit their different national laws and corporate regulatory frameworks. The PCAOB standards, however, are only used within one nation, the United States and, therefore, do not need to confer flexibility on the auditor to respond to other, non-U.S. jurisdictional requirements. Paragraph 43 of ISA 700 discusses the auditor's report prescribed by law or regulation. In the United States, PCAOB AU 534 does not contain this section. ISA 710 addresses reporting in other jurisdictions that are different to the United States, including requirements that are not covered by the auditor's report. For example, if the prior period financial statements have been revised and reissued with a new auditor's report, the auditor should obtain sufficient audit evidence that the corresponding figures agree with the revised financial statements. This is addressed in a separate section.

Auditor's Signature

The auditor's report should be signed. However, there is currently an unresolved controversy both in the United States and separately in the EU as to whether the partner's name or just the firm name should be used. Because the issue is unresolved, we add no further discussion here.

Date of the Auditor's Report

This is covered in paragraph 52 of ISA 700. The auditor should date the report on the financial statements no earlier than the date on which the auditor obtained sufficient appropriate audit evidence on which they base their opinion on the financial statements. ISA 700 states that sufficient appropriate audit evidence should include evidence that the entity's complete set of financial statements have been prepared and that those with the responsibility for doing so have asserted that they have taken responsibility for them.

The date of the auditor's report informs the reader that the auditor has considered the effect of events and transactions of which the auditor became aware and that occurred *up to the auditor's report date.* The auditor's report also includes the party addressed by the report, consistent with the standard for reporting. The auditor's responsibility for events and transactions between yearend and the auditor's report date is addressed in ISA 560 "Subsequent Events." If the auditor perceives that there are problems, then the auditor may not be in a position to provide an unqualified opinion.

Types of Auditor's Reports

There are four types of reports that can be given by an auditor. These are:

- Standard unmodified opinion
- Qualified opinion

- Disclaimer of opinion
- Adverse opinion

Standard Unmodified Opinion

The auditor should give a standard unmodified opinion when the auditor feels that the financial statements give a true and fair view (or present fairly in all material respects). To give a standard unqualified opinion, the auditor must be satisfied with respect to the following, namely:

- The financial information has been prepared using acceptable accounting policies, which have been consistently applied.
- The financial information complies with relevant regulations and statutory requirements.
- The view presented by the financial information as a whole is consistent with the auditor's knowledge of the business of the entity.
- There is adequate disclosure of all material matters relevant to the proper presentation of the financial statements.

An auditor may not be able to express an unmodified opinion when either of the following circumstances exists and, in the auditor's judgment, is material to the financial statements:

- There is a limitation on the scope of the auditor's work.
- There is a disagreement with management regarding the acceptability of the accounting policies selected, the method of their application, or the adequacy of financial statement disclosures.

An auditor's report which represents a standard unmodified opinion is also required to state that any changes in accounting principles or in the method of their application and their effects have been properly determined and disclosed in the financial statements.

Qualified Opinion

A qualified opinion should be expressed when the auditor concludes that an unmodified opinion cannot be expressed and that the effect of any disagreement with management that causes the auditor to issue a qualified opinion is material. A qualified opinion is expressed as fairly presenting the financial statement followed by *except for,* which clause is, in turn, followed by a discussion of the exceptions.

Disclaimer of Opinion

A disclaimer of opinion should be expressed when the possible effect of a limitation on the scope of the audit is considered so material and pervasive that the auditor is not able to obtain sufficient appropriate audit evidence and, accordingly, is unable to express an opinion on the financial statements. Paragraph 18 of ISA 701 requires that the auditor's report should describe the limitation and indicate the possible adjustments to the financial statements that might have been determined to be necessary had the limitation not existed.

ISA 705, paragraphs 9 and 10, requires the auditor to disclaim an opinion in certain circumstances. This could be when the auditor concludes that it is not possible to form an opinion on the financial statements. This could be due to a number of factors including, but not limited to, interaction of a number of uncertainties and their possible cumulative effect on the financial statements. In the United States, PCAOB AU 508 does not include this requirement; this is based on the ASB's initially and now PCAOB's view that a disclaimer of opinion is appropriate only when the auditor is not able to obtain sufficient appropriate audit evidence. The PCAOB could presume that the guidance in paragraph 30 of PCAOB's AU 508 entitled *Reports on Audited Financial Statements,* as amended, is appropriate in these circumstances. PCAOB AU 508 includes this guidance. There is also another difference. Paragraph 13(b) (1) of ISA 705 *requires* the auditor to withdraw from the audit when the auditor is unable to obtain sufficient appropriate audit evidence, and the auditor concludes that the possible effects on the financial statements of undetected misstatements, if any, could be both material and pervasive with the result that a qualification of the opinion would be inadequate to communicate the gravity of the situation. We reviewed PCAOBs AS numbers 1 to 17 and other PCAOB's AU standards and find no reference to the discussion of situations *requiring* auditors to withdraw from an audit. The paragraph 13b of ISA 705 states as follows:

If the auditor concludes that the possible effects on the financial statements of undetected misstatements, if any, could be both material and pervasive so that a qualification of the opinion would be inadequate to communicate the gravity of the situation, the auditor shall

1. Withdraw from the audit, where practicable and possible under applicable law or regulation or
2. If withdrawal from the audit before issuing the auditor's report is not practicable or possible, disclaim an opinion on the financial statements.

Hence, we conclude that this is a major difference between PCAOB and ISA. However, we note that PCAOB AU 561, *Subsequent Discovery of Facts Existing at the Date of the Auditor's Report*, changes this requirement so that the auditor should only *consider* withdrawal from the engagement under such circumstances. Paragraph 4 of AU 561 states that "when the auditor becomes aware of information which relates to financial statements reported on by him but not known to him at the date of his report, and which is of such a nature that the auditor would have investigated it had it come to the auditor's attention during the course of the audit the auditor should, as soon as practicable undertake to determine whether the information is reliable and whether the facts existed at the date of his report. In this connection, the auditor should discuss the matter with his client and whatever management levels the auditor deems appropriate,...." As can be seen, there is no reference to withdrawing from the audit. The ASB initially, and now PCAOB, apparently presumes that, in the United States, the auditor should not be required to withdraw from an engagement but, rather, should consider whether to withdraw or disclaim an opinion

An example which could also justify a disclaimer of opinion could be limitation of scope. For our immediate purposes, a scope limitation might include a refusal by client management to allow the auditor to audit some portion of the client entity's assets. In the United States, auditing standards allow an auditor to accept an audit knowing that a limitation of scope exists and then provide a qualified audit report noting that the financial statements are presented fairly except for the limitation in scope. However, we note an important point: namely, the United States is significantly different from most European countries. In most European countries, the auditor would not be allowed to accept an audit with a limitation of scope.

Adverse Opinion

An adverse opinion should be expressed when the effect of a disagreement is so material and pervasive to the financial statements that the auditor concludes that just a qualification of the report may not be adequate to disclose the misleading or incomplete nature of the financial statements. The auditor may disagree with management about matters such as the acceptability of accounting policies selected, the method of their application, or the adequacy of disclosures in the financial statements. However, such disagreements may not be material. Paragraph 8 of ISA 705, entitled *Modifications to the Independent Auditor's Report* states that an adverse opinion should be provided only if such disagreements are perceived to be material to the financial statements individually or in the aggregate. Ordinarily this information would be set out in a separate paragraph preceding the opinion or disclaimer of opinion on the financial statements and may include a reference to a more extensive discussion, if any, in a note to the financial statements. (Please note that the relevant standard on this was ISA 701 entitled *Modifications to the Independent Auditor's Report*. This is now superceded. Effective December 15, 2009, the relevant standard is ISA 705 entitled *Modifications to the Independent Auditor's Report*.)

The "Modified" Report

An audit report can be *modified* to include qualified, disclaimer, and adverse reports. ISA 705 allows the auditor, in certain circumstances, to *modify* the audit report by adding an *emphasis of matter* paragraph to highlight a matter affecting the financial statements. The addition of such an emphasis of matter paragraph should not affect the auditor's opinion according to ISA 705. The paragraph should be included *after* the paragraph containing the auditor's opinion but before the section on any other reporting responsibilities, if any. The emphasis of matter paragraph should refer to the fact that the auditor's opinion is not qualified in this respect. A note in the financial statements is advised to more extensively discuss the matter.

When should the report be modified? The auditor can modify the report if there is a financial uncertainty problem. An uncertainty is defined (paragraph 5 of ISA 705) as a matter whose outcome depends on future actions or events not under the direct control of the entity but that may affect the financial statements. In this instance, the auditor according to ISA 705 should consider modifying the report by adding a paragraph discussing the uncertainty and stating that the resolution of the uncertainty is dependent upon future events that could affect the financial statements.

Paragraph 8 of ISA 701 provides an example of an emphasis of matter paragraph for a significant uncertainty as follows:

> Without qualifying our opinion we draw attention to Note X to the financial statements. The Company is the defendant in a lawsuit alleging infringement of certain patent rights and claiming royalties and punitive damages. The Company has filed a counter action, and preliminary hearings and discovery proceedings on both actions are in progress. The ultimate outcome of the matter cannot presently be determined, and no provision for any liability that may result has been made in the financial statements.

Issues Relating to Other Information in Annual Reports

ISA 720 states that the auditor should read the other information in documents containing audited financial statements) to identify material inconsistencies or material misstatements of fact with the audited financial statements. What is *other information* (refer paragraph 2, ISA 720)? Other information includes documents such as an annual report, a report by the management or the board of directors on operations, financial summary or highlights, employment data, planned capital expenditures, financial ratios, names of officers and directors among other information required by law, regulation, or custom. The auditor is required to look for material inconsistencies created by other information. There are two issues: material inconsistencies and material misstatements of fact. These will be considered individually.

What is a Material Inconsistency?

Paragraph 3 of ISA 720 notes that a material inconsistency exists when other information contradicts information contained in the audited financial statements. In paragraph 3 it is noted that a material inconsistency is something that could raise doubts about the audit conclusions drawn from audit evidence obtained and, possibly, about the basis for the auditor's opinion on the financial statements. In some circumstances the auditor may have a statutory obligation to report specifically on this other information. In other circumstances, the auditor may have no such obligation. However, in paragraph 6 of ISA 720, it is noted that even when the auditor has no obligation, it is imperative for the auditor to determine whether the audited financial statements or the other information needs to be amended. If the auditor believes an amendment is necessary in the other information and the client refuses to make the amendment, the auditor should consider including an emphasis of matter paragraph describing the material inconsistency or taking other action. If an amendment is necessary for the audited financial statements and the entity refuses to allow it, the auditor should express a qualified or adverse opinion (refer paragraphs 11, 12, and 13 for this discussion).

What is Material Misstatement of Fact?

Paragraph 15 of ISA 720 defines material misstatements of fact as relating to information not related to matters appearing in the financial statements that is incorrectly stated or presented. Paragraph 16 ISA 720 notes that, if the auditor becomes aware that the other information appears to include a material misstatement of fact, the auditor should discuss the matter with the company's management; if the auditor still considers there is an apparent misstatement of fact, the auditor should request that management consult with a qualified third party, such as the entity's legal counsel, and consider the advice received. If management still refuses to correct the misstatement, the auditor should take appropriate action that could include notifying those charged with governance in writing of the auditor's concern regarding the other information and also offer legal advice to prevent future law suits.

Up to now in the discussion, there were no significant differences (according to our observation) between the ISA and PCAOB in the discussion on audit reports. The ASB has roughly the same recommendations. However, there are minor differences. The purposes of the differences, as identified by an AICPA report (http://www.aicpa.org/interestareas/frc/auditattest/downloadabledocuments/clarity/substantive_differences_isa_gass.pdf) is to limit the auditor's responsibilities. There are the issues in the PCAOB standards that are not found in the ISA:

- Clarifying that the *auditor's opinion* is the opinion on the financial statements (PCAOB AU 623)
- Deleting the phrase *either by law, regulation, or custom* from the definition of other information to avoid confusion with required supplementary information (PCAOB AU 558)
- Adding the phrase *other matter* to clarify the report modification (PCAOB's AU 508)

ISA 720 requires the auditor to make appropriate arrangements with those charged with governance to report material misstatements and inconsistencies. However, there is one difference. The correction of material misstatements in ISA 720 relates to the date of the auditor's report. However, the ASB initially and now the PCAOB (PCAOB's AU 530 *Dating of the Independent Auditor's Report*) determined that the report release date rather than the auditor's report date would be more appropriate for the U.S. environment. Since the release date may be later than the report date, the audit firms in the United States have a longer time frame to evaluate the consequences of material misstatements and inconsistencies.

Subsequent Events

Auditors are required to perform audit procedures to determine what is referred to as subsequent events. Subsequent events are transactions and other pertinent events that occurred after the balance sheet date and which affect the fair presentation or disclosure of the statements being audited. ISA 560 entitled *Subsequent Events* provides a definition. Subsequent events are defined in paragraph 3 as events after the balance sheet date that deals with the treatment in financial statements of events, both favorable and unfavorable, that occur between the date of the financial statements and the date when the financial statements are authorized for issue (Paragraph 3 of ISB 560 entitled *Subsequent Events*)."When, after the financial statements are issued, the auditor becomes aware of a fact which existed at the date of the auditor's report and which, if known at that date, may have caused the auditor to modify the auditor's report, the auditor should discuss the matter with management and should take the appropriate action in the circumstances," according to paragraph 15 of ISA 560. Paragraph 16 of ISA 560 notes that when the management revises the financial statements, the auditor should carry out the audit procedures necessary in the circumstances, the purpose being to review the steps taken by the management to ensure that anyone in receipt of the previously issued financial statements together with the auditor's report is aware of the situation. The auditor should also inform the management that a new report will be issued. The audit procedures referred to should be extended to the new auditor's report. Paragraph 27 states that the new report should include an *emphasis of matter* paragraph referring to a note in the financial statements that more extensively discusses the reason for the revision of the previously issued financial statements. The new auditor's report should be dated no earlier than the date of the approval of the revised financial statements. "Date of approval of the financial statements is the date on which those with the recognized authority assert that they have prepared the entity's complete set of financial statements, including the related notes, and that they have taken responsibility for them" (refer paragraph 4 of ISA 560, *Subsequent events*). ISA 560 notes that local regulations of some countries require the auditor to restrict the audit procedures regarding the revised financial statements to the effects of the subsequent events that necessitated the revision only. In such cases the new auditor's report should contain a statement to that effect.

At this juncture, there are important differences that should be recognized.

Differences in Definition of Subsequent Events

In essence, paragraph 1 of ISA 560 defines subsequent events to include both events occurring between the date of the financial statements and the date of the auditor's report and facts that become known to the auditor after the date of the auditor's report. In the U.S. PCAOB AU 560 entitled *Subsequent events* includes separate definitions for *subsequent events* which are discussed in the section on subsequent events. AU 560 clearly states that for each category, the auditors' responsibility is different and clearly distinguishes the auditor's responsibility for each. ISA does not go into this in detail (that is separate definitions), nor does it clearly distinguish the auditors' responsibilities for each.

Differences With Respect to Dates

As mentioned above, paragraph 5 of ISA 560 defines the date the financial statements are issued as the date the audited financial statements are available to third parties. However, this is addressed in AS 3 paragraphs 14 and 15. There is no significant difference between ISA (ISA 560) and PCAOB (AS 3) with respect to dating and issuing of audited financial statements to third parties.

Conflict With Laws Regarding Dating of the Financial Statements

Internationally, many European countries have laws that prohibit the management from revising the financial statements to include the effects of subsequent events. The implication is that subsequent events relate to the next period and should be treated as such. Hence paragraph 12 of ISA 560 has a reference to laws and regulations and notes that the auditor should include subsequent events and dual date the audited financial statements (release and issue dates) if the local laws do not prohibit reporting of subsequent events. In the United States, there is no such prohibition by law. Hence the equivalent paragraph (13) of (PCAOB AU 560) does not have any reference to law or regulation. This is totally omitted.

Requirement of New Auditor's Reports

Paragraph 12 of ISA 560 requires the auditor to provide a new or revised auditor's report including the subsequent events (if there is no conflict with local laws). This should include an emphasis of matter paragraph that discusses the auditor's procedures and note that these procedures were restricted solely to the revision of the financial statements. If management does not amend the financial statements to include the subsequent events, then the auditor is required to include an emphasis of matter paragraph and express a qualified opinion or even an adverse opinion depending on the significance of the events on the financial statements (contingent on no conflict with the local country's laws). This is not included in the PCAOB's AU 560. This is because it is uncommon in the United States to provide a new or revised auditor's report that includes an emphasis of matter paragraph (Refer PCAOB AU 560).

PCAOB AU 390 entitled *Consideration of Omitted Procedures after the Report Date* addresses this. Paragraph 7 of AU 390 states that, if the auditor is unable to apply the previously omitted procedures or alternative procedures to test the impact of discovered subsequent events, then the auditor should consult an attorney to determine an appropriate course of action concerning the auditor's responsibilities to its client. This also applies to regulatory authorities, if any, having jurisdiction over the client, and persons relying or likely to rely on his/her report. There is a clear and telling difference. The ISA, it appears, insist on a qualified or adverse auditor's report with an emphasis of matter paragraph if there is no restriction by local laws. The PCAOB leaves this open ended, leaving the appropriate course of action to the auditor after consulting an attorney.

Types of Subsequent Events

Paragraph 3 of ISA 560 identifies two types of subsequent events. These include the following:

- Those that provide evidence of conditions that existed at the date of the financial statements. This type requires adjustment to the financial statements. Some examples provided by Hayes et al. are settlement of litigation at an amount different from the amount recorded on the books. Other examples are sale of investments at a price below cost.

- Those that are indicative of conditions that arose after the date of the financial statements. This type of material requires disclosure in the notes to the financial statements, but no adjustment in the financial statements is required. Examples provided by Hayes et al. are a decline in the market value of securities held for temporary investment or resale; a decline in the market value of inventory as a consequence of government action; and an uninsured loss of inventories as a result of a fire.

In the case of both of these, if the event is material, and the client did not adjust their financial statements, the auditor should include an emphasis of matter paragraph in a revised auditor's statement (if there is no restriction by local laws). Whether the financial statements are revised depends on whether the subsequent event(s) falls into the (a) or (b) category noted earlier. If the management refuses, the auditor should include the emphasis of matter paragraph in either a qualified or, in rarer circumstances, an adverse report. In the United States, PCAOB 560 does not address this. But the PCAOB's AU 390 leaves it open ended for the auditor, stating (paragraph 3) that "he should consult his attorney to determine an appropriate course of action concerning his responsibilities to his client." It is interesting that nowhere in ISA is there a reference to consulting attorneys.

Issues Relating to Going Concern Status of the Firm

In certain cases, an uncertainty may be so grave as to potentially impact the survival of the company in the foreseeable future. This is referred to as a going concern problem. ISA allows the auditor to modify the report in the presence of going concern uncertainties as well. Paragraph 9 notes that the addition of a paragraph emphasizing a going concern problem is adequate to meet the auditor's reporting responsibilities regarding such matters. However, in rare cases, such as situations involving multiple uncertainties, the auditor could issue a disclaimer of opinion instead of adding an emphasis of matter paragraph.

ISA 570 entitled Going Concern is premised on the assumption that the management has a responsibility to assess the entity's ability to continue as a going concern, regardless of whether the financial reporting framework being applied requires management to do so. ISA 570 specifically states that one of the auditor's objectives is to obtain sufficient evidence regarding the appropriateness of management's use of the going concern assumption in the preparation of the financial statements (paragraphs 1 and 2). PCAOB AU 341 requires the auditor to evaluate whether there is substantial doubt about the entity's ability to continue as a going concern for a reasonable period of time (paragraph 2). ISA 570 requires consideration of the going concern assumption throughout the engagement. An AICPA report (http://www.aicpa.org/InterestAreas/FRC/AuditAttest/DownloadableDocuments/Clarity/Substantive_Differences_ISA_GASS.pdf) states that in planning the audit, the auditor is required to consider whether there are events or conditions that may cast significant doubt on the entity's ability to continue as a going concern and to remain alert throughout the audit for evidence of such events or conditions. Here, there is a significant difference with the PCAOB AU 341. PCAOB AU 341 does *not* require the auditor to design audit procedures solely to identify such events and conditions. It requires the auditor to consider whether the results of other procedures performed during the course of the engagement identify conditions and events that, when considered in the aggregate, indicate there could be substantial doubt about the entity's ability to continue as a going concern. However, there is no material difference with the original standard by ASB except for the wording. The wording is important and is repeated here.

> The auditor's evaluation is based on his or her knowledge of relevant conditions and events that exist at or have occurred prior to the date of the auditor's report. Information about such conditions or events is obtained from the application of auditing procedures planned and performed to achieve audit objectives that are related to management's assertions embodied in the financial statements being audited. (PCAOB AU 341, paragraph 3)

There is no requirement to specifically test for going concern. Rather, the implication is that if results of other tests indicate the possibility of a going concern uncertainty the auditor should consider this when deciding on the report to be issued.

In essence, U.S. auditing standards are different in that the auditor is not required to specifically design and use procedures for testing the going concern status of the client. This only becomes a concern if the results of other procedures indicate there could be a going concern problem.

Under ISA if management decides that a going concern problem exists, then paragraph 10 of ISA 570 requires the auditor to discuss with management why the auditor believes a going concern paragraph should be added to the auditor's report. There is an important difference with PCAOB AU 341. AU 341 does not contain these explicit requirements. Rather when the auditor believes there is substantial doubt about the entity's ability to continue as a going concern, the auditor is required to consider the management's plans for dealing with the adverse effects of the conditions and events that led to the auditor's belief. In our opinion the ISA is more proactive in that the auditor is required to discuss with management the reasons for the going concern qualification. In the case of U.S. standards, if the auditor through other tests feels a going concern modified report has to be issued, they are first required to ask management their plans with special focus on extenuating factors, such as good news items, that could mitigate the going concern uncertainty threat. This difference could be due to the unique history of the United States with respect to going concern reporting. In the 1980s there was considerable opposition to the qualified going concern report with letters to the ASB that a qualified report had adverse consequences especially with respect to stock market prices. The ASB came up with a modified report and also required auditors to consider extenuating circumstances in the form of good news items in order to placate the opposition.

As regards the period of assessment, the approaches differ. Where there is substantial doubt about the entity's ability to continue as a going concern, ISA 570 requires the auditor to consider the same period as that used by management in making its assessment, a period of at least, but not limited to, twelve months from the balance sheet date. In the United

States, the PCAOB's AU 341 requires the auditor to consider a period of time not to exceed one year beyond the date of the financial statements being audited. What happens if there is a delay in the signature or approval of the financial statements by the management after the balance sheet date? ISA 570 considers this to be important. The ISA requests the auditor to specifically consider the reasons for the delay. If the delay is related to events or conditions relating to the going concern assessment, the auditor should consider performing additional audit procedures to evaluate the effect on the auditor's conclusion regarding the existence of the going concern uncertainty. The ASB does not contain similar guidance. In essence if there is a delay, under ISA the auditor is required to perform procedures to test for going concern during the period covered by the delay. The PCAOB does not cover this issue at all. The question is, is this important with respect to legal ramifications? We leave this issue to the reader.

Conclusions

The audit report is the key outcome of the audit. Without it, the investors and creditors and interested others are left wondering about the credibility of the financial statements and other related information in the annual reports. Accordingly, this chapter provides important information to the reader about the different audit reports that could be issued by auditors in the United States and in countries that conform to ISA. This information makes the audit reports interpretable. In addition, the contrasts drawn between ASB/PCAOB and ISA standard-based audit reports enables the reader to better understand how audit reports issued in one country may differ from those issued in another.

This chapter, then, is *almost* a capstone chapter to this book. What remains to be presented is information about other ways that audit regulation may differ depending on the nations within which the auditor conducts their audit. It is also important to briefly describe other things that may affect the reader's understanding of audit reports issued in different places. That information is discussed in the next, final chapter.

Appendix: Discussion of Fair Presentation Frameworks versus Compliance Frameworks

The purpose of financial statements is to fulfill the information needs of its users. The financial reporting framework used is based on the jurisdiction in which the entity and its users exist. Two main and competing styles of reporting frameworks are:

- fair presentation frameworks (also known as conceptual frameworks); and
- compliance frameworks (also known as rules-based framework).

Fair Presentation Framework

Fazal (2013) notes that a fair presentation framework requires compliance with the provisions of the framework, but, in addition, Fazal acknowledges that:

- in achieving fair presentation, the management might have to make additional disclosures that are not specifically required by the framework; and
- in extremely rare circumstances, it might be necessary to depart from the requirements of the framework to achieve fair presentation in the financial statements of the entity's financial position and performance.

Compliance Framework

Compliance frameworks require compliance with the provisions of the framework, that is, strict obedience to instructions is required, and the ones preparing financial statements have no choice but to follow the requirements of the framework. Compliance frameworks do not allow any room or flexibility as is given under fair presentation frameworks.

Fazal notes that fair presentation frameworks require compliance but still allow for alternatives that can achieve more relevant and reliable presentation of financial statements even if management has to make additions or go against the requirements of the framework. In the compliance framework, no such leverage is given, and under this framework, complete compliance is required under any condition.

CHAPTER 12

Final Considerations About Auditing

In this chapter, we discuss why corporate governance and differences in the international regulation of auditing practice are of importance. This chapter discusses so-called "meta-issues", issues above and beyond the specific auditing standards used. Specifically, we discuss:

- corporate governance and its implications for auditors;
- auditor regulation in different venues;
- financial reporting standards (International Financial Reporting Standards [IFRS], Generally Accepted Accounting Principles [GAAP]) and their implications for understanding audited financial statements; and
- implications for researchers, practitioners, and students.

Investopedia defines corporate governance as:

The system of rules, practices, and processes by which a company is directed and controlled. Corporate governance essentially involves balancing the interests of the many stakeholders in a company—these include its shareholders, management, customers, suppliers, financiers, government, and the community. Because corporate governance also provides the framework for achieving a company's objectives, it encompasses practically every sphere of management, from action plans and internal controls to performance measurement and corporate disclosure.

Source: http://www.investopedia.com/terms/c/corporate governance.asp

There are many definitions of corporate governance which incorporate the issues discussed above. A much cited, although fairly narrow definition of corporate governance is given by Shleifer and Vishny (1997). Their definition emphasizes the separation of ownership and control in corporations. They define corporate governance as dealing with "the ways in which the suppliers of finance to corporations assure themselves of getting a return on their investment."

1. *What should the user of this book know about corporate governance structures with particular reference to differences in international corporate governance structures?*

Corporate governance has been the subject of a great deal of discussion for years. Such scandals as Enron and WorldCom in the United States and others overseas have raised questions as to *how could this have happened?* The remedy, which impacted both auditors and corporate management in the United States, was conceived to be the Sarbanes-Oxley Act (SOX) of 2002, which has been discussed in prior chapters but will be repeated here. In essence though, SOX seeks to strengthen corporate governance systems in response to corporate failures. However, there have been arguments that the costs of implementation far exceed the benefits. And it is important to note that no matter how well a governance system is designed, fraud could still be perpetrated if parties collude.

The general topic of corporate governance is much too broad for discussion in this book. For example, different nations have different company laws. Further, there is no national company law in the United States. Instead, each of the 50 states has its own company law. With respect to the European Union, these laws are described by Qfinance.com as "the body of legislation that relates to the formation, status, conduct, and *corporate governance*" http://europa.eu/ legislation_summaries/internal_market/businesses/company_law/ l26016_en.htm. The Qfinance.com link also provides a good summary of different administrative arrangements found in the European Union member state company laws. Specifically, it summarizes the responsibilities of EU-wide company boards that have two tier systems (management boards and supervisory boards) and one tier systems (just supervisory boards). Summaries of company law for other entities, state-based (as in the case of the United States) or national (as in the case of each of the countries in the European Union), can be found elsewhere.

In addition to the company law itself, it is also important to understand the different penalty arrangements that exist for discovered violations of these laws. Further, the ability of the regulator to discover violations of required corporate governance practices, their willingness to attempt to sanction discovered violations, and the ability of the potentially sanctioned firms to fight back successfully, given different legal codes (some are more investor-friendly than others) and differing cultural acceptance of law violations (some cultures are more severe than others, in part depending on the nature of the law violation) make this a difficult topic to pursue here. To underscore this difficulty, we note that the ISA have been adopted in whole or in part in well over 100 nations. Accordingly, we note that it is in the interest of the reader to understand the corporate governance practices of the client entities that they are most interested in.

Whereas corporate governance practices may follow general trends within particular countries, practices that outwardly conform to the laws of those nations, the reality of how a corporate entity is actually governed may be different than that of general practice. For example, firms in different nations may differ based on how closely the firm's voting rights of a firm's stock equals the cash flow rights of a firm's stock. In some nations, for example, Taiwan, some shares of stock only have rights to receive dividend distributions but cannot vote for members of the board of directors. These investors are said to have cash flow rights. Rights to vote for members of the board of directors are reserved to a kind of stock that specifically has that right, that is, voting rights. This has implications for control of the corporation and the ability of all the shareholders to correct situations that are perceived to be undesirable. In some nations, there are supervisory boards of directors and *regular* boards of directors (the so-called two tier director system mentioned above). In others, for example, Germany, representatives of the workers are guaranteed a position on the boards of directors. Finding out just how closely the corporate entity's actual practices are to the legal requirements of the nation or the supranational entity (e.g., the European Union as mentioned earlier as well) it is domiciled in is likely to be extremely difficult. *Because these are legal, not auditing standard-based, questions,* we only suggest ways to approach them. Standards that affect auditors' behavior are only relevant when the standards require the auditor to report things or not report things that contravene the law.

Auditors, though, are in a much better position to find out how an entity is actually run. Auditors may find that the reality of having worker representation differs from the ideal of having worker representation on the board, in that a review of the board of director minutes shows that the worker representative is no more supportive of worker interests than others on the board. Further, unlike students, managers of other entities, and researchers, the auditor may interact on a daily basis with the entity's management. In addition, the auditors must develop an understanding of the entity. Accordingly, the auditor will certainly have the ability to develop an understanding of the corporate governance of the firm because of these activities. These were discussed in earlier chapters. In addition, the auditor must know what the legal requirements are for corporate governance practices in the country that entity is domiciled in (its legal home). The auditor must also understand the legal obligations of the auditor with respect to reporting any violation of legal governance arrangements to external (outside the entity) governmental agencies. These requirements may differ widely between jurisdictions (nations). Auditors, of course, should always know whether they have the obligation—or whether it just is prudent—to consult with legal counsel before reporting any reportable governance infraction to higher authorities in a particular jurisdiction. Legal standards always trump auditing standards set forth by the ISA or the PCAOB or the AICPA ASB. As a standard setter, the ISA differs notably from the PCAOB or even the AICPA ASB in that the ISA seeks to establish uniform auditing standards across over 100 national entities. Accordingly, while PCAOB and AICPA ASB standards can clearly be tailored to meet national legal obligations imposed on the auditing profession,

ISA standards cannot. This does not prevent, however, individual nations (e.g., the Union of South Africa) from adopting most ISA but rejecting or substituting its own variant of some ISA. The same is true for the United Kingdom and Germany as well. The German standards, for example, are set by the Institut der Wirtschaftsprüfer (IDW). It tailors ISA to address differences that arise due to regulatory and legal requirements specific to Germany. The United Kingdom standards are set by the Auditing Practices Board part of the Financial Reporting Council. It also tailors ISA to meet local legal and regulatory requirements. The key takeaway from this discussion therefore is that managers, students, and researchers should use this book as a general guide for comparing ISA, PCAOB, and AICPA ASB standards. Specific differences from the ISA may exist within different countries. Accordingly, depending on the circumstances, the reader may wish to seek expert guidance on national adaptations of auditing standards adopted within specific countries.

Individuals who are seeking to understand or judge the auditor's performance should develop resources relevant to answering the questions they may have about auditing and auditor performance as well as about issues pertinent to the governance of corporations in different countries. Developing these answers, though, is costly— in terms of time if not necessarily in dollars or euros. Accordingly, readers should ask themselves whether they have enough reason to seek the answer to the questions they have. Accordingly, we pose the following questions:

- What are the legally acceptable corporate governance practices in a nation of interest?
- What are the auditor's legal reporting obligations; should the auditor have uncovered a difference between the way a corporate entity actually governs itself and the way it is legally required to govern itself?
- What are the differences between ISA and national adaptations of ISA to meet specific national legal and regulatory requirements such as exist in the Union of South Africa, Germany, and the United Kingdom?

2. *What should the user of this book know about regulation of auditing within countries of interest?*

In this book, we have presented an overview of auditing with a discussion of three different sources of auditing standards: The ISA, the AICPA ASB standards, and the PCAOB standards. We have discussed the similarities and differences primarily between the ISA and PCAOB standards in order to enhance the reader's understanding of what it means when Auditor A in Country A conducts an audit according to the ISA whereas Auditor A in Country B conducts an audit according to PCAOB standards. The AICPA ASB standards were referred to when we thought referring to them would be of particular interest. Even so, the setting of auditing standards is one aspect of auditing regulation. The standards provide guidelines (some more restrictive than others) for auditor behavior. Standards, by themselves, though, will not always govern auditor behavior. It is not to be expected that just because a standard, a guideline for behavior, exists that the auditor will automatically follow the standards. Auditors may stray because of human error or willful noncompliance with the standards. We noted early on in this book that the PCAOB was created in the SOX of 2002 because of the furor that greeted the revelation of the Enron and other scandals. In the aftermath of the financial crisis that began in 2008, the European Union was also moved to rethink regulation of auditing. Accordingly, how auditors are regulated is an additional issue that the user of this book should think about. Specifically, *what mechanisms are in place to help ensure that auditors follow the standards in place, whether ISA, PCAOB standards AICPA ASB standards, or all three?* Describing the various regulatory initiatives in place or contemplated is beyond the scope of this book. In this section, however, we do suggest various questions the reader may pose to themselves in deciding whether to research this important topic further. The questions are:

- How is the auditing profession regulated in reader's nation? (Note, different nations—including nations within the European Union—have different auditing regulatory bodies. The

United Kingdom, for example, has the Auditing Inspection Unit part of the Financial Regulatory Council, and Germany has the WPK (Wirtschaftsprüferkammer, also known as the Chamber of Public Accountants), whereas Japan has the Japanese Institute of Certified Public Accountants (JICPA). The last named oversees the process in which audit firms undergo review by their peer firms.

- ○ Regulation of auditors includes ways to gather information about the quality of audits conducted by the auditor. The reader might, therefore, be interested in learning:
  - —Is an auditor's work *inspected* or *doublechecked* by either the national regulatory agency (e.g., the PCAOB or in the United Kingdom, the Audit Inspection Unit of the Financial Reporting Council) or, in other nations, private regulatory agencies (e.g., in the United States, the AICPA has the wherewithal to conduct audit quality peer reviews for auditors of nonpublic companies, whereas in Japan, the Japanese Institute of Certified Public Accountants orchestrates audit firm peer reviews)
  - —How thorough are the audit inspection routines if they are conducted?
  - —What is the range of penalties that may be imposed on an auditor? For example, in the United States, forbidding an auditing firm from conducting audits would seriously impair the potential financial health of that firm. On the other hand, the audit firm could just be penalized with a fine or receive just a reprimand.
  - —Does the regulatory body publish inspection reports on the audit firms specifically or more generally. The PCAOB does, as do other nations like Canada and the United Kingdom.
- When considering the differences between two audit firms, would it make sense to read the PCAOB or other regulatory body inspection reports?
- Is there evidence that the audit firm or firms of interest to the reader have improved their audit practice quality over time?

The information mentioned in the preceding paragraphs may be of use to students, managers and researchers if they wanted to come to an understanding on just how credible the audit reports that accompany the financial statements are. On the surface, at least, jurisdictions that impose stricter penalties for failure to acceptably follow the auditing standards may have better quality audits performed.

3. *What should the reader of this book know about the financial accounting standards used in creating the financial statements? How do differences between sources (e.g., IFRS versus U.S. GAAP) affect the financial statements and affect the reader's understanding of audit opinions delivered on IFRS-based financial statements versus U.S. GAAP-based financial statements?*

Financial accounting standards, too, are beyond the remit of this book. The correctness of application of the standards to accounting transactions, though, are an essential part of what the auditors strive to understand as they begin their work with the client accounting records and accounting system. In the United States, all publicly listed companies must use the U.S.-based GAAP in preparing financial statements. GAAP consists of sets of rules for recognizing revenue, recording depreciation on assets both owned and used by the entity to generate revenue, recording leases as either operating leases (basically, treating a leased property as if it was being *rented*) or recording leases as capital leases (basically, treating a leased property as if it was *owned*). While GAAP is unique to the United States, and all financial statements prepared in the United States must be prepared in a manner consistent with the rules of GAAP, financial statements prepared in a large part of the rest of the world must be prepared in accordance with IFRS.* The two sets of financial accounting rules are *not identical.* That said, there is some overlap between the sets of rules. In addition, there has been a lot of talk in the last few years

---

* There are different versions of IFRS that are used. Some countries require adaptations of IFRS, and therefore, not all countries that seem to use IFRS are using exactly the same set of accounting principles/rules as others that seem to be using IFRS.

about harmonizing U.S. GAAP with IFRS, essentially by having the U.S. financial statement preparers adopt IFRS. So far, that has not happened. There remains a great deal of debate over the wisdom of converting U.S. companies to IFRS users.

There are several important reasons why the use of IFRS is resisted in the United States. The one of most interest here is that, although the AICPA has designated IFRS rules as "high quality" financial accounting standards, IFRS permits managers to exercise much more discretion in making accounting judgments than does U.S. GAAP. Given this, auditors looking at accounting records compiled using IFRS will have less ability to challenge management's choices than they would in the United States, where the more precise (i.e., rule-bound) U.S. standards are more likely to prescribe accounting choices for the managers. Given that this is the case, two companies, one using IFRS and one using U.S. GAAP, with exactly the same transactions, may report very different financial results. Given that one company was headquartered in a country where IFRS use was required and the other in the United States where GAAP use was required, both companies would have received unmodified or *clean* opinions on their very different financial statements. If both companies were required to conform to U.S. GAAP, the situation would be different. This may have resulted in the auditor qualifying the audit opinion of one of the companies. For the readers of this book, then, it is important to keep in mind that, even in the areas where ISA and PCAOB and ASB auditing standards are in effect identical, the financial statements attested to may be very different but still able to receive the *good* or *unqualified* or *unmodified* opinion from the respective auditors.

This information may be of use to managers, researchers, and students because it helps them better understand that accounting and auditing are complicated matters. To better understand the intersection between auditing and accounting issues will require further exploration of the differences between the kinds of accounting standards discussed in this section. There are many resources for developing this kind of understanding, for example, examining the books referenced on this Internet page: http://www.businessexpertpress. com/taxonomy/term/18.

Conclusion

The purpose of this conclusion is not just to summarize the contents of this chapter but to link this final chapter with key issues discussed in the earlier chapters of this book. In this chapter, we provided different definitions of auditing; namely from investopedia.com and a popularly cited definition by Shleifer and Vishny. In addition, ISA 260 entitled *Communications of audit matters with those charged with governance* states that governance is the term used to describe the role of persons entrusted with the supervision, control, and direction of an entity. Depending on the jurisdiction, the responsibility for corporate governance could vary between different parties such as the board of directors, audit committee, and other supervisory committees. ISA requires the auditor to determine those persons to be charged with governance. The auditing profession has a very important role to play especially in providing guidance on steps taken to improve corporate governance and reducing opportunities to commit accounting fraud. As noted in ISA 260, the auditor does not have direct corporate governance responsibility. The auditor's primary role is to check whether the financial information given to investors is reliable in a sound corporate governance setting.

However, the fact remains that corporate governance failures could occur. One reaction to corporate governance failures has been to focus on public companies' internal controls. There is a difference between PCAOB standards and the ISA. First, under SOX, the PCAOB requires the auditor to understand the role of internal controls as part of the audit and test the effectiveness of internal controls over financial reporting. It also requires that the auditor do a separate report on the effectiveness of internal controls. ISAs also require auditors to focus on understanding internal controls as part of the audit.

For corporate governance to be effective it is important that the auditor is, and is perceived to be, independent of the client. However, there is a difference between SOX/PCAOB and the ISA. (We state SOX/PCAOB because it is in both SOX and in PCAOB.) SOX/PCAOB adopted a rules-driven approach, which sets out prohibited services and requires pre-approval by the audit committee of nonaudit services. The EU 8th Directive (and the ISA) apply a threats and safeguards approach (this means that if the auditor thinks there is a threat, the auditor should assess whether the threat is significant. Then take action to remove or mitigate it.) The AICPA has a similar approach, called the Conceptual Framework, for use when specific ethics guidance is not provided. There are minor variations in implementing corporate governance.

Finally, we note that the cost of accounting and audit failures are immense. Audit failures result in increased skepticism by corporate and organizational stakeholders, higher rates of litigation, and investor losses, and also pose a threat to the very survival of auditors and the companies they audit. The differences between the PCAOB and ISA standards range from small to large. Collectively, these differences pose challenges to students of auditing in that they may impact the individual's ability to appreciate the importance of financial statements audited under one set of standards as opposed to the other set of standards explored here. Understanding the differences between PCAOB and ISA requirements are therefore important to all interested parties.

About the Authors

Asokan Anandarajan is a professor of accounting and accounting information systems at the School of Management, New Jersey Institute of Technology, based in Newark, New Jersey. He has an MBA and MPhil from Cranfield University, UK and a PhD in accounting from Drexel University, Philadelphia. His research interests relate to earnings management and expectation gap auditing standards. He has published in many peer reviewed research journals including *Accounting Horizons, Auditing: A Journal of Practice and Theory, Accounting and Finance, Advances in Accounting, Behavioral Research in Accounting, International Journal of Intelligent Systems in Accounting, Finance and Management, and Research in Accounting Regulation* among others, He is a Chartered Management Accountant (UK) and worked at Hewlett Packard (UK) prior to joining academia.

Gary Kleinman has taught auditing for many years at both undergraduate and master's levels. He teaches in the School of Business at Montclair State University. He has a CPA license and obtained his PhD from Rutgers University, Newark, New Jersey. In addition, Dr. Kleinman has an extensive research background, writing about auditing, auditor judgment, auditor independence, auditor behavior, and statistical sampling in auditing. Some of his many research articles, on auditing and other topics, have appeared in the *Journal of Accounting, Auditing and Finance,* the *Journal of International Accounting Research, Review of Quantitative Finance and Accounting, Research in Accounting Regulation, and in Accounting, Economics and Law: A Convivium.* In addition to writing many journal articles, Dr. Kleinman has also coauthored two previous books on auditing, one an academically oriented book and the other a practitioner-oriented text concerning PCAOB and SEC standards on auditing.

References

Allen, C. October 2010. "Comparing the Ethics Codes: AICPA and IFAC." *Journal of Accountancy* 210, no. 4, pp. 24–32.

AICPA (American Institute of Certified Public Accountants). 2014. *Substantive Differences Between the International Standards on Auditing and Generally Accepted Auditing Standards*. http://www.aicpa.org/InterestAreas/FRC/ AuditAttest/DownloadableDocuments/Clarity/Substantive_Differences_ ISA_GASS.pdf

AICPA. 2014. AICPA Code of Ethics, Section 0.300.010.01, p. 4.

AICPA. September 1983. AU Section 334. *Related Parties*.

AICPA. 2011. AU-C Section 550. *Related Parties*.

ASB. AU-C Section 530. *Auditing Sampling*.

Benjamin, M. April 8, 2002. "Cardboard Board: Too Often, Corporate Directors Are Mere Decoration." U.S. News & World Report, 28, 30.

Bily v. Arthur Young and Co., 834 P.2d 745 (California 1992).

Citizens State Bank v. Timm, Schmidt and Co., 335 N.W. 2d 361 (Wisconsin 1983).

Cohen Commission. 1978. The Commission on Auditors' Responsibilities: Report, Conclusions and Recommendations. New York: American Institute of Certified Public Accountants Publication.

Credit Alliance Corp v. Arthur Andersen and Co., 483 N.E. 2d 110 (New York 1985).

Dingell Commission. Securities and Exchange Commission Act of 1987, H.R. 2600.

Dodd-Frank Wall Street Reform and Consumer Protection Act of 2010, Pub 111-203. H.R. 4173.

ESM Government Securities v. Alexander Grant and Co., U.S. Court of Appeals, Eleventh Circuit 820F, 2nd 352 (1985).

European Council Commission. 2002. Eighth Company Directive 84/253/EEC.

European Economic Commission. 2005. *A Study on Systems of Civil Liability of Statutory Auditors in the Context of a Single Market for Auditing Services in the European Union*. http://ec.europa.eu/internal_market/auditing/docs/ liability/auditliability_en.pdf

Fazal, H. 2013. *Accounting Concepts and Policies, Audit Assurance, Auditing. Association of Chartered and Certified Accountants (ACCA)*, F-8. pakaccountants.com/difference-fair-presentation-vs-compliance-framework/

Hayes, R., R. Dassen, A. Schilder, and P. Wallage. 2005. *Principles of Auditing: An Introduction to International Standards on Auditing*. 2nd ed. New York: FT Prentice Hall

Herzfeld v. Laventhol, Krekstein, Horwarth and Horwarth, Transfer Binder CCH FED Sec. Law Reporter #94,574, at 95,999 (S.D.N.Y. May 29, 1974).

IAASB (International Auditing and Assurance Standards Board). 2014. *Implementation of the Clarified International Standards on Auditing*. http://www.ifac.org/publications-resources/implementation-clarified-international-standards-auditing-isas

IFAC (International Federation of Accountants). Section 290. *Code of Ethics for Professional Accountants*. New York: IFAC. http://www.aicpa.org/InterestAreas/FRC/AuditAttest/DownloadableDocuments/Clarity/Substantive_Differences_ISA_GASS.pdf

IFAC. Compliance Program. www.ifac.org/about-ifac/membership/compliance-program

IFRS (International Financial Reporting Standards) 10. *Consolidation—Special Purpose Entities* (IFRS 2011 publication).

ISA (International Standard on Auditing) No. 200. *Objective and General Principles Governing an Audit of Financial Statements* (ISA 2006 publication).

ISA (International Standard on Auditing) No. 200. *Objective and General Principles Governing an Audit of Financial Statements* (IFAC publication).

ISA (International Standard on Auditing) No. 200. *Overall Objectives of the Independent Auditor and the Conduct of an Audit in Accordance with International Standards on Auditing* (IFAC December 15, 2009 publication).

ISA (International Standard on Auditing) No. 210. *Agreeing the Terms of Audit Engagements* (IFAC December 15, 2009 publication). http://www.ifac.org/sites/default/files/downloads/a009-2010-iaasb-handbook-isa-210.pdf

ISA (International Standard on Auditing) No. 220. *Quality Control for Audits of Historical Financial information* (IFAC December 15, 2009 publication).

ISA (International Standard on Auditing) No. 230. *Audit Documentation* (IFAC December 15, 2009 publication).

ISA (International Standard on Auditing) No. 240. *The Auditor's Responsibilities Relating to Fraud in an Audit of Financial Statements* (IFAC December 15, 2009 publication).

ISA (International Standard on Auditing) No. 260. *Communication of Audit Matters with Those Charged with Governance* (ISA December 15, 2009 publication).

ISA (International Standard on Auditing) No. 265. *Communicating Deficiencies in Internal Control to Those Charged with Governance and Management* (ISA Publication).

ISA (International Standard on Auditing) No. 300. *Planning an Audit of Financial Statements* (IFAC December 15, 2009 publication). http://www.ifac.org/sites/default/files/downloads/a016-2010-iaasb-handbook-isa-300.pdf

ISA (International Standard on Auditing) No. 315. *Identifying and Assessing the Risks of Material Misstatement Through Understanding the Entity and its Environment* (IFAC December 15, 2009 publication) http://www.ifac.org/sites/default/files/downloads/a017-2010-iaasb-handbook-isa-315.pdf

ISA (International Standard on Auditing) No. 315. *Understanding the Entity and its Environment and Assessing the Risks of Material Misstatement* (IFAC December 15, 2009 publication).

ISA (International Standard on Auditing) No. 315. *Understanding the Entity and its Environment and Assessing the Risks of Material Misstatement* (IFAC publication).

ISA (International Standard on Auditing) No. 330. *The Auditor's Procedures in Response to Assessed Risks.* (IFAC 2005).

ISA (International Standard on Auditing) No. 330. *The Auditor's Procedures in Response to Assessed Risks* (ISA 2009).

ISA (International Standard on Auditing) No. 330. *The Auditor's Response to Assessed Risks.* http://www.ifac.org/sites/default/files/downloads/a019-2010-iaasb-handbook-isa-330.pdf

ISA (International Standard on Auditing) No. 500. *Audit Evidence* (IFAC December 15, 2009 publication). http://www.ifac.org/sites/default/files/downloads/a022-2010-iaasb-handbook-isa-500.pdf

ISA (International Standard on Auditing) No. 501. *Audit Evidence—Specific Considerations for Selected items* (IFAC December 15, 2009 publication).

ISA (International Standard on Auditing) No. 510. *Initial Audit Engagements—Opening Balances.* http://www.ifac.org/sites/default/files/downloads/a025-2010-iaasb-handbook-isa-510.pdf

ISA (International Standard on Auditing) No. 520. *Analytical Procedures* (IFAC 2004 publication).

ISA (International Standard on Auditing) No. 530. *Audit Sampling and Other Testing Procedures* (ISA Publication).

ISA (International Standard on Auditing) No. 550. *Related Parties* (IFAC publication).

ISA (International Standard on Auditing) No. 550. *Related Parties.* http://www.frc.org.uk/Our-Work/Publications/APB/550-Related-parties.aspx

ISA (International Standard on Auditing) No. 560. *Subsequent Events* (IFAC publication).

ISA (International Standard on Auditing) No. 560. *Subsequent Events* (ISA publication).

ISA (International Standard on Auditing) No. 570. *Going Concern* (IFAC publication).

ISA (International Standard on Auditing) No. 570. *Going Concern* (ISA publication).

ISA (International Standard on Auditing) No. 580. *Written Representations* (IFAC publication).

ISA (International Standard on Auditing) No. 600. *Special Considerations— Audits of Group Financial Statements* (IFAC publication) (Including the Work of Component Auditors). http://www.ifac.org/sites/default/files/downloads/ a033-2010-iaasb-handbook-isa-600.pdf

ISA (International Standard on Auditing) No. 610. *Using the Work of Internal Auditors.* http://ifac.org/sites/default/files/downloads/a034-2010-iaasb -handbook-isa-610.pdf

ISA (International Standard on Auditing) No. 620. *Using the Work of an Auditor's Expert* (IFAC publication). http://ifac.org/sites/default/files/downloads/ a035-2010-iaasb-handbook-isa-620.pdf

ISA (International Standard on Auditing) No. 700. *Forming an Opinion and Reporting Financial Statements.* http://www.ifac.org/sites/default/files/ downloads/a036-2010-iaasb-handbook-isa-700.pdf

ISA (International Standard on Auditing) No. 700. *The Independent Auditor's Report on a Complete Set of General Purpose Financial Statements* (ISA 2006 publication).

ISA (International Standard on Auditing) No. 701. *Modifications to the Independent Auditor's Report* (ISA 2006).

ISA (International Standard on Auditing) No. 705. *Modifications to the Opinion in the Independent Auditor's Report.* (ISA Publication)

ISA (International Standard on Auditing) No. 710. *Comparatives.* (ISA Publication).

ISA (International Standard on Auditing) No. 720. *The Auditor's Responsibilities Relating to Other Information in Documents Containing Audited Financial Statements* (ISA publication).

ISQC (International Standard on Quality Control) 1. *Quality Control for Firms that Perform Audits and Reviews of Historical Financial Information, and Other Assurance and Related Service Agreements* (ISA June 15, 2006).

Kleinman, G., B. Lin, and D. Palmon. 2014. "Audit Quality: Cross-National Comparison of Regulatory Regimes." *Journal of Accounting, Auditing and Finance* 29, no. 1, 61–87.

Lindberg, D.L., and D. Seifert. April 2011. "A Comparison of U.S. Auditing Standards with International Standards on Auditing: Moving towards Convergence." *The CPA Journal* 81, no. 4.

Marden, R.E., R.K. Edwards, and W.D. Stout. 2003. "The CEO/CFO Certification Requirement." *The CPA Journal.* http://www.nysscpa.org/ cpajournal/2003/0703/features/f073603.htm

Mosco, A., G. Bruner, and M. Zielsman. June 2014. "Heads Up—PCAOB Adopts New Requirements for Auditing Related Parties, Significant Unusual

Transactions, and Other Matters." *IAS Plus* 21, no. 6. Deloitte Touche. http:// www.iasplus.com/en/publications/us/heads-up/2014/pcaob-requirements

PCAOB (Public Company Accounting Oversight Board). AS No. 1. *References in Auditors' Reports to the Standards of the Public Company Accounting Oversight Board*. PCAOB release no. 2003-025.

PCAOB (Public Company Accounting Oversight Board). AS No. 3. *Audit Documentation*. PCAOB release no. 2004-006.

PCAOB (Public Company Accounting Oversight Board). AS No. 5. *An Audit of Internal Control Over Financial Reporting That Is Integrated With An Audit of Financial Statements*. PCAOB release no. 2007-005A.

PCAOB (Public Company Accounting Oversight Board). AS No. 8. *Audit Risk*. PCAOB release no. 2010-004.

PCAOB (Public Company Accounting Oversight Board). AS No. 11. *Consideration of Materiality in Planning and Performing an Audit*. PCAOB release no. 2010-004.

PCAOB (Public Company Accounting Oversight Board). AS No. 12. *Identifying and Assessing Risks of Material Misstatement*. PCAOB release no. 2010-004.

PCAOB (Public Company Accounting Oversight Board). AS No. 13. *The Auditor's Responses to the Risks of Material Misstatement*. PCAOB release no. 2010-004.

PCAOB (Public Company Accounting Oversight Board). AS No.14. *Evaluating Audit Results*. PCAOB release no. 2010-004.

PCAOB (Public Company Accounting Standards Board). AS No. 15. *Audit Evidence*. PCAOB release no. 2010-004.

PCAOB (Public Company Accounting Oversight Board). June 2014. AS No. 18. *Related Party Transactions*. PCAOB release no. 2014-002.

PCAOB (Public Company Accounting Oversight Board). AU Section 220. *Independence*.

PCAOB (Public Company Accounting Oversight Board). AU Section 315. *Communications between Predecessor and Successor Auditors*. PCAOB release no. 2010-004.

PCAOB (Public Company Accounting Oversight Board). AU Section 316. *Consideration of Fraud in a Financial Statement Audit*. PCAOB release no. 2010-004.

PCAOB (Public Company Accounting Oversight Board). AU Section 325. *Communications about Control Deficiencies in an Audit of Financial Statements*. PCAOB release no. 2007-005A.

PCAOB (Public Company Accounting Oversight Board). 2010. AU Section 329. *Substantive Analytical Procedures*. PCAOB release no. 2010-004.

PCAOB (Public Company Accounting Oversight Board). AU Section 330. *The Confirmation Process*. PCAOB release no. 2010-004

PCAOB (Public Company Accounting Oversight Board). AU Section 336. *Using the Work of a Specialist*. PCAOB release no. 2010-004.

PCAOB (Public Company Accounting Oversight Board). AU Section 341. *The Auditor's Consideration of an Entity's Ability to Continue as a Going Concern.* PCAOB release 2010-004.

PCAOB (Public Company Accounting Oversight Board). AU Section 350. *Audit Sampling.*

PCAOB (Public Company Accounting Oversight Board). AU Section 390. *Consideration of Omitted Procedures after the Report Date.* PCAOB release 2007-005A.

PCAOB (Public Company Accounting Oversight Board). AU Section 508. *Reports on Audited Financial Statements.* PCAOB release 2007-005A.

PCAOB (Public Company Accounting Oversight Board). AU Section 530. *Dating of the Auditor's Report* PCAOB release No. 2010-004.

PCAOB (Public Company Accounting Oversight Board). AU Section 534. *Reporting on Financial Statements for Use in Other Countries.*

PCAOB (Public Company Accounting Oversight Board). AU Section 543. *Part of Audit Performed by Other Independent Auditors.* PCAOB release no. 2007-005A.

PCAOB (Public Company Accounting Oversight Board). AU Section 558. *Required Supplementary Information.*

PCAOB (Public Company Accounting Oversight Board). AU Section 560. *Subsequent Events* PCAOB release.

PCAOB (Public Company Accounting Oversight Board). AU Section 623. *Special Reports* PCAOB release.

PCAOB (Public Company Accounting Oversight Board). AU Section 625. *Reports on the Application of Accounting Principles.*

PCAOB (Public Company Accounting Oversight Board). Rule 3500T. *Interim Ethics Standards.*

PCAOB (Public Company Accounting Oversight Board). Rule 3502. *Responsibility Not to Knowingly or Recklessly Contribute to Violations.*

PCAOB (Public Company Accounting Oversight Board). Rules 3521. *Contingent Fees.*

PCAOB (Public Company Accounting Oversight Board). Rules 3522. *Tax Transactions.*

PCAOB (Public Company Accounting Oversight Board). Rules 3523. *Tax Services for Persons in Financial Reporting Oversight Roles.*

PCAOB (Public Company Accounting Oversight Board). Rules 3524. *Audit Committee Pre-approval of Certain Tax Services.*

Rittenberg, L.E., B.J. Schwieger, and K.M. Johnstone. 2008. *Auditing: A Business Risk Approach.* 6th ed. Mason, OH: Thomson Southwestern.

Rosenblum Inc v. Adler, 461 A.2d. 138 (New Jersey 1983).

Roussey, R. 1999. "The Development of International Standards on Auditing." *The CPA Journal* 69, no. 10, pp. 14–20

Sarbanes Oxley Act of 2002, Public Company Accounting Reform and Investor Protection Act, Pub. L. 107-204, 116 stat.745.

Schwarcz, S.L. 2002. "Enron and the Use and Abuse of Special Purpose Entities in Corporate Structures." *University of Cincinnati Law Review* 70, pp. 1309–18

Securities Act of 1933, 33Act 48 Stat. 74, Enacted May 21, 1933.

Securities Exchange Act of 1934, 73-291, 48 Stat. 881, Enacted June 6, 1934.

Shleifer, A., and R.W. Vishny. 1997. "A Survey of Corporate Governance." *The Journal of Finance* 52, no. 2, pp. 737–83.

SAS (Statement of Auditing Standards) No. 39. *Audit Sampling* (AICPA Professional Standards, Vol. 1, AU section 350).

SAS (Statement of Auditing Standards) No. 99. *Consideration of Fraud in a Financial Statement Audit* (AICPA 2002 publication).

Treadway Commission. 1987. Report of the National Commission on Fraudulent Financial Reporting. Publication of the National Commission on Fraudulent Financial Reporting.

Ultramares Corporation v. Touche. 174 N.E. 441 (New York 1931).

Index

Material weaknesses in internal
   control over financial
   reporting, 154–156
Multinational corporations, 3

Negligence, 27, 28
Netherlands, legal liability of auditors
   in, 47, 48
New York Stock Exchange (NYSE),
   54
Nonaudit services to audit clients,
   74–79
Nonsampling risk, 207
Nonstatistical sampling technique,
   203, 204

Operational audits, 11, 15
Ordinary negligence, 27
Oxley, Michael G., 53

PCAOB. *See* Public Company
   Accounting Oversight Board
Permanent documentation, 216–218
Planning of audit, 128
   issues regarding
      partner rotation, 121, 122
      using work of an expert,
         125–127
      using work of another auditor,
         122–125
   objectives in, 107–114
   related party transactions (RPTs)
      (*see* Related party transactions
      (RPTs))
Portugal, legal liability of auditors in,
   48, 49
Professional behavior, 65
Projecting errors, 207–209
Project misstatement results as per
   PCAOB AU 350, 212
Public Company Accounting
   Oversight Board (PCAOB),
   1–5, 12, 14–16, 18, 22,
   54–56, 59, 60, 62, 63, 67, 79,
   80, 82–84, 95, 98, 99, 129,
   136, 138, 156, 162, 163, 177,
   193, 200, 211, 268, 269

AS 3, 222
AS 5, 130, 131, 138, 153, 155,
   160, 161
AS 12, 168, 169, 174
AS 14, 169
AU 329, 164, 168, 174, 175
AU 330, 110
AU 334, 115
AU 336, 108, 127
AU 341, 228, 253
AU 350, 195, 208, 212
AU 560, 250
difference between
   GAAS standards and, 90–92
   ISA standards and, 86–90,
      116–121
expansion of authority in 2010, 85
Interim Standard AU 220, 69
operation of, 85, 86
-related party standard, 114
related party transactions (*see*
   Related party transactions
   (RPTs))
Rule 3502, 81
Rule 3521, 80
Rule 3522(a), 80, 81
Rule 3522(b), 81
Rule 3524, 81
setting standards, procedure of,
   85, 86

Qualified opinion, 243

Random number tables, 199
Ratio analysis, 169, 170
Reasonableness testing, 170
Recruitment of senior management
   for assurance client may, 78,
   79
Regulation of auditors
   recent developments in United
      States and other countries,
      53–57
Related party transactions (RPTs),
   114–127
   categories of
      audit procedures associated with,
         117, 118

OTHER TITLES IN OUR FINANCIAL ACCOUNTING AND AUDITING COLLECTION

Scott Showalter, NC State University and
Jan Williams, University of Tennessee, Collection Editors

FORTHCOMING IN THIS COLLECTION

Announcing the Business Expert Press Digital Library

Concise e-books business students need for classroom and research

This book can also be purchased in an e-book collection by your library as

- a one-time purchase,
- that is owned forever,
- allows for simultaneous readers,
- has no restrictions on printing, and
- can be downloaded as PDFs from within the library community.

Our digital library collections are a great solution to beat the rising cost of textbooks. E-books can be loaded into their course management systems or onto student's e-book readers.
The **Business Expert Press** digital libraries are very affordable, with no obligation to buy in future years. For more information, please visit **www.businessexpertpress.com/librarians**. To set up a trial in the United States, please contact **Adam Chesler** at *adam.chesler@businessexpertpress.com*, for all other regions, contact **Nicole Lee** at *nicole.lee@igroupnet.com*.

www.ingramcontent.com/pod-product-compliance
Lightning Source LLC
Chambersburg PA
CBHW052107230326
41599CB00054B/4276